Democracy and Diversity

Democracy and Diversity

India and the American Experience

Edited by

K. Shankar Bajpai

OXFORD

UNIVERSITY PRESS

YMCA Library Building, Jai Singh Road, New Delhi 110 001

Oxford University Press is a department of the University of Oxford.
It furthers the University's objective of excellence in research,
scholarship, and education by publishing worldwide in

Oxford   New York

Auckland   Cape Town   Dar es Salaam   Hong Kong   Karachi   Kuala Lumpur
Madrid   Melbourne   Mexico City   Nairobi   New Delhi   Shanghai   Taipei   Toronto

With offices in

Argentina   Austria   Brazil   Chile   Czech Republic   France   Greece   Guatemala
Hungary   Italy   Japan   Poland   Portugal   Singapore   South Korea   Switzerland
Thailand   Turkey   Ukraine   Vietnam

Published in India by Oxford University Press, New Delhi

First published 2007

ISBN-13: 978-019-568368-4
ISBN-10: 019-568368-4

Typeset in Calisto MT 10.5/12.5, S.R.Enterprises, New Delhi
Printed in India at Deunique, New Delhi-110 018
Published by Oxford University Press
YMCA Library Building, Jai Singh Road, New Delhi 110 001

To the memory of Bashiruddin Ahmed, Austin Ranney, and Aaron Wildavsky, who encouraged the idea of this study, sought to improve its contents, but were lost to it and to us far too soon.

Contents

Tables and Figures

FIGURES

Preface

K. Shankar Bajpai

The eight essays written for this volume look at some of the issues that are straining the institutions, mechanisms, and practice of democracy because of the pressures of population diversity, as experienced in India and the United States (henceforth US). Why these two countries, and why these particular issues?

India usually elicits the attention of the world (or even of its own intellective classes) for its problems and disasters, while its successes are underestimated or overlooked, yet its political evolution since Independence has been one of the most impressive achievements in history. A billion people, too many still too poor and barely literate, practising every religion under the sun and speaking countless languages—the basic facts are well-known, but their implications overlooked. There is simply no parallel to such a state anywhere, ever; so many diversities of race, religion, language, region, ways of life, and in such huge numbers, have never been comprehended within that system of self-government known as democracy.

This accomplishment is all the more remarkable for defying the long-advanced theories of both political scientists, that hold democracy dependent on a certain modicum of social homogeneity, and of the colonial rulers, who believed the country could not survive the loss of the cementing force they attributed to their own control. Contrary to such beliefs, within a couple of decades India effectively compressed the processes of democratization that took generations, even centuries, and usually civil wars or revolutions, in other states. In addition to empowering, extensively if still incompletely, the vast previously under-privileged elements of society, this evolution has also gone a long way towards consolidating a unique nationhood. How and why this has happened has not been systematically examined by scholars who can draw instructive conceptual and practical conclusions.

The formidable problems India still faces call for such studies, which could provide lessons for India itself, and also pointers for other states and societies grappling with the challenges of diversity. It is a growing phenomenon of our times to find groups of people who feel conscious of a distinctive cultural identity, be it based on race, language, or other cultural determinant, seeking a distinctive political identity, either within an existing state framework or by opting out of it, (such as Canada, Belgium, and Spain). Why did Yugoslavia break up, and with such terrible violence, when India, which certainly went through as bloody a strife at the time of Partition, and has hardly been free of outbursts since, manages to consolidate itself both as a nation and as what *The Economist* once called 'the world's most improbable democracy'? A large part of the answer lies in cultural explanations, and in what constitutes the sense of nationhood among different peoples, but political and governmental practices and institutions play a vital role.

Short of outright secessionism, groups seeking some special consideration based on what they feel is a distinctive identity more or less different from their fellow citizens, may use—or disrupt—the political process to obtain benefits ranging from schools of their own to states of their own, with greater autonomy in specific fields. Several ways of dealing with such pressures have been employed, from increasing the powers of local government or of constituent units in a federal structure, to judicial intervention or such devices as affirmative action, or electoral laws, and gerrymandering. Our contributors were asked to examine a few of the problems India has faced and how it has dealt with them, bearing in mind any comparable experiences in the US.

The elements that shape the distinctive ways of life of the groups constituting a plural society raise numerous specific problems when meeting varying preferences for the personal practice and national role of religions, for the language of education and of transacting business, both private and official, obtaining privileges or even rights from the state, and influencing public policy, and so on. Such centrifugal tendencies, however, also raise the broad question of what constitutes nationhood, which in turn involves the definition of a state.

What, in our day and age, constitutes a state? It, of course, continues to be the only legitimate source of organized force within a defined territory, as well as the unit of international interaction, but as the embodiment of a nation's sovereignty it has undergone enormous changes. Freedom in internal affairs has long since ceased to be absolute, not only to the extent of voluntary surrender of sovereignty by acceptance of international obligations, but even where a particular state feels sure it can do what it wants without any outside involvement. Much has already been written about the erosion of national frontiers and sovereignty by modern economic forces, such as the flow of billions of currency across continents at the press of a button, or by the need to meet environmental or drug threats, or to combat terrorism. Beyond that, many of the world's leading powers are now developing a theory of the international right of humanitarian intervention. Clearly, things change, and practices that were acceptable by 'the civilized world' as necessary for state building in the past, now cause abhorrence and moral or political, if not economic or military, interference. The sovereign is no longer free to do whatever he wants even within his recognized jurisdiction—for example, he cannot massacre his people without provoking international reaction. But the use of force to preserve nationhood cannot be relegated to the past.

It is here that what might seem a matter of international law and practice becomes relevant to the consolidation of nationhood. India has faced violent challenges to its unity, partly indigenous and partly externally managed, and has resorted to the use of force—in Kashmir, Punjab, and some Northeastern states—to much international criticism. These cases clearly included more or less reprehensible departures from democratic norms, at least in the violence inflicted on human rights. Countries which once had to resort to the most extreme use of force—America's nationhood was, after all, practically consolidated by the bloodiest Civil War in history—today condemn anything similar as unacceptable, but clearly the use of force to preserve the nation remains a legitimate instrument of the state.

Moreover, in India as a whole, reliance on democracy to resolve such issues has become so well established that diverse communities have by and large been given confidence in finding the life they want within the broader unity of India. Consider four of the biggest challenges India has faced in this context. The very first movement towards secessionism is now almost forgotten: Tamil Nadu, which seemed soon after India's Independence to be pressing for states' rights verging on separation, soon became a key player in the central government, thanks to wise political leadership both in Delhi and in the State. Punjab was involved in far more violence but, again, is one of the most robust players on the national scene. Kashmir and, less prominent but in some ways even more difficult, parts of India's Northeast, persist, greatly due to external instigation and management but with undeniable internal discontent, requiring heavy use of military force. There is again a search for political solutions to retrieve the acquiescence of the local people in the Indian nexus, but both these parts of present-day India cannot but raise questions of the kind of nationhood that can encompass such diversities.

These are defined areas of specific 'ethnicity'; beyond them is the geographically and numerically vast problem of India's Muslims, now at some 140 million, the world's second largest Muslim population. When this book was first conceived, over a decade ago, India's management of diversities had so many successes that it seemed well on the way to exemplifying a new kind of nation. Even more disturbing than the persistent militancy in Kashmir and the Northeast, which clearly feed on internal discontents, is the communal violence that erupted in Gujarat in 2002, reviving concerns which had seemed part of history. The half-full-glass view of the Gujarat crisis can certainly find it reassuring that it was confined to one state and, far from spreading to other areas—as it so easily would have if it was part of a national trend—actually woke others up to the vital importance of constantly tending India's pluralism. The half-empty-glass view cannot, however, be dismissed as invalid in asking whether what has worked so far can serve India's needs in the future. The participants in this project have been fully conscious of this need for fresh answers.

Whether there is any validity to the theory that democracy and the market economy have perfected all forms of political and economic evolution, and 'ended history', is arguable to say the least, but there can surely be no question that the evolution of nations is nowhere near complete. There is a strong element of opposition to the concept of the nation state (which has probably caused more bloodshed than any other form of political organization). India is perhaps the first major instance of a multicultural or civilizational state, almost a multinational state. It is what western Europe strives to become, what various regional groupings like the Association of Southeast Asian Nations (ASEAN) seek to approximate, what might have saved Yugoslavia or the Soviet Union if the component units of these states could have enjoyed that overarching sense of belonging to something more satisfying than their particularisms.

This sense of unity in India has always been hard to define, and indeed doubted even by well-intentioned observers. The arguments used by the Indian nationalists in the struggle for independence seem rhetorical, even poetical or mystical, compared to, say, the cold logic of the proponents of Partition. Still, the concept of India has been a cementing force throughout history. Whereas in the US, the constituent units first strengthened their own individuality and power and then grew into a sense of unity; in India the notion of unity was the most compelling motivation in the struggle for independence, the particularisms becoming active subsequently.

How far the experience of one state or society can be helpful to another is debatable, even when they are closely similar. In India and the US, the most basic factors—historical, cultural, economic—are so different, that the possibilities for useful comparisons between the two would seem remote. Moreover, in the foreseeable future, India cannot hope to apply to its problems anything like the material resources available in the US. Above all, the role of, and public attitudes towards the government are completely different.

In India, government is almost all-pervasive, affecting most aspects of society and the lives of citizens individually: it is to government that Indians turn to for solutions. In the US, government affects far more of society or individual life than was envisaged by the founding fathers, or is welcome by many of their descendants. That in itself has intensified criticism of governmental activity, and the strong tradition is still the norm of an American turning to the government almost as a last resort.

But if India needs more non-governmental initiative and responsibility to shape its social and political environment, the US has surely found that many of the problems of American society are intractable without effective government action. The balance appropriate to each country has to be found through the larger dynamics at work within the state, but some essential challenges each has faced have mutually instructive similarities. Minority rights provides one obvious example. What in America is called 'affirmative action' and in India 'reservations' has had some successes, many failures, and an increasing number of unforeseen results. The ways in which the federal government and black leaders used the federal judicial system was instrumental in bringing about changes in the US faster and more effectively than any other method could have been. Indeed, the role of the America judiciary, most particularly the US Supreme Court, in the formation and continuing evolution of the American polity, can provide a wealth of material relevant to India. Many of the conflicts between states' rights and federal powers have been sorted out in the US, but many remain or keep arising, as they have been doing in India. While much more has been done at the local government level in the US than in India, there are surprising similarities in the problems of coping with needs which each country is facing. The emphasis in the last decade has been on state and local authorities in the US taking care of responsibilities previously built up within the federal system and this has cast burdens not dissimilar to what the local authorities in India have to bear. The tax base for financing institutions and solutions in the US, and the role of the private sector there, are of course enormous compared to India's, but so too are the demands and expectations of society.

The US has, no doubt, unified almost as extensive a range of ethnic and other diversities as India, but mainly because it has had a dominant culture to which all newcomers aspired (apart from the unifying effect of economic opportunities which, for instance, encourage a common language). Without going into the question of whether it still does or does not have a dominant culture, the US today has a more accommodative approach to its components 'doing their own thing', and has become increasingly attentive to group rights over and above its traditional concentration on individual rights. It is, in any case, the only democracy anything like the same size and complexity as India.

Moreover, the problems US faced in forging both the mechanics and the sense of nationhood, though now relegated to history, were not dissimilar to India's continuing effort to accommodate particularisms. It was more than a question of the states' rights versus a strong federal regime: while the US doubtlessly enjoyed the advantages of a common language, much common cultural heritage, and even some rough homogeneity of racial types (African–Americans, Hispanics, and now various Asians excepted), 'the way of life' developed in different regions, even in various parts of states, and the distinct social and cultural habits and attitudes of people could easily have led to a far more diversified totality than the one fused by the Civil War.

India's diversities are, of course, far more varied, historically rooted, and, in many ways, harder to emulsify, much less homogenize, but it is precisely the deliberate preference for letting diversities go their own way (within limits) that makes the Indian experience so interesting and instructive. Whereas the US has one law, till recently (and still mainly) one language and so on, India has so far not only allowed a separate Muslim law, or all kinds of tribal customs, but has developed even stronger unity while letting a multiplicity of languages flourish—twenty-two officially recognized by the Constitution, which means that they are the languages of official use in different constituent states of the Union, which have the right to communicate in them with each other and with the Union.

Ultimately, it may all be said to come down to a people's approach to nationhood: what is it that makes them prefer, or at least accept, living together with differences? Because it has no parallel in history, India was long considered too varied to remain a unity. Even many Indians, while denouncing British prophecies that they would fall apart as imperialistic tactics of 'divide and rule' had the uneasy, if unexpressed, fears that they were true, which led the founding fathers to go in for what is now considered an over-powerful federal centre. How far Delhi's powers have served India's nationhood, even if too often abused, and provocative of avoidable challenges, is an endless debate. Even in the US, with its currently ever-more popular tradition of mistrusting federal governmental activity, it is clear that some states would still be resisting change and accommodation but for the pressure of Washington—for example, would Mississippi have otherwise accepted legal desegregation? In India too, the social as well as economic backwardness of some regions can only be tackled because of Delhi's exertions. In other words, federal activism is useful and necessary and the real question in India, as in the US, is how the pulls and pressures of states' rights can be accommodated.

Whenever India runs into political difficulties, a chorus of criticism of its Constitution arises, specifically of the suitability of the parliamentary system,—and within it of the 'first-past-the-post electoral system'—for stable, effective, and representative government. It is hardly possible to conceive of any basic recasting of India's Constitution: in present or foreseeable circumstances neither a high-standard constituent assembly nor the sort of broad ideological harmony such as India had when its existing Constitution was framed are to be expected. The preference expressed for a presidential form of government usually turns out to be a yearning for a strong, decisive executive authority. Nevertheless, a serious examination of the issues that lead to the endless debate in India, and also of the successes, failures, and problems of the presidential system in the US, should suggest how institutions and devices can be developed to strengthen democratic functioning, if only by bringing out the difficulties of the US presidential system and the weakness of its executive.

In short, the needs of reconciliation or containment of increasingly varied, conflicting, and demanding group interests is heightening pressures on existing governance in both India and in America. Those at work in a highly industrialized, technologically advanced, and increasingly information-based society are obviously different from what is at work in one that is immensely varied, unevenly developed, and resource-scarce. Yet the American experience has considerable relevance to India's needs and, surprising as it may seem to those who have difficulty in taking India seriously, this is mutual.

There are indeed far more aspects of democratic arrangements and practices in India and the US needing mutual attention than could possibly be considered in a limited and essentially arbitrarily selective survey such as is attempted here. Nor was it intended to try to come to direct comparisons but rather for the authors to approach their subjects in relation to one country, bearing in mind some of the relevant, contrasting, or similar points in the other. As to why some subjects were chosen and not others, two considerations prevailed: we wanted to bring together the optimum number of scholars, half from India and half from the US, who could between them cover a sufficiently illustrative range of issues without becoming too large a group, so that they could work together comfortably and with significant cooperation. As always, funding imposes its own limitations, but the first determinant was practical interaction. Secondly, the choice of participants was naturally linked to their individual areas of interest and expertise in the subjects we wanted included.

We were extremely fortunate in evoking the interest of an impressive number of outstanding scholars, both in the US and in India, making it excitingly difficult to pick the eight authors.

Our idea was to pick out some of the issues crucial to the management of diversity as illustrating the broader range, and at the same time getting the benefit of world-class scholars who had not applied themselves to the subject in relation to India.

I wanted, in particular, to attract the attention of American scholars who have contributed so much to the study of state and society without ever writing about India: I felt that the depth of their expertise combined with their freshness of approach to India, would both give the study of India in this context its long delayed due and stimulate the new thinking needed within India. The choice of Indians was in one sense simpler: there was no lack of specialists on any of our problems, but almost none had had any chance of looking at the US. We, therefore, arranged for the Americans to spend time in India and the Indians in the US, and to get all eight together to compare notes at least twice, apart from their bilateral interactions.

The result was what is offered here. Arend Lijphart agreed to provide a broad overview; the project took so much longer than originally expected that it would have been unfair to keep from the world his first observations, which we agreed should be published as they were as 'The Puzzle of Indian Democracy', but his further involvement in our endeavour has given us the benefit of more of his thinking here. The one feature of the experience of the US and of India that comes first to mind as being similar is the provision of special treatment for the disadvantaged. Nathan Glazer was an obvious choice, all the more welcome because, for all his long personal involvement with India, he had not written on our problems. Each of the four Indians had worked on subjects connected with those we assigned them but agreed to address them after familiarizing themselves with the US handling of the related issue. Language was taken for granted in the US till lately, and is still a problem only in limited areas, but it is creating pressures in India; Neera Chandhoke undertook this study. Modern democracies are inseparable from modern political parties, which are also important in negotiating ethnic or other group demands; E. Sridharan devotes his contribution to this role. What the local government can do at everyday levels was another evident area of enquiry, and is here presented by Professor deSouza.

A special explanation is called for in regard to the work of Alfred Stepan and his colleagues, Juan J. Linz and Yogendra Yadav. Stepan was originally going to work on federal issues while Linz was studying the whole question of India's nationhood. Al Stepan, in fact, greatly extended his visits to India to look at both aspects, and worked closely together with Yogendra Yadav and his remarkable statistical samplings of public attitudes and opinions. Linz also spent several weeks in India personally and became familiar in India, and on a visit to Oxford, with Yogendra Yadav's work and all three agreed, to our great pleasure, to pool their talents, wisdom, and knowledge to do a combined study highly revealing about India's sense of nationhood.

This whole project originated as far back as the late 1980s, when, after retiring as India's Ambassador to the US, I was a Visiting Professor at the University of California, Berkeley. I was invited on the basis of my involvement in international affairs, but that most stimulating of environments, both in the university and in the town, gave me the chance to reflect on a lifelong concern: how does one govern India? I had the good fortune of working—and relaxing—with Berkeley's galaxy of experts, thinkers, and talkers, especially with some who were not quite sure where India was on the map but knew all there is to know on problems of governance in the US and elsewhere. Six scholars whose friendship is largely responsible for this project—without any blame for the inadequacies I brought to it—must be given my first thanks. Austin Ranney, the Chairman of the Political Science Department, who had presided over my two lectures as Regents' Professor and then arranged for me to go back for three marvellous years; his pleasure when I told him the work was finally with the printers was alas short-lived, and all involved here deeply regret his tragic passing away. Equally encouraging was Nelson Polsby, who first shared his wit and knowledge and then gave me the hospitality of the Institute of Government Studies, and who made me feel that my thoughts were not unworthy of attention. Aaron Wildavsky, whose amazing mind seemed to be working away even if he were merely waiting to cross a street, was another guru—I cannot adequately convey how much I owe him or how much I miss him. Ray Wolfinger and Bruce Cain added to my sense of being on to something worth pursuing. As for thirty years and happily still today, Robert Scalapino, who first arranged for my assignment to the university, was a constant encouragement— He with the other five friends I have mentioned, helped me work up a project to put to the Ford Foundation. Its alacrity in accepting the project showed once again its extraordinary commitment to furthering good causes in relation to India; this was even more evident in its extraordinary patience in regard to the project, supporting what must be the longest gestating project in its history. We have worked through three successive Directors of its India office—David Arnold, Gowher Rizvi, and G. Balachander with perseverance; they will agree that our thanks to them are owed even more to their most helpful programme officers—Mark Robinson for many years and then Bishnu Mohapatra.

It is the Foundation's practice to ensure that a project is lodged in an institution. While ours originated in Berkeley, an Indian sponsor was needed. We were fortunate to find one in the University of Pennsylvania Institute for the Advanced Study of India; without claiming its endorsement of any of the views expressed in this volume, we are all grateful for its assistance.

Above all, this book is due to its contributors; it is impossible to acknowledge adequately the time, effort, and devotion they have given to it.

And, of course, what is a book without a publisher? The ready interest of the Oxford University Press, stimulated by Dominic Byatt and sustained by his colleagues in Delhi, was as flattering as it is fruitful; we hope the reader, whatever faults he may find with our contents, will thank them as much as we do, for their advice, improvements, and patience.

Abbreviations

ACLU	American Civil Liberties Union
ADMK	Anna Dravida Munnetra Kazhagam
AFL–CIO	American Federation of Labour and Congress of Industrial Organizations
AIADMK	All India Anna Dravida Munnetra Kazhagam
AICC	All India Congress Committee
ASEAN	Association of Southeast Asian Nations
BDR	Bundesrepublik Deutschland (West Germany)
BJP	Bharatiya Janata Party
BJS	Bharatiya Jana Sangh
BSP	Bahujan Samaj Party
CPI	Communist Party of India
CPI (M)	Communist Party of India (Marxist)
CSDS	Centre for the Study of Developing Societies
CWC	Congress Working Committee
DCC	District Congress Committee
DDR	Deutsche Demokratische Republik (East Germany)
DK	Dravida Kazhagam
DMK	Dravida Munnetra Kazhagam
ELA	English Language Amendment
EO	English Only
EU	European Union
FPTP	first-past-the-post
HVP	Haryana Vikas Party
IAS	Indian Administrative Service
LCP	Loktantrik Congress Party
MBC	Most Backward Class
MKSS	Mazdoor Kisan Shakti Sangathan
MP	Member of Parliament
MPLADS	MP Local Area Development Scheme
NCP	Nationalist Congress Party

NCRWC	National Commission to Review the Working of the Constitution
NCSCST	National Commission for SCs and STs
NDA	National Democratic Alliance
NES	National Election Study
NGO	Non-Governmental Organization
NSCN (I–M)	Nationalist Socialist Council of Nagalim (Isaac –Muivah)
OBC	Other Backward Class
OE	Official English
OECD	Organization for Economic Cooperation and Development
PCC	Pradesh Congress Committee
PEPSU	Patiala and East Punjab States Union
PR	Proportional Representation
PRI	Panchayati Raj Institution
RDA	Rural Development Agency
RSS	Rashtriya Swayamsevak Sangh
SC	Scheduled Caste
SDSA	State of Democracy in South Asia
SEC	State Election Commission
SHG	Self-help Group
ST	Scheduled Tribe
STV	single transferable vote
TMC	Tamil Maanila Congress
US	United States
VHP	Vishwa Hindu Parishad
WVS	World Values Survey

1

Introduction
The Importance of India–United States Comparison for Political Science

Arend Lijphart

India and the US are the world's largest—that is, most populous—democracies by far. One does not have to be a political scientist to appreciate that this fact makes the two countries especially important and worthy of special attention; it is something that can be readily understood by the average 'man in the street'. And a lay person with slightly above-average intellectual curiosity can also easily understand that it makes the two countries especially worth comparing and provides a special opportunity for lessons that the two may be able to learn from each other.

If these conclusions are obvious to lay people, they should be even more obvious to political scientists; in fact, it would be reasonable to expect that comparative studies of India and the US would abound in political science. However, such comparisons are extremely rare. Let me first briefly address the question of how the dearth of India–US comparisons can be explained. Second, I shall discuss the more important question of why such comparisons are of special significance to political science—including, but also going beyond, the obvious reasons stated above.

THE DEARTH OF COMPARATIVE INDIA–US STUDIES

The basic fact is clear: political science has produced very few comparative analyses of the Indian and American governmental and political systems. There are a handful of minor exceptions—

mainly narrowly focused articles and monographs—but I believe that I can state unequivocally, and without insulting the few authors involved, that none of these are comparable in scope, depth, and scholarly significance to the present volume. This is one of the situations where the adage that 'the exceptions (that is, the paucity of exceptions) prove the rule' nicely applies: where we would expect hundreds of examples of comparative studies focusing on India and the US, and dozens of major volumes, only a handful of minor examples exist. This volume is therefore a truly pioneering study that is of unusual significance for political science. It is probably indicative of the past failures of political scientists that the initiative for the book was taken by a diplomat-turned-scholar, K. Shankar Bajpai, instead of a purely academic political scientist. It is our hope, of course, that the book will mark a turning point for political science, and that it will inspire our fellow political scientists to undertake more comparisons of Indian and American government and politics in the future.

I shall discuss below why population size is an extremely important and powerful explanatory variable in political analyses and why it makes India–US comparisons particularly important, but size is also one explanation of why, in practice, such comparisons have been rare. The first explanation is that citizens and policy-makers in large countries tend to be inward-looking and less aware of and concerned about foreign countries and developments than small countries. As a native of one small country, the Netherlands, I remember the following illustrative anecdote: there was a short period in the 1950s when the Dutch cabinet had not the conventional one, but two ministers in charge of its foreign affairs. This occurred for party-political reasons—an additional portfolio had to be created to satisfy the demands of all the parties in a new cabinet coalition—but a frequent joke at the time was that two foreign ministers were needed because, for a small country like the Netherlands, the rest of the world was so large that one minister could not possibly handle all of it! There is some truth to this joke: the balance of domestic versus foreign interests and events is necessarily different in large and small countries.

This inward-looking tendency in large countries applies to political scientists, too, and it makes them less likely to do comparative work. Among today's American political scientists, my estimate is that more than a third, and probably close to half, are 'Americanists' who study aspects of American politics and American politics only. An additional reason—and a reason that is more respectable in scholarly terms—is that at least some of these Americanists actually do engage in comparative studies but that these focus on within-country comparisons: comparisons of the different states, regions, ethnic groups, religions, and so on, that the highly diverse US has in abundance. Indian political scientists are, if anything, even more narrowly focused on their own country—a tendency reinforced by their lack of adequate resources for doing research on other countries.

The counterpoint to the above assertions is that we should logically expect both citizens and political scientists in smaller countries to be more outward-looking and, in fact, to give special attention to the largest countries. This is only partly the case, however. In comparative studies of the industrialized democracies (largely coinciding with the members of the Organization for Economic Cooperation and Development [OECD)], the US is often included, but certainly not always. The reason is that in some crucial respects the US is too different from the other industrialized democracies. For instance, comparative analyses of the formation of coalition governments usually do not include the US, because coalition formation in a presidential system of government is fundamentally different from that in parliamentary systems. Also, the American electoral and party systems—especially the prevalence of primary elections and the strict two-party system (consisting of two large, but uncohesive parties, and without significant third parties)—are unique and make them difficult to compare with electoral and party systems in other democracies.

As far as the specific comparison of India and the US is concerned, when I have informally asked some of my colleagues whether they could explain the dearth of such comparisons, their most frequent speculative answer has been the big difference in levels of economic development. This seems a plausible explanation to me, too. But it is not a justification—unless one is an economic determinist. Moreover, the essence of comparative analysis—a subject to which I shall return below—is to study comparable cases, that is, cases that are similar in a large number of respects but differ in others. Therefore, there is no reason why comparative study of countries at different levels of development should be precluded.

There are two additional speculative explanations—both plausible, although partly contradictory—of why India has not been included in more comparative analyses. One is that, among developing countries, it is the only Asian or African country that has been democratic for a long time—more than half a century. The only other developing country with a similarly strong record of stable democracy is Costa Rica in Latin America, a much smaller country with a population of about 4 million. On the other hand, outside observers have tended not to take India's democracy seriously because, given the frequent failure of democracy in other developing and ethnically divided countries in Asia and Africa, they jumped to the conclusion that democracy in as large, poor, and religiously and ethnically diverse a country as India was 'too good to be true'—and therefore likely not to be true. The 1975–7 Emergency reinforced this bias, although, while it was certainly a non-democratic interlude, it only lasted a year-and-a-half and was followed by the restoration of full democracy.

In my own work on consociational democracy, I have experienced a striking example of the problem that political scientists have not sufficiently studied India in comparative terms. Consociational or power-sharing theory holds that democracy is possible in deeply divided societies but only if their type of democracy is consociational: that is, characterized by (1) grand coalition governments that include representatives of all major linguistic and religious groups, (2) cultural autonomy for these groups, (3) proportionality in political representation and civil service appointments, and (4) a minority veto with regard to vital minority rights and autonomy. In contrast, under majoritarian winner-take-all democracy—characterized by the concentration of power in bare-majority one-party governments, centralized power, a disproportional electoral system, and absolute majority rule—consociational theory regards stable democracy in deeply divided societies as highly unlikely. In other words, consociational theory maintains that power-sharing is a necessary, although not sufficient, condition for democracy in deeply divided countries. I started my work on this subject with a case study of the religiously divided but stable, and clearly consociational, Netherlands, published in 1968. Next, I discovered and analysed a number of similar consociational systems in Europe—Belgium, Switzerland, and Austria). Consociationalism became a widely accepted paradigm that was used by a host of other comparativist scholars for the interpretation of many other political systems, large and small—from tiny Liechtenstein to even the European Union (EU).

India, however, was never subjected to a similar thorough analysis. Hence, before I became involved in direct research on India myself, the only evidence that I had to classify India consisted of a few rather cursory and superficial assessments by Indian experts and comparative scholars that India was either a completely deviant case for consociational theory (a majoritarian but stable democracy) or a partly deviant case (stable democracy in a partly majoritarian and partly consociational system). Only when, in connection with the project that has resulted in the present volume edited by Ambassador Bajpai, I undertook an extended study trip to India in 1993 in order to do my own research focused on interviews with social scientists and policy-makers and the study of original documents and reports, I finally discovered that India was not a deviant case at all. In the article in which I reported my findings, I wrote that 'the evidence clearly shows that India has always had a power-sharing system of democracy' and that India was therefore not a deviant case but 'an impressive confirming case' (Lijphart 1996: 259). My conclusion could have been stated even more strongly: in comparison with the other clear cases of consociational democracy, India has deeper religious and linguistic divisions and also possesses the four basic features of power-sharing in a more thorough fashion.[1] It is therefore not only a clear case of a power-sharing democracy, but one of the most

---

[1]   Let me briefly describe how India's democracy fits the four components of the consociational model: (1) Broad linguistic, religious, and regional representation in the cabinet has resulted from the internally coalitional nature of the Congress party in the early decades and, more recently, from inter-party coalitions in which very large numbers of parties have participated. (2) Autonomy for linguistic and religious minorities has taken three forms: the federal system in which state and linguistic boundaries largely coincide, the right of religious and linguistic groups to run their own schools with full state financial support, and separate personal laws for Hindus, Muslims, and smaller religious minorities. (3) In spite of the plurality method of election, there has been a high degree of proportionality in political representation as a result of the Congress's deliberate inclusion of religious and linguistic minorities (especially important in the early decades), the fact that the plurality

important and interesting cases in the democratic world of the judicious, and effective use of many consociational practices. That it took several decades to discover this basic fact about India shows a truly astonishing failure to examine the world's largest democracy from a comparative perspective.

THE SIZE FACTOR IN COMPARATIVE POLITICS

I see two enormously important reasons why Indian and American democracies should be studied not only comparatively but specifically in comparison with each other: the crucial effects of population size as an explanatory variable and the fact that India and the US can be regarded as comparable cases in many respects and therefore as outstanding candidates for comparative analysis.

Why is size such an important variable in political analysis? One reason has to do with the link between the fields of comparative politics and foreign policy. In the international arena, large countries are likely to be the more powerful countries and therefore more worthy of study than smaller countries, and the very largest and most populous countries are likely to be hegemons in their geographical areas. The influence of large countries in international affairs was undoubtedly the main reason why, in traditional political science prior to the behavioural revolution of the 1950s, comparative politics in the US tended to focus on the British, French, German, and Soviet political systems. Especially to the extent that political scientists serve as advisers to policy-makers, this is still a perfectly legitimate reason for paying special attention to what is happening in the larger, and especially the largest, countries.

---

rule does not disfavour geographically concentrated minorities, the 'reserved seats' for the Scheduled Castes (SCs) and Scheduled Tribes (STs), and the 'reservations' that have benefited these scheduled groups and the Other Backward Classes (OBCs) with regard to public service employment and university admissions. (4) Finally, good examples of the informal minority veto in India are the 1965 agreement by the central government that Hindi would not be made the exclusive official language without the approval of the major non-Hindi-speaking regions, and the Muslim minority's successful attempt in the 1980s to reverse the Supreme Court's decision in the Shah Bano case which was seen as an attack on Muslim personal law.

What should be emphasized, however, is that a country's size has many weighty consequences in addition to its effect on the country's stature in the international arena. One obvious consequence of large population size is that it makes the political and policy-making system of a country more complex. In their classic study *Size and Democracy*, Dahl and Tufte (1973: 40), reach the following conclusions after a thorough evaluation of the evidence: 'Other things being equal . . . the larger a country, the greater the number of organizations and subunits it will contain, and the greater the number of organized interests or interest groups it will contain.' This means that among democracies, *ceteris paribus*, 'the larger the country, the more complex its policy-making processes will be.'[2] We can add to this that the larger a country, the larger the number of religious, ethnic, and linguistic groups it is likely to have. Moreover, larger states are also more likely to conduct active foreign policies—adding a further load on governmental management and decision-making. For all these reasons, large states are considerably more difficult to manage than small states.

A final salient element of the size variable is that, in Dahl and Tufte's (1973: 37) words, 'the larger country, the more decentralized its government, whether federal or not.' In my own thirty-six-nation study *Patterns of Democracy*, I found that large population size was clearly related to both federalism and decentralization (Lijphart 1999: 185–99, 252). What is true of larger democracies generally, applies to the two largest, India and the US, with a vengeance: both are enormously complex political systems with very large and diverse numbers of interest groups as well as ethnic and religious groups, and heavy burdens on their decision-making apparatuses. And the diversity and size of their populations make federalism a virtual necessity for them.[3]

---

[2] A slightly countervailing factor, reducing this complexity, is that large countries are less likely to suffer interference in their internal affairs by other countries.

[3] At the same time, of course, there are a number of important differences between the two federalisms. While the US and India are both clearly federal systems, the American system is more decentralized; India's federalism is complemented by non-territorial autonomy in the form of the separate personal laws and minority schools mentioned earlier; India's frequent creation of new states has shown a more dynamic

In addition, what makes size such a critically important parameter is that the range of variation on it is truly huge. There are several countries which are members of the United Nations (UN) with populations below 100,000. Such countries have less than 0.01 per cent of the population of India's. Moreover, the range of population sizes is extremely skewed. In my *Patterns of Democracy*, I examine thirty-six stable democracies, defined as all countries with a minimum population of 250,000, which, as of 1996, had been continuously democratic for about twenty years. India and the US are by far the largest; next are Japan and Germany, but with steeply lower population numbers—less than half and less than a third, respectively, of the population of the US. India's population is larger than that of the other thirty-five countries combined. And the sum of the populations of India and the US is almost twice the combined populations of the other thirty-four countries. At the other end of the range, large numbers of smaller countries are concentrated: the median population of the thirty-six democracies is below 8 million; three countries— the Bahamas, Barbados, and Iceland—barely meet the minimum criterion of 250,000 inhabitants (Lijphart 1999: 56).

As I mentioned earlier, traditional comparative politics until the 1950s focused almost exclusively on comparisons of the larger, mainly European, countries. This tendency came in for increasing criticism, and it was one of the principal weaknesses of the field highlighted in Macridis's (1955) well-known critique of the field. Coinciding with the behavioural revolution, a major effort was now made to include smaller countries in comparative analyses. For instance, the Smaller European Democracies project, launched in the 1960s by Stein Rokkan, Robert A. Dahl, Hans Daalder, and Val R. Lorwin, aimed at thorough analyses of the political systems of about a dozen smaller European countries (the Nordic and Benelux countries, Ireland, Austria, and Switzerland).

The Smaller European Democracies project and similar efforts were very successful in making smaller countries available for comparative analysis and in encouraging studies based on

---

form of federalism; and the two federations differed in their initial purposes—in Alfred Stepan's (2001: 320, italics added) terminology, the contrast is between the American '*coming* together' and India's '*holding* together' origin of federalism.

larger numbers of cases—a major advantage for comparativists trying to establish general propositions about political phenomena, especially because, when the number of cases exceeds about fifteen or twenty, they can start using statistical techniques and controls. However, because there are many more small than large countries, a necessary drawback is that comparative analysis has come to be dominated by the smaller countries. This problem has often been tacitly disregarded, and sometimes the size variable has even been explicitly treated as irrelevant. A striking example is Kenneth Janda's (1980) collection of data on political parties in fifty-three countries around the world. Because parties in each of these countries were covered so painstakingly, he had to limit the number of countries included in his mammoth compilation. For instance, he was unable to cover all of the Scandinavian and Benelux countries, but instead of resolving this problem by choosing the larger countries, he simply drew lots. That is how tiny Iceland was selected instead of Norway, and tiny Luxembourg instead of Belgium.

More recent comparative analyses based on relatively large numbers of cases have not made this mistake. For instance, in my comparative thirty-six-nation study *Patterns of Democracy*, when I examine the policy consequences of different types of democracy, I consistently control for the effect of different population sizes (Lijphart 1999: 262–300). What must be recognized, however, is that a fundamental problem remains. Because the distribution of values on the size variable is so extremely skewed to the smaller populations, I followed the standard operating procedure of using logged population numbers. The logarithm of 100,000 to the base 10 is 5; of one million it is 6; and of India's roughly one billion population, it is 9. This compressed distribution is now manageable for statistical manipulations—but it also obviously hides the big differences that exist in the real world.

In short, if we want to take the variable of population size, and especially the effects of very large sizes, seriously—as we should—we have no alternative but to single out the very large countries for special attention and comparative analysis. It would be wonderful if we had a few more cases of democracies with very large populations of the same order of magnitude as India and the US. We can hope that China and Indonesia will be candidates in the future—but this will be a distant future if we want to study not just large democracies, but large *long-term* democracies. For the time being, our only option is the India–US comparison, and this makes the comparative study of the Indian and American political systems so vitally important.

Furthermore, it is important to emphasize that two-country comparisons should not be denigrated as merely an acceptable, but second-rate, solution under less than ideal circumstances. Political scientists, as well as other social scientists and historians, have used them successfully for a long time. The late Stein Rokkan (1970: 52, italics in the original) was a especially strong advocate of what he called 'the strategy of *paired comparisons*', and he wrote that 'students of comparative political development have found the method of paired [comparisons and] contrasts of great value, both as a device in the ordering and evaluation of data, and as a procedure in the generation of hypotheses and insights.' One important example that he noted was the well-known analysis of political modernization in Japan and Turkey, the two non-western countries that, as of the 1960s, had gone farthest in the direction of modernization, but whose developmental paths showed significant differences (Ward and Rustow 1964). Rokkan's (1970: 118) suggestion that a paired comparison of the consociational Netherlands and Switzerland would open 'fascinating possibilities of comparative historical analysis' inspired Hans Daalder (1973) to do exactly this kind of study. In recent years, economists have been strongly interested in paired comparisons of economic developments in India and China: two countries that are similar in size—they are 'Asia's giants' (Wolf 2005)—and stage of economic development, but that follow divergent development strategies and operate under sharply different political systems (for recent examples, see Sáez 2004 and Sinha 2005). The paired comparison of Indian and American democracy therefore belongs to a long and venerable tradition in political science and the social sciences.

INDIA AND THE UNITED STATES AS COMPARABLE CASES

The basic problem confronting political and social scientists who study large units like national political systems is: many variables, small number of cases. In order to solve or ameliorate this problem, the comparative method is often used; its essence is to focus the analysis on *comparable* cases, that is, cases that are similar in a large number of important characteristics which one wants to treat as constants, but dissimilar as far as those variables are concerned which one wants to relate to each other (Lijphart 1971). The Scandinavian democracies provide an ideal example of comparable cases because they have similar cultures, political institutions, geographic locations, and population sizes. On the other side of the globe, the three Southern Cone countries are almost equally perfect comparable cases, except that they differ more on the size variable. For each of these sets of countries, if we observe differences between countries, we know that these differences cannot be attributed to cultural, political–institutional, and geographic factors—which very helpfully narrows the number of possible explanations.

India and the US obviously do not meet the same standard of comparability, but they actually do have a number of important characteristics in common. I would therefore argue that, according to slightly more lenient criteria, they also qualify as comparable cases. I have already repeatedly emphasized their similarly large populations. Some of their basic political institutions are also similar: federalism, a virtual necessity in very large countries; the plurality, single-member district system of elections; and judicial review with activist courts. They are also both highly diverse societies, although the religious and ethnic divisions in India are deeper and sharper than in the US. As far as their main dissimilarities are concerned—the level of socio-economic development and two key political institutions—the differences are large: India has a parliamentary system of government in contrast with the American presidential system; on the spectrum of party systems, India's extreme multiparty system is at one end and the American strict two-party system at the opposite end; and India is the poorest among the long-term democracies, while the US is one of the richest. However, in spite of the latter contrast and in spite of the fact that socio-economic inequalities tend to go down as economic development goes up, India and the US are strikingly similar— and strikingly different from most other democracies—not only in their high degrees of inequality of incomes and wealth, but also in their remarkable public tolerance for these inequalities.

The mixture of similarities and differences offers great opportunities for comparative analysis and also for lessons that the two countries can learn from each other. There are many such explicit and implicit lessons in the substantive chapters that follow, including my own. I would like to highlight one of these lessons here. Earlier in this Introduction, I mentioned my article on India as a consociational democracy; my argument was that India had been able to maintain its democratic system of government in spite of its deep social divisions because it used power-sharing rules and institutions to an almost perfect extent. I wrote this analysis in the mid-1990s, and at that time I expressed concern about signs that India's consociationalism was weakening and that, as a result, its democratic system was being endangered. In particular, I noted the shift in the Congress party and Congress cabinets from broadly representative and consensual to more centralized and hierarchical relationships, as well as the weakening of the federal system as a result of the increasing use of President's Rule for partisan purposes (Lijphart 1996: 263–5).

More than ten years later, I can note with satisfaction that my fears were largely unfounded. Cabinets have become multiparty coalition cabinets—in fact, multiparty coalitions that are extreme in comparative terms, with more than a dozen parties, and at one time as many as twenty-three parties, participating—which are generally just as broad and inclusive of most geographic, linguistic, and religious interests as the Congress cabinets in the first two decades of India's democracy. And federalism has rebounded as President's Rule has faded away. These developments show a flexibility and dynamism in Indian politics that contrasts sharply with the static, even stagnant, condition of American political institutions. My interpretation is that this institutional flexibility in India can be attributed largely to its parliamentary system and to its shift to multipartism. Among the many lessons to be learned from the India–US comparison, this may be one of the most important.

REFERENCES

Daalder, Hans, 'Building Consociational Nations', in S. N. Eisenstadt and Stein Rokkan, eds, *Building States and Nations: Analyses by Region*, vol. 2, Beverly Hills: Sage, 1973, pp. 14–31.

Dahl, Robert A. and Edward R. Tufte, *Size and Democracy*, Stanford: Stanford University Press, 1973.

Janda, Kenneth, *Political Parties: A Cross-National Survey*, New York: Free Press, 1980.

Lijphart, Arend, 'Comparative Politics and the Comparative Method', *American Political Science Review*, vol. 65 (3), September 1971, pp. 682–93.

——'The Puzzle of Indian Democracy: A Consociational Interpretation', *American Political Science Review*, vol. 90 (2), June 1996, pp. 258–68.

——*Patterns of Democracy: Government Forms and Performance in Thirty-Six Countries*, New Haven: Yale University Press, 1999.

Macridis, Roy C., *The Study of Comparative Government*, New York: Random House, 1955.

Rokkan, Stein, *Citizens, Elections, Parties: Approaches to the Comparative Study of the Processes of Development*, Oslo: Universitetsforlaget, 1970.

Sáez, Lawrence, *Banking Reform in India and China*, New York: Palgrave Macmillan, 2004.

Sinha, Aseema, 'Political Foundations of Market-Enhancing Federalism: Theoretical Lessons from India and China', *Comparative Politics*, vol. 37 (3), April 2005, pp. 337–56.

Stepan, Alfred, *Arguing Comparative Politics,* Oxford: Oxford University Press, 2001.

Ward, Robert E., and Dankwart E. Rustow, eds, *Political Modernization in Japan and Turkey*, Princeton: Princeton University Press, 1964.

Wolf, Martin, 'Asia's Giants Take Different Routes', *Financial Times*, 22 February 2005.

2

Democratic Institutions and Ethnic/ Religious Pluralism
Can India and the United States Learn from each other—and from the Smaller Democracies?

Arend Lijphart

INTRODUCTION

Religious, cultural, linguistic, ethnic, and racial divisions have long been regarded as a major problem for democratic governments. Writing in 1861, John Stuart Mill's conclusion in *Considerations on Representative Government* was that 'free institutions are next to impossible in a country made up of different nationalities. Among a people without fellow-feeling, especially if they read and speak different languages, the united public opinion, necessary to the working of representative government, cannot exist' (chapter 16). Mill wrote before any full democracies existed anywhere in the world,[1] and, instead of speaking of democratic institutions, he used the terms 'free institutions' and 'representative government'.

---

[1] This statement is contrary to Samuel P. Huntington's (1991) argument that the first wave of democratization began as early as 1828, but he uses a much too lenient definition of 'universal' suffrage: the right to vote for at least 50 per cent of adult males. According to a strict definition of universal suffrage, New Zealand became the world's first democracy—and the only democracy in the nineteenth century— when it gave the right to vote to all of its citizens, including women

However, his proposition applies to democracy, too: free and representative institutions are not necessarily fully democratic ones, but democracy does entail both of these characteristics. Mill's proposition can therefore be stated in modern terms as follows: In multi-ethnic societies (countries with 'different nationalities') democracy is very difficult—in fact, almost impossible—to achieve and maintain, and democracy is completely impossible if societies are not only multi-ethnic but also multilingual.

In spite of the fact that, when democracy was established in many countries in the twentieth century, there were several examples of multi-ethnic and multilingual democracies—in Canada and Belgium, for instance—Mill's extreme views were rarely challenged. It was not until the 1960s, more than a hundred years after the publication of Mill's *Considerations on Representative Government*, that consociational scholars began to explain why some deeply divided countries had been able to maintain democracy: democracy can have many different institutional forms and arrangements, and some of these are much more suitable than others for deeply divided societies. Sir Arthur Lewis (1965) was the pioneering theorist. In his book on the failure of democracy in the ethnically divided West African countries, he pointed out that this failure was not at all inevitable, and that democracy could work satisfactorily if three key institutions were adopted: broad coalition governments, proportional representation (PR), and federalism. Several other scholars have extended and refined the theory of consociational democracy from the late 1960s onwards (see, for instance, Lehmbruch 1967; Huyse 1970; McRae 1974; Steiner 1974; Lijphart 1977; Messarra 1983).

In this chapter, I shall use the analytical framework of my *Patterns of Democracy: Government Forms and Performance in Thirty-Six Democracies* (Lijphart 1999) to compare and contrast the democratic institutions developed by the world's most populous democracies,

---

and the Maori ethnic minority, in 1893. In the US, often called 'the world's oldest democracy'—indeed, Huntington (1991, p. 16) explicitly states that it was 'the United States [that] began the first wave of democratization'—universal suffrage was not firmly established until the passage of the Voting Rights Act in 1965. This means that, strictly speaking, India is an older democracy, dating from the first national elections in 1951–2 (but interrupted in the 1975–7 Emergency), than the US.

India and the US, to manage the many divisions in their societies: How similar or how different are their political institutions and how similar or how different are their societal divisions? How do they differ from the other, smaller, democracies? And do the answers to these questions imply any practical lessons that they can learn from each other—and perhaps from the smaller democracies as well?

THE MAJORITARIAN–CONSENSUS CONTRAST

In *Patterns of Democracy*, I show that the main institutional rules and practices of modern democracies—such as the organization and operation of executives, legislatures, party systems, electoral systems, interest groups, and the relationships between central and lower-level governments—can all be measured on scales from majoritarianism at one end to consensus on the other. This contrast is based on radically different interpretations of the basic definition of democracy as 'government by and for the people': who will do the governing and to whose interests should the government be responsive when the people are in disagreement and have divergent preferences? One answer is: the majority of the people. The alternative is: as many people as possible. These two answers typify the two basic models of democracy: majoritarian and consensus. The majoritarian model concentrates political power in the hands of the majority, whereas the consensus model tries to share, disperse, and limit power in a variety of ways.

Ten differences with regard to political institutions and practices can be deduced from these two contrasting principles. Since the ten majoritarian characteristics are derived from the same principle and hence are logically connected, we would expect them to occur together in the real world. The same applies to the ten consensus elements. Comparative analysis largely confirms these expectations—with one major exception: the majoritarian as well as the consensus characteristics cluster along two clearly separate dimensions.

The first cluster, which I call the *executives–parties dimension*, groups together five characteristics of the arrangement of executive power and of the electoral, party, and interest group systems. I shall formulate them in terms of dichotomous contrasts between the majoritarian and consensus models, but it is important to emphasize that they are all variables on which particular countries may be at either end of the continuum or anywhere in between. The majoritarian characteristic is listed first in each case: (1) majoritarian and disproportional electoral systems versus PR (2) two-party versus multi-party systems; (3) concentration of executive power in single-party majority cabinets versus executive power-sharing in broad multiparty coalitions; (4) executive–legislative relations in which the executive is dominant versus executive-legislative balance of power; and (5) pluralist interest group systems with free-for-all competition among groups versus coordinated and corporatist interest group systems aimed at compromise and concertation.

The first four elements are structurally connected: according to the well-known Duverger's (1964) Law, plurality elections discriminate against small parties and encourage a two-party system with a majority party; this tends to lead to the formation of one-party cabinets and to the cabinet's predominance over the legislature. Conversely, PR tends to lead to multipartism, multipartism to coalition cabinets, and coalition cabinets to more balanced executive–legislative power relations. The connection between these four elements and the interest group system is mainly cultural. Katzenstein (1985: 32, 157) speaks of an 'ideology of social partnership' and the absence of a 'winner-take-all mentality' in consensus democracies; this political culture provides the indirect link between corporatism and the other characteristics of consensus democracy.

The five differences in the second cluster, the *federal–unitary dimension*, are the following—the majoritarian/unitary characteristics being listed first: (1) unitary and centralized government versus federal and decentralized government; (2) concentration of legislative power in a unicameral legislature versus division of legislative power between two equally strong but differently constituted houses; (3) flexible constitutions that can be amended by simple majorities versus rigid constitutions that can be changed only by extraordinary majorities; (4) systems in which legislatures have the final word on the constitutionality of their own legislation versus systems in which laws are subject to a judicial review of their constitutionality by supreme or constitutional courts;

and (5) central banks that are dependent on the executive versus independent central banks.

The connections among the first four of these variables can be regarded as functional. As theorists of federalism have long argued, the main purpose of federalism is to promote and protect a decentralized system of government, and this goal requires a division of power guaranteed by a rigid constitution and further protected by judicial review and a strong federal chamber in a bicameral legislature (Friedrich 1950: 189–221; Elazar 1968; Duchacek 1970). Their link with strong central banks can be explained in terms of the fact that diffusion of power takes place mainly by means of institutional separation: division of power between separate federal and state institutions, two separate chambers in the legislature, and separate and independent high courts and central banks. This explanation also provides a reason for the existence of the two separate dimensions. The first dimension of consensus democracy is also characterized by diffusion of power, but here it mainly assumes the form of shared power instead of separate institutions: multiparty face-to-face interactions within cabinets, legislatures, and legislative committees, and in concertation meetings between governments and interest groups (Crepaz 2002: 173–6).

INDIA AND THE UNITED STATES ON THE CONCEPTUAL MAP OF DEMOCRACY

The two-dimensional pattern formed by the ten institutional variables allows us to summarize where individual countries are situated between majoritarian and consensus democracy. Their values on each of the two sets of five variables can be averaged so as to form just two summary values,[2] and these can be used to place each of the democracies on the two-dimensional conceptual map of democracy shown in Figure 2.1. The horizontal axis represents

[2]   In order to arrive at the average of the five variables in each of the two clusters, they first had to be standardized (so as to have a mean of 0 and a standard deviation of 1), because they were originally measured on quite different scales. After averaging these standardized variables, the resulting averages were standardized again so that each unit on the two axes represents one standard deviation.

Figure 2.1: The Two-Dimensional Conceptual Map of Democracy

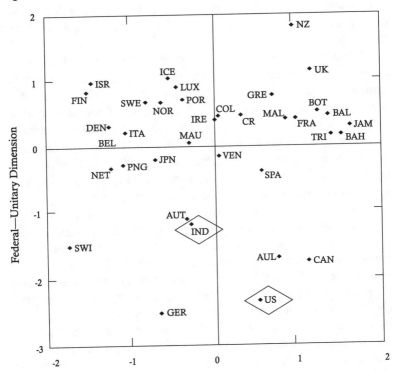

Note: The countries are identified by the first three characters of their
English names, except that AUL means Australia, AUT Austria,
CR Costa Rica, JPN Japan, NZ New Zealand, PNG Papua New
Guinea, UK United Kingdom, and US United States.

Source: Author's own construction based on his earlier work in *Patterns
of Democracy: Government Forms and Performance in Thirty-Six
Countries*, New Haven: Yale University Press, 1999, p. 248,
Fig. 14.1.

the executive–parties dimension and the vertical axis the federal–
unitary dimension. Each unit on these axes represents one
standard deviation; high values indicate majoritarianism and low
values, consensus. Thirty-six countries are included; the period
covered for each country is from the first election after 1945, or
the first election after democratization or re-democratization,

until 1996, which was the cutoff date for my study.[3] India (from re-democratization in 1977 until 1996) and the US (1946–96), the democracies on which this chapter focuses, are highlighted on the map.

Although far away from each other on the geographical map, on the conceptual map India and the US are clearly not very distant from each other. They are both located on the lower—federal— part of the map and, while on different sides of the vertical axis, they are both relatively close to this axis. Only federal Australia and Canada are closer to the US than India is, and federal Germany is approximately equidistant. India is very close to Austria—yet another federal democracy—and surrounded at greater distances by a rough circle of countries that includes the US.

Are India and the US in the 'correct' location in terms of the explanations of why some democracies are more majoritarian and others are more consensus-oriented? There are three causal explanations that emerge from an inspection of the distribution of countries in Figure 2.1 and that are also statistically significant (Lijphart 1999: 250–3). First, there is a clear relationship between the type of democracy and the degree of societal heterogeneity or—to use the term that I shall use henceforth—the degree to which countries are *plural societies*. Countries can be classified as plural, semi-plural, and non-plural societies. This three-fold classification is based on the depth of cleavages between and within ethnic, religious, and other groups and the degree to which these groups differentiate themselves organizationally.

With only one exception, Trinidad and Tobago, the nine plural societies among the thirty-six countries in Figure 2.1 are also linguistically divided. India, with its more than a dozen officially recognized languages is an extreme case, and Papua New Guinea is even more fragmented along linguistic lines. The population of Mauritius is about two-third of Indian and one-third of African descent; the Indian community is a microcosm of the linguistic and religious divisions of India. The other plural societies are Belgium, Canada, Israel, Spain, and Switzerland. I classify the US as semi-plural, as well as Austria, Colombia, Finland, France,

---

[3]   My criteria for inclusion are continuous democracy between 1977 and 1996 and a population size of at least 250,000.

Germany, Italy, Luxembourg, and the Netherlands. The remaining eighteen countries are non-plural—which obviously does not mean that they are completely homogeneous: most of them are religiously divided to at least some extent and most contain one or more small minorities.

In Figure 2.1, as we move from the top right-hand corner to the bottom left-hand corner, we find semi-plural and plural societies with increasing frequency: the more divided countries are likely to be the more consensual and federal democracies. There are some notable exceptions—for instance, plural Trinidad in the upper right-hand quadrant and non-plural Japan in the bottom left-hand quadrant—but in general the relationship is very strong. The second explanation for the location of the democracies on the conceptual map is population size. As we move from the top to the bottom in Figure 2.1, population size tends to go up: on the federal–unitary dimension, smaller countries are likely to be more unitary and larger countries to be more federal. Clearly deviant cases here are the strongly unitary United Kingdom (UK) with its population of around 60 million and a very strongly federal Switzerland with a population of less than 8 million.

The third explanation is the influence of the British political heritage. The countries that have been British colonies or dependencies and the UK itself are mainly located on the right-hand side in Figure 2.1. The most striking exception is Israel, which spurned the Westminster tradition of the former ruler of the Mandate of Palestine. In spite of their British heritage, India, Mauritius, and Papua New Guinea (formerly ruled by Australia, itself a former British colony) are on the left-hand side. What also unites these four countries, however, is that they are plural societies, suggesting that a high degree of pluralism can override the effect of British political traditions.

The first two explanations are also justifications. It makes sense for plural and semi-plural societies to adopt consensual democratic institutions and practices in order to be able to deal with their internal divisions as effectively and peacefully as possible. It also makes more sense for large countries, rather than small ones, to take advantage of federal-type institutions. The third explanation is not a justification: in fact, the British political heritage may well interfere with what countries need on the basis of internal divisions and population size.

In terms of the above three explanations, where would we expect India and the US to be located on the conceptual map of democracy? Because their societies are, respectively, plural and semi-plural, the first explanation predicts that both should be below the diagonal that runs from the top left-hand corner to the bottom right-hand corner; this is the triangle AEG in the stylized version of the conceptual map shown in Figure 2.2. The second explanation predicts that, because they are both large countries, they belong in the bottom half of the map; the rectangle HDEG. And the third explanation predicts that they should be in the right-hand half of the map: rectangle BCEF. All three explanations are satisfied in the small triangle KEF. And it is exactly in this triangle that the US is located, but not India—although India is only just outside the triangle. More relevant is the location predicted by the first two explanations that can also be regarded as justifications; this is the larger area of the trapezoid HKEFG. And India is within this area—in fact, almost exactly in its centre.

The apparent conclusions are that (1) the democratic institutions of both India and the US are appropriate for their population sizes and their internal divisions, (2) these institutions are roughly similar to each other, and (3) consequently, there is not much that the two countries can learn from each other. The first of these tentative conclusions could be stated much more strongly for the case of India: the kinds of democratic institutions it has are more than just appropriate—they are indispensable. India's extremely deep linguistic and religious cleavages make the country, according to John Stuart Mill's judgment cited earlier, a poor candidate for a viable democracy. As I have argued elsewhere, however, its consociational institutions—broadly inclusive cabinets, linguistic federalism, religious autonomy, proportional participation, and minority veto rights—which are very similar to the institutions of consensus democracy, have allowed democracy to survive since 1947 with only the brief interruption of the 1975–7 Emergency (Lijphart 1996). But this should not be taken to mean that India's democratic institutions are ideal and cannot be improved. The same applies to the US. The second and third tentative conclusions are also premature and incomplete, as I shall argue in more detail henceforth.

Figure 2.2: Areas of the Conceptual Map of Democracy where Countries like India and the United States are likely to be located

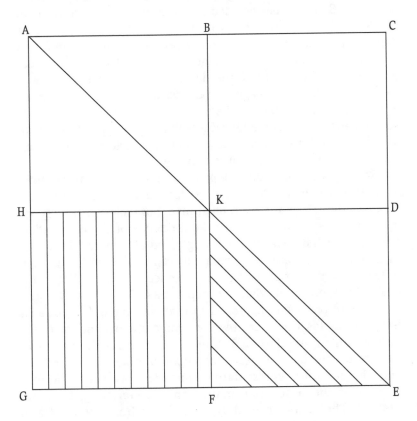

Source: Author's own construction.

MORE DETAILED COMPARISONS: THE FEDERAL–UNITARY DIMENSION

One problem with the three explanations for the placement of India and the US on the conceptual map of democracy is that they predict reasonably well where they are located in relation to the other thirty-four democracies, but much less well where they are located compared with each other. First, since India is a plural society and the US only semi-plural, India should be at a greater distance from the diagonal AKE in Figure 2.2 (or the diagonal from –2,+2 to +2,–2 in Figure 2.1) than the US. But the opposite is true. This discrepancy cannot be resolved by arguing that the US should be regarded as more of a plural society than India. To be sure, American society is highly diverse, but its degree of ethnic, linguistic, and religious pluralism cannot be compared to that of India (Vanhanen 1991: 137–41). A much closer parallel to India would be the nascent EU, especially as far as its many different languages are concerned, but India's religious antagonisms are stronger than western Europe's—and much stronger than those in the US (Rudolph and Rudolph 2002: 53–4). There can be little doubt that among the world's democracies, India is the most extreme plural society.

Second, because India's population is more than three times as large as America's, we would expect India to be below instead of above the US on the conceptual map, but their actual locations are the reverse. Third, because the influence of British political traditions on India was much stronger and also more recent than in the American case, we would expect India to be to the right instead of to the left of the US on the conceptual map—but that is again the opposite of what the map shows.

A more promising approach to resolving these discrepancies is to take a closer look at how the democratic institutions of the two countries are classified. Table 2.1 provides the values of each of the ten basic institutional variables for India and the US, and also for four representative countries located in the four corners of the conceptual map: Canada, Germany, UK, and Finland. The period covered by Table 2.1 is from about 1945 to the middle of 1996 for five of the countries (1946–96 in the case of the US), but from 1977, the end of the Emergency, to mid-1996 for India.

Let us take a look at the federal–unitary dimension first. Of the five variables in this dimension, four are based on relatively rough five-fold or four-fold classifications, from the most federalist to the most unitary characteristics (with values ranging from a high of 5.0 or 4.0 to a low of 1.0). The last variable, the degree of central bank independence, is a more precise measure (ranging in theory from 1 to 0, and in practice from 0.69 to 0.17) designed by several teams of economists. As Table 2.1 shows, the US has a higher federalist score than India on four of the five variables; in fact, on the first four, it has the highest possible score. The one

Table 2.1: Institutional Characteristics of 36 Democracies (Averages) and of India, the United States, Canada, Germany, the United Kingdom, and Finland (c. 1945–96*)

	IND	US	CAN	GER	UK	FIN
Executives–Parties Dimension**	0.29	–0.54	–1.12	0.67	–1.21	1.53
Eff. no. of parl. parties	4.11	2.40	2.37	2.93	2.11	5.03
Min. w. one-p. cab's (%)	52.5	81.2	91.0	36.2	96.7	12.8
Executive dominance	2.08	1.00	4.90	2.82	5.52	1.24
Electoral disprop. (%)	11.38	14.91	11.72	2.52	10.33	2.93
Interest group pluralism	2.30	3.31	3.56	1.38	3.38	1.31
Federal–Unitary Dimension**	1.22	2.36	1.78	2.52	–1.12	–0.84
Federalism/decentral.	4.5	5.0	5.0	5.0	1.0	2.0
Bicameralism	3.0	4.0	3.0	4.0	2.5	1.0
Constitutional rigidity	3.0	4.0	4.0	3.5	1.0	3.0
Judicial review	4.0	4.0	3.3	4.0	1.0	1.0
Central bank indep.	0.35	0.56	0.52	0.69	0.31	0.28

Notes: *The data for India are based on the 1977–96 period.
**High values indicate consensus/federalism and low values majoritarianism/unitary government (the reverse of the, equally arbitrary, signs given to the two dimensions in Figure 2.1).
Source: Based on data in Lijphart 1999, pp. 312–14.

exception is judicial review where both countries are in the category of the strongest and most active judicial review. No one is likely to disagree with this judgment as far as the US is concerned, but it may be somewhat more controversial for India because India's courts were not very assertive in their early days. However, as Carl Baar (1992) argues, from 1977 on, they have become 'the world's most active judiciary' (see also Sorabjee 2000: 177–9). And the Indian Supreme Court is described by Gadbois (1987: 137–8) as 'the closest analogue—not just non-Western analogue—to the American Supreme Court as both a policy-making and politically important institution.'

With regard to bicameralism, constitutional rigidity, and central bank independence, there is no doubt about the accuracy of the higher score for the US either. The two houses of India's parliament are asymmetrical, that is, the Lok Sabha has considerably more power than the Rajya Sabha; and they are only moderately incongruent, that is, the smaller states are given only slightly more representation in the Rajya Sabha than their populations would warrant. In contrast, the US Senate and House of Representatives are almost completely symmetrical in terms of power, and equal state representation in the Senate entails extreme over-representation of the smaller states. Some provisions of India's lengthy Constitution can be changed by regular majorities in both houses, others by absolute majorities of all members of the two houses, and yet others only by two-thirds majorities plus approval by the legislatures of half of the states. The last group contains key provisions like the division of power between central and state governments, and it is the rule for amending these that places the Indian Constitution among the relatively rigid ones. But it is clearly not as rigid as the US Constitution, which is probably the most rigid and difficult Constitution to change in the world. And India's central bank clearly does not have the power and stature of the American 'Fed'.[4]

FEDERALISM IN INDIA AND THE UNITED STATES

I do have serious second thoughts about my scoring of the remaining variable in the federal–unitary dimension: the degree of federalism and decentralization. My five-fold classification is based on an initial distinction between formally federal and formally unitary systems, and I then divide each of these categories into

---

[4]   The 'Fed' is among the world's strongest and most independent banks, together with the Swiss, German, Canadian, and Austrian central banks. The score on this variable for India is an average of two different indices that happen to be in close agreement: an index, designed by Alex Cukierman et al. (1992), representing the legal independence of the central banks (0.34), and an index based on the turnover rate of central bank governors in the 1980s, based on the assumption that a high turnover rate indicates low central bank independence in practice (0.35); see Lijphart 1999, pp. 235–9.

centralized and decentralized subclasses; in practice, most, but not all, federal systems are also relatively decentralized, and most, but not all, unitary systems are relatively centralized. To these four categories I add the intermediate category of semi-federal systems for a few democracies that cannot be unambiguously classified as either federal or unitary.

India and the US are both federal systems, and the US also clearly has a decentralized system of government, which gives it the maximum score of 5.0. However, I judged India to be in an intermediate position between centralization and decentralization and meriting only an intermediate score of 4.5—in line with Wheare's (1964: 28) often cited conclusion that both the Constitution of India and its governmental practices are only 'quasi-federal' instead of fully federal. In particular, the frequent use of so-called President's Rule for partisan purposes detracts from strong federalism: the Constitution gives the central government the right to dismiss state governments and to replace them with direct rule from the centre for the purpose of dealing with grave emergencies, but in practice President's Rule has been used mainly by the central government to remove state governments controlled by other parties and to call new state elections in the hope of winning these (Tummala 1996: 378–82).

The intermediate category of semi-federal systems (with a score of 3.0), mentioned earlier, includes countries like Spain, which has granted extensive autonomy to Catalonia, the Basque Country, and Galicia, and later to other regions as well, without, however, becoming a formally federal state. It also includes democracies that Robert A. Dahl has called 'sociologically federal' (cited in Verba 1967: 126), and which may also be called non-territorially federal, like the Netherlands, Belgium, and Israel. The central governments of these countries have long recognized, heavily subsidized, and delegated power to private associations with important semi-public functions, especially in the fields of education and culture, established by the major religious and ideological groups in these societies. This description also fits India in two important respects: not only as far as educational autonomy is concerned but also with regard to the system of separate 'personal laws'—laws on marriage, divorce, custody and adoption of children, and inheritance—for different religious groups. India can therefore be considered both formally federal and 'sociologically' federal.

The crucial feature of educational autonomy is not just the right of religious groups, and religious minorities in particular, to set up and run their own schools, but the ability to make this right effective through full government financial support of these schools. Dutch and Belgian religious minorities had to fight hard to obtain this right, and, while full educational autonomy was granted in the Netherlands in 1917, it was not instituted in Belgium until 1958. In India, however, the Constitution provided this right from the outset. Article 30 states that 'all minorities, whether based on religion or language, shall have the right to establish and administer educational institutions of their choice', and more important, that 'the State shall not, in granting aid to educational institutions, discriminate against any educational institution on the ground that it is under the management of a minority, whether based on religion or language.' In the US, the principle of separation of church and state has prevented the development of this kind of educational autonomy.

Separate personal laws for Hindus, Muslims, and smaller religious minorities already existed under British rule, and they were carried forward and sometimes amended or replaced by similar new laws in independent India. Examples are the 1955 Hindu Marriage Act, the 1956 Hindu Succession (that is, inheritance) Act, the 1937 Muslim Personal Law (Shariat) Application Act, the 1939 Dissolution of Muslim Marriages Act, and the 1872 Indian Christian Marriage Act (Fyzee 1964; Engineer 1987). These statutes were enacted by parliamentary majorities but, when intended for one of the minorities, were drafted in conformity with the minority's wishes. For instance, after the controversial 1985 Shah Bano decision by the Supreme Court (involving the right of a divorced Muslim woman to financial support from her former husband), a new Muslim Women (Protection of Right on Divorce) Act was adopted in 1986, largely in line with the wishes of the Muslim Personal Law Board. And the new 1993 Christian Marriage Act was proposed by the government after extensive consultations with and the final approval of all Christian churches.

The Constituent Assembly explicitly considered the question of whether separate personal laws ought to be continued in independent, democratic India. An amendment to the draft Constitution was proposed that would have ended this form of religious autonomy: 'The Union or the State shall not undertake any legislation or pass any law ... applicable to some particular community or communities and no other' (cited in Luthera 1964: 83). Significantly, such a clause was *not* included in the Constitution. A year later, law minister B.R. Ambedkar, replying to accusations of discrimination on the ground of religion during a parliamentary debate, again emphatically endorsed the principle of minority personal laws: 'The Constitution permits us to treat different communities differently and if we treat them differently, nobody can charge the Government with practising discrimination' (cited in Luthera 1964: 86).

There is no direct parallel to these personal laws in the US, although it is worth noting that laws concerning marriage, divorce, adoption, inheritance, and so on are mainly state rather than federal laws in the US, and that they can be quite different in different states. For example, the right of first cousins to marry each other and the right of lesbians and gays to adopt their partners' children diverge from state to state to an extreme extent. The one state that has a high concentration of members of a small religious minority—Utah, where Mormons make up about 70 per cent of the population and about 90 per cent of the state legislature—effectively bans such adoptions. So do Florida and Mississippi. By contrast, three states specifically allow lesbians and gays to adopt their partners' children: California, Connecticut, and Vermont. Most other states take intermediate positions on this matter (Goode 2002). Utah is one of five states that permit first-cousin marriages only when these couples will not bear children; two states have other restrictions, and twenty-four states ban first-cousin marriages entirely. In contrast, nineteen states allow it without any restrictions (Grady 2002). But, of course, Utah's state laws and those of any other state are subject to overall federal constitutional principles, and personal laws adopted by the state cannot violate, for instance, the 'equal protection' clause of the US Constitution. It is also worth noting that marriage ceremonies in the US are commonly conducted by religious functionaries, and that such marriages have full legal effect.

In addition to India's formal, territorial federalism being supplemented with non-territorial sociological federalism, its territorial federalism is also particularly significant because it does much more than decentralize power: state and linguistic boundaries coincide to a large extent, and India's federal system thus provides a high degree of autonomy for the many linguistic groups in the country—as the similar linguistic federalism does in Belgium, Canada, and Switzerland. The British colonial rulers of India drew the administrative divisions of the country without much regard for linguistic or cultural cohesion. The Congress movement was opposed to this policy and committed itself to a thorough redrawing of the boundaries along linguistic lines; from 1921 onwards, it also based its own organization on linguistically homogeneous units, the so-called Pradesh Committees. Jawaharlal Nehru and other Congress leaders had second thoughts, however, and the Constituent Assembly, following the advice of its Linguistic Provinces Commission, decided not to incorporate the linguistic principle into the new Constitution.

Pressures from below forced a complete change of policy in the 1950s. After the state of Madras was divided into the separate Tamil-speaking and Telugu-speaking states of Tamil Nadu and Andhra Pradesh in 1953, the States Reorganization Commission embraced the linguistic principle and recommended drastic revisions in state boundaries along linguistic lines in 1955. These were quickly implemented in 1956, followed by the creation of several additional states in later years. The leadership's initial fears that linguistic federalism would strengthen fissiparous tendencies[5] have not been realized, and India's linguistic federalism is now regarded as largely successful by most observers. In the words of Rajni Kothari (1970: 115), the 'rationalizing [of] the political map of India' has made language 'a cementing and integrating influence' instead of a 'force for division.'

A third special feature of India's federalism is that it is a dynamic and flexible instrument that has been used more and more for the purpose of giving autonomy to other types of minorities, too. The new state of Punjab was formed in 1966 for

---

[5]   Such fears have also been expressed by social scientists who have argued that democratic stability depends on cross-cutting cleavages and therefore also requires that federal boundaries cut across ethnic and linguistic boundaries (see especially, Lipset 1960). In addition to India, good examples of the beneficial effect that the coincidence of federal and ethnic-linguistic can have are Switzerland, Belgium, Canada, and Nigeria (Lijphart 1995, pp. 861–2).

both linguistic and religious reasons. In the 1970s and 1980s, several new states were created, especially in the northeast of the country, for ethnic groups that did not have a separate linguistic identity. And in one recent year, 2000, three more new states of this kind were carved out of the existing large states of Uttar Pradesh, Bihar, and Madhya Pradesh.

The above three special aspects of the Indian federal system—sociological, linguistic, and dynamic federalism—make the system unusually meaningful and significant. In retrospect, therefore, I think that I made a mistake when I did not credit India with the highest federal ranking of 5.0—the same that I gave to the US (see Table 2.1). I moved Israel, the Netherlands, and Belgium (before it became a federal state in 1993) from one of the unitary categories, with values of 1.0 and 2.0, to the intermediate semi-federal category with a value of 3.0 on account of their sociological federalism. For the same reason, India should have been upgraded from 4.5 to the maximum of 5.0, or possibly even an above-scale 5.5 or 6.0. This would have given India a higher overall federalist score and would have moved it to a slightly lower location on the conceptual map of democracy in Figure 2.1, but not as far down as the US because of the latter's higher scores on bicameralism, constitutional rigidity, and central bank independence.

FEDERAL COMPARISONS AND PRACTICAL LESSONS

Do the above comparisons yield any practical lessons that the world's two largest democracies, which are also the largest federal democracies, can learn from each other? Linguistic federalism is not a relevant option for the US because it has one dominant language and because its small minority linguistic groups are not geographically concentrated. Neither is the possibility of separate personal laws for different religious groups, although, as already noted, personal laws do differ from state to state in the US. On this issue, however, India may be able to learn a lesson from the American example of state autonomy combined with federal constitutional supremacy: a possible compromise between Indians who want to maintain separate personal laws in their present status and those who seek to replace them with a uniform civil code would be their retention with the proviso that basic civil rights, especially the principle of equality, cannot be infringed, and that the Supreme Court, or possibly some kind of special tribunal, will have the authority to decide on alleged violations of these rights (Bhargava 2000; Hasan 2000).

India's model of sociological federalism in the form of educational autonomy for religious and other groups is a model that is worth considering seriously by the US. I may be especially sympathetic to this model because I have personally observed its very successful operation in the Netherlands—perhaps a more persuasive model for the US because the Netherlands, unlike India, is a mainly Christian nation. Instituted in 1917, it gave all schools, public and private, equal financial support from the state in proportion to their enrolments. Although the new law was primarily designed to accommodate the main religious groups (Catholics and Protestants) and their religious schools, it was formulated in neutral language and allowed any group to establish and run schools as long as basic educational standards would be observed. As a result, it has also long been taken advantage of by small secular groups interested in particular educational philosophies to establish, for instance, Montessori schools. More recently, quite a few non-Christian religious schools have also been set up: about thirty Muslim, six Hindu, and a few other non-Christian schools. The law maintains the state's neutrality with regard to religion just as much as the principle of the separation of church and state does, but in a manner that is fairer and more sensitive to minority concerns.

Because federal systems are particularly suitable for large and diverse countries, should India try to emulate the US with regard to the three federalist aspects on which the US is more strongly federal? The answer is probably yes as far as central bank independence is concerned. Especially in the last fifteen years or so, most scholars and policy-makers have come to agree that strong central banks are essential for sound monetary policy, and many democracies have strengthened their central banks a great deal, notably the UK where until 1997 the Bank of England used to be a subservient branch of the executive. The new central bank created by the EU is among the world's strongest and most independent central banks. India has already given its central bank greater independence since the early days of independence. Alex Cukierman and his collaborators (1992: 387) give India an 0.25 score on legal central bank independence in the 1950s, but a higher rating of 0.34 for the 1960s, 1970s, and 1980s. However, in comparison with other democracies, and especially with other federal democracies, this is still a relatively weak score.[6]

As far as bicameralism and judicial review are concerned, we should not jump to the conclusion that more is necessarily better. One aspect of strong bicameralism in federal systems is the over-representation of small states in the federal chamber of the legislature—which can be justified on the basis of the federal principle that states as well as individuals deserve political representation, but which also violates the principle of one-person, one-vote to at least some extent. In the US, over-representation in the Senate has become extreme: in 1996, 50 per cent of the most favourably represented voters (those in the smaller states) elected 83.8 per cent of the US Senators. The corresponding figure for the Rajya Sabha in India is only 56.8 per cent (Lijphart 1999: 208).

The best compromise between the conflicting federal and democratic principles, it seems to me, is to have some, but not too much over-representation for small states. Certainly, the federal principle that states should be represented does not mandate *equal* state representation (Stepan 2001: 341–3). In addition to India, examples of modest over-representation but not equal representation are Germany, Canada, and Austria. If the Indian model appears to be too radical for the US, the German model may be more suitable: each German *Land* has a minimum of three and a maximum of six members in the *Bundesrat*, depending on the size of its population.[7]

The second aspect of strong bicameralism is symmetrical bicameralism, meaning that the two houses of the legislature have

6   As already indicated in note 4, the 0.35 rating for India in Table 2.1 is an average in which the Cukierman *et al.* (1992) score is one of two components. The highest Cukierman *et al.* rating is for federal Germany: 0.69 (which is also the average score for Germany in Table 2.1). No similar ratings are available for the 1990s, but the second index for India—based on the turnover rate of central bank governors— was the same in the 1990s as in the 1980s: there were three turnovers in each decade.

7   My advice may be influenced by the fact that I am a severely under- represented Californian: California has more than 10 per cent of the total population of the US, but only 2 per cent representation in the Senate.

equal power. This is a rare occurrence in modern democracies: usually, the first chamber or lower house is more powerful than the second chamber or upper (federal) chamber, as is the case in India. The US Congress is an exception, not only because its two houses are roughly equal in power but also because the Senate is arguably even somewhat more important than the House of Representatives as a result of its special powers over treaties and appointments. There is one crucial reason why the American model is not appropriate for India. In a parliamentary system, it may be very difficult to form and maintain a cabinet if the cabinet has to have the confidence of each of two different chambers, if these chambers, as is usually the case in federal democracies, are also differently constituted. Therefore, symmetrical bicameralism is perfectly appropriate for a federal democracy that is also a presidential system like the US, but not for a federal and parliamentary system like India.

For amending the constitutions of both India and the US (in the Indian case, the most important provisions of the constitution), the first step is approval by two-thirds majorities in both houses of the national legislature; however, the second step is significantly different in the two countries: approval by half of the state legislatures in India versus three-fourths of the states in the US. As a result of this difference, the Indian Constitution has been amended much more frequently than the American Constitution. Which rule is preferable? First, it is worth emphasizing again that more is not necessarily better, because this would mean that the best Constitution would be a completely rigid and unamendable— something that no constitutional expert would advocate. Second, if institutional reforms are desirable in the two countries, as I argue in this chapter, then it is better to have moderate instead of extreme constitutional rigidity.

Finally, as already noted, both India and the US have a strong and active judicial review, and I have classified both of them in the highest category (see Table 2.1). Within this category, there are still significant differences. In particular, the German Constitutional Court has been extremely activist: from 1951 to 1990, it invalidated almost 5 per cent of all federal laws (Landfried 1995: 308). The Supreme Courts of India and the US have operated well below this excessive degree of judicial activism, although during the 1990s the conservative US Supreme Court majority has become increasingly activist; indeed, many critics have faulted it for its imperious and arrogant stance on many controversial issues, typified by the blatantly partisan Bush v. Gore decision in December 2000 (Dershowitz 2001).

A related issue is the respective sizes of the two courts: twenty-six justices in India (since 1986) but only nine in the US (since the late nineteenth century). There is a curious discrepancy in American democracy between the principle of divided and limited power that is embodied in having a strong High Court with the right of judicial review on one hand and a high degree of concentration of power within the court on the other. Power is concentrated in only nine justices—and frequently in a five-member court majority—who, moreover, enjoy life tenure. The considerably larger Indian Supreme Court with justices who have to retire at age sixty-five appears to be the wiser and more balanced approach. Larger court membership also offers better opportunities for broad representation of different ethnic and religious groups in heterogeneous societies.

MORE DETAILED COMPARISONS: THE EXECUTIVES–PARTIES DIMENSION

Let us now turn to an examination of the executive–parties dimension. On this dimension, as Table 2.1 shows, India is more consensual with regard to all except one of the variables. The differences between the two countries that appear in the table are roughly in accordance with the judgments of knowledgeable observers; therefore, we do not need to go into all of the complexities of operationalization and the exact details of the measurements.

The one variable on which the US is more consensual than India is executive dominance. The American system of executive-legislative relations is one of overall balance, not so much because the president is a weak executive as because Congress is an extraordinarily strong legislature; the US Congress and the Swiss parliament can be regarded as the world's two strongest national legislatures. Compared with the US, India has a clearly stronger executive (cabinet) and weaker legislative branch.

The more striking difference with regard to executive–legislative relations between the two countries is that India has a parliamentary and the US a presidential system of government. Juan Linz's (1990, 1994) indictment of presidentialism has found strong support among comparative politics experts. He argues that presidential democracy is prone to failure because of serious institutional deficiencies such as the fixed terms of office which make the government very rigid, the tendency to executive–legislative deadlock, and paralysis resulting from the coexistence of two branches that are separately elected and can both claim democratic legitimacy, the zero-sum or winner-take-all nature of presidential elections, and the encouragement of the politics of personality instead of a politics of competing parties and party programmes. Both the winner-take-all rule and the fact that executive power is concentrated in one person are serious obstacles to minority representation in divided societies. The US has never had an African-American, Hispanic, female, or Jewish president, and only one Catholic president. Presidential government has its advocates in India (see Noorani 1989; Sathe 1991; Kashyap 1993), but this aspect of the American system is clearly not a good model for India to follow.

With regard to the effective number of parliamentary parties (a measure that takes both the number of parties and their sizes into consideration, counting large parties more heavily than small ones), the averages in Table 2.1 show that India has a multiparty system and the US close to a two-party system.[8] What the Indian average conceals is that, beginning with the 1989 election, the party system has been transformed from a dominant-party system to a multiparty system and, in comparative terms, a rather extreme multiparty system (deSouza 2000: 211–16). The first and second columns of Table 2.2 show the effective numbers of parties separately for the years before and after 1989. Because the table also updates this information to the middle of 2001, these two periods are roughly equal in length: 1977–89 and 1989–2001. The third column reports the figures for the entire twenty-four-year period from 1977 to 2001; and, for purposes of comparison, the

[8]   In computing the effective number of parties, I also made an adjustment for uncohesive and/or factionalized parties, such as the Congress party in India and the Democrats in the US, counting such parties as, roughly, one-and-a-half parties. This explains why the effective number of parties in the US is 2.40 in Table 2.1 instead of the approximately 2.00 that one would expect in an almost pure two-party system.

fourth and fifth columns repeat the information on India and the US from Table 2.1. The average number of 5.66 parties in the five elections in the more recent period is approximately twice the average of 2.82 in the three elections in the earlier period.

Table 2.2: Effective Numbers of Political Parties, Minimal Winning One-Party Cabinets (Per Cent), and Electoral Disproportionality in India and the United States in Various Periods

	India 1977–89 (three elections)	India 1989–2001 (five elections)	India 1977–2001	India 1977–96	US 1946–96
Eff. no. of parl. parties	2.82	5.66	4.60	4.11	2.40
Min. w. one-p. cab's (%)	58.4	23.4	41.7	52.5	81.2
Electoral disprop. (%)	15.56	7.41	10.47	11.38	14.91

Source: Based on data in Lijphart 1999, pp. 312–14, election results reported by the Election Commission of India, and information provided by E. Sridharan.

At the same time, minority cabinets (which are counted as the equivalents of oversized cabinets because of their similar inter-party bargaining patterns) and coalition cabinets have become more and more common in India: the proportion of minimal winning one-party cabinets declined from 58.4 to 23.4 per cent, as Table 2.2 shows. In contrast, the much higher score for American cabinets, 81.2 per cent, reflects the fact that they are almost always purely one-party cabinets and often also majority (minimal winning) cabinets, except in periods of 'divided government' when the presidency and one or both houses of Congress are controlled by different parties. Neither the Indian nor the American interest group system can be called corporatist, but India is at least somewhat more corporatist, notably in the field of agriculture.

Elections and Electoral Systems in India and the United States

The big differences in the Indian and American party systems and types of cabinets are surprising because such differences tend to be driven by differences in the electoral system; Duverger's Law, mentioned earlier, predicts that plurality first-past-the-post (FPTP) systems will lead to two-party systems and one-party majority government, whereas PR tends to produce multiparty systems and coalition or minority cabinets—but both India and the US use FPTP electoral systems! Moreover, as the last three columns of Table 2.2 show, overall electoral disproportionality is lower in India, both in the 1977–96 period and in the somewhat longer 1977–2001 period, than in the US, but the difference is not great. PR systems typically yield electoral disproportionalities between about 1 and 4 per cent, and the Indian and American percentages are well above 10 per cent. Here again, however, the overall percentages for India conceal major differences between the 1977–89 and 1989–2001 period. The 15.56 per cent disproportionality in the three elections in the earlier period was more than twice as high as the 7.41 per cent in the five elections of the later period, mainly because from 1989 on there was no longer a party that benefited from extreme over-representation. But the 7.41 per cent is, of course, still considerably higher than what PR systems tend to produce.

My measure of disproportionality is the index proposed by Michael Gallagher (1991). It calculates the difference between the vote share and seat share of each party and then averages these differences in such a way that large deviations are counted much more heavily than small ones. The disproportionality of PR elections tends to be not only lower than that of FPTP elections but also tends to vary little from election to election. In contrast, the disproportionality of FPTP elections tends to vary a great deal. In the Indian elections from 1977 to 1999, the highest disproportionality was 18.76 per cent in 1984 and the lowest was 6.30 in 1991.

The American case is more complicated: because the US is a presidential system, the American index of disproportionality is based on both House of Representatives elections and presidential elections. The former tends to be relatively low in spite of the FPTP election method: an average of 4.90 in the 1946–94 congressional elections, with a high of 9.23 and a low of 0.50 per cent. The main explanation of this unusual phenomenon is the existence of primary elections in the US; primaries are an almost exclusively American phenomenon, almost never used in other democracies. In most FPTP systems, a major portion of the disproportionality of elections is caused by small parties that remain unrepresented or are severely under-represented; there are very few of these in the US because primary elections give strong incentives for dissidents to try their luck in one of the major party primaries instead of establishing separate small parties. In addition, state laws tend to discriminate against small parties (Lawson 1987). However, its presidential elections give the US a high overall level of disproportionality after all. Presidential elections are inherently disproportional because the winning candidate wins a 100 per cent seat share—that is, the one 'seat' that is at stake—with a vote share rarely exceeding 55 to 60 per cent, and the US is no exception.

One may well argue that both the Indian and the American electoral disproportionalities are overstated because they are concerned exclusively with the representation of political parties. What is arguably more important in plural and semi-plural societies is the representation of ethnic, religious, and other minorities, and both India and the US have special rules in their electoral systems to provide for the representation of specified minorities and, in particular, the minorities that have suffered the greatest discrimination: the SCs (untouchables) in India and African-Americans in the US (Vanhanen 1991: 135–7). India has used a system of 'reserved seats' for the SCs and STs ever since its first national election in 1951–2: in about a fifth of the parliamentary election districts, only members of these groups are allowed to be candidates, thus guaranteeing that a member of the specified group is elected (Sridharan 2002b). The comparable method in the US, since the late 1960s, has been 'affirmative gerrymandering': drawing election districts in such a way that African-Americans or Hispanics constitute majorities in these districts, which makes the election of representatives belonging to these ethnic minorities more likely.

ELECTORAL SYSTEM COMPARISONS AND PRACTICAL LESSONS

Reserved seats and affirmative gerrymandering are examples of what I have called attempts to achieve 'proportionality by non-PR methods' in a previous study (Lijphart 1986). What such methods promise is the best of both worlds: both minority representation and the advantages of more effective decision-making and greater accountability offered by FPTP. But it is a promise on which they cannot deliver. First of all, they are meant to counter discrimination but are themselves inherently discriminatory in the sense of giving advantages only to certain specified groups to the exclusion of all other minority groups. In contrast, the beauty of PR is not only that it provides proportionality and minority representation, but that it allows *any* minority to be represented and that it is therefore completely even-handed, non-discriminatory, and flexible. Moreover, time appears to be running out for affirmative gerrymandering in the US. In the most recent significant Supreme Court decision—*Easley* v. *Cromartie* in April 2001—only five of the nine justices found it to be constitutional, and then only as long as race was only one factor, and not the predominant factor, in deciding how the district boundaries were drawn. In the longer run, it would therefore be much wiser for African-American and Latino political leaders to support the adoption of PR in congressional elections, as proposed, for instance, by the US Representatives Cynthia McKinney and Mel Watt.

That the advantages of FPTP and two-party systems have been greatly overrated is becoming more and more widely acknowledged. Lowell's (1896: 70–4) 'axiom in politics' that FPTP, two-party systems, and one-party majority governments are needed for effective policy-making was not questioned for many decades, but is certainly no longer the unchallenged conventional wisdom. The comparative empirical evidence shows, for instance, the majoritarian democracies are not at all better at macro-economic decision-making and the control of violence than consensus democracies (Lijphart 1999: 258–74). There remains the undoubtedly important question of accountability and identifiability, and here, almost by definition, FPTP, two-party systems, and one-party cabinets have the edge. If one party is in power and has a governing majority, it can be given credit or blame for specific policies and also for how successfully government policies are implemented. When there are coalition cabinets and/or minority cabinets, it is obviously much more difficult to identify who is responsible.

However, the critical questions that should be asked are: what is the purpose of accountability, and does the greater accountability in majoritarian systems achieve this purpose? The primary purpose, clearly, is to keep the government in line with voters' preferences. But when the relative distances between governments and the median voters are measured on a left–right scale, it turns out that the distance is actually smaller—to a statistically significant degree—in consensus than in majoritarian democracies (Lijphart 1999: 287–8; Powell 2000). Another problem with the accountability argument is that, while in majoritarian democracies it is easy to identify the incumbent one-party government as the agent responsible for government policy, it is in practice difficult for the voters—that is, for the majority of the voters—to remove this government. In Britain since 1945, for instance, all re-elected governments were re-elected in spite of the fact that majorities of the voters voted for opposition parties. An even more serious, albeit relatively rare, problem is that a government can be elected or re-elected in spite of having received fewer votes than its main rival, as happened in Britain in 1951, in New Zealand in 1978 and 1981, and in the US in 2000.

Furthermore, as Moosbrugger (2001) points out, the accountability of one-party majority governments is a two-edged sword: it allows citizens to know and judge who is responsible for government policies but it also provides a clear and tempting target for interest-group pressure. Therefore, especially when special interests are strong and well-organized and when the public interest has only weakly organized defenders, it may be easier for multiparty coalition governments with their diffuse accountability to make decisions favouring the public interest over special interests than it is for highly accountable one-party governments.

Finally, all of the pro-FPTP arguments apply more to an idealized version of majoritarian democracy than to real-world cases of FPTP-based systems such as India and the US. In the latter, responsibility for government policy can rarely be assigned to specific parties because of the separation of powers, frequent divided government, and the uncohesiveness of the two major parties. In India, FPTP has not led to one-party majority governments in recent years, and India can therefore be said to be saddled with the disadvantages of both FPTP and PR: high electoral disproportionality and also coalition and minority cabinets. Moreover, as Sridharan (2002a) has argued, coalitions under PR are likely to be more stable and effective than coalitions in an FPTP system under PR:

Partner parties in a coalition need not fear that a shift in popular support (future vote share) towards one of their partners will decimate them in terms of seats...However, in the FPTP system, a relatively small shift in vote share can provoke a huge shift in seats. This will inevitably create a much great degree of tension between coalition partners in an FPTP system than under PR..., and hence make for the greater instability of such coalitions.

As far as the electoral system is concerned, the two large democracies can learn more from the smaller democracies than from each other. Among the thirty-six democracies studied in my *Patterns of Democracy* (Lijphart 1999), the next largest, Japan, uses a combination of FPTP and PR, and twenty-two of the remaining thirty-three democracies use PR; when we exclude the eight smallest of these countries (with populations under two million), PR is used by nineteen out of twenty-five democracies. Most experts agree with the following conclusion by Diamond (1999: 104; see also Vanhanen 1987):

If any generalization about institutional design is sustainable..., it is that majoritarian systems are ill-advised for countries with deep ethnic, regional, religious, or other emotional and polarizing divisions. Where cleavage groups are sharply defined and group identities (and intergroup insecurities and suspicions) deeply felt, the overriding imperative is to avoid broad and indefinite exclusion from power of any significant group.

The only major scholarly dissenter is Horowitz (1991) who advocates a majority-preferential (alternative vote) system as used for the election of the federal House of Representatives in Australia. But his arguments have not found much scholarly support; only Australian political scientist Benjamin Reilly (2001) has come to his defence— and only with significant qualifications.[9] It is also worth noting that, while Horowitz is critical of PR, he is equally critical of FPTP. In fact, I cannot think of even one major comparative politics expert who explicitly believes in the superiority of FPTP for divided societies.

A major obstacle to the adoption of PR by India and the US is the strength of the British political heritage in both countries. However, both countries have at least some experience with the single transferable vote (STV) form of PR. It is used in India for the election of the Rajya Sabha by members of the state legislative

---

[9]   For instance, Reilly (2001) dissents from Horowitz's (1991) advocacy of the alternative vote for the key case of South Africa.

assemblies. In the US, it has been used for local elections in about a dozen cities, including New York City and Cincinnati, and is currently still used in Cambridge, Massachusetts. New Zealand's shift from FPTP to PR in 1996 shows that British traditions are not an insuperable obstacle. And even in Britain itself, PR is no longer a rarity: it was introduced for Northern Ireland elections in the 1970s, and its use has recently been extended to the election of the Scottish and Welsh regional assemblies, the London city council, and the British representatives to the European Parliament.

The British political heritage may be more difficult to overcome in India and the US because large countries tend to be inward-looking and self-absorbed. One example is that American political scientists who are experts on American government tend to react with horror to the suggestion that PR should be introduced because they fear that PR and multipartism would set American racial, ethnic, and other groups apart from and against each other—apparently oblivious of the fact that comparativists have found the opposite to be the general pattern. Institutional conservatism can also be bolstered by constitutional rigidity. Abolishing the US presidential college—the last such electoral college (in presidential and semi-presidential systems) in the world after Finland and Argentina abolished theirs in the early 1990s—will be very difficult because of the two-thirds and three-fourths requirements for constitutional amendment as well as the over-representation of small states in the Senate.

On the other hand, there is no constitutional rule that mandates FPTP and that prohibits PR for the election of the House of Representatives. Representative Cynthia McKinney's proposal, the Voters' Choice Act, referred to earlier, is to amend the congressional statute that requires single-member districts, and to allow states to use multi-member districts if they apply PR or semi-proportional systems in these districts. Her plan envisages the gradual introduction of PR, first in some states and then in others—a possibility that is clearly permitted by the Constitution and that appears to be an additional favourable factor for the introduction of PR. Mel Watt's Choice of Voting Systems Act is a similar proposal. The only constitutional limitation is that the seats in the House of Representatives are apportioned to the states (Article I, Section II), that PR requires at least two and preferably more seats per district, and that seven small states have only one representative and therefore can only be single-member non-PR districts. But the same pattern occurs in other mainly PR countries, such as Switzerland where the smallest cantons constitute single-member non-PR districts for the election of the National Council. The resistance to PR in the US can clearly not be blamed on the rigidity of the Constitution—which leaves us with the paradox that the US is a highly dynamic and innovative society but has an extremely static and conservative political culture.

The Constitution of India is also largely silent on the issue of FPTP versus PR. The election clauses (Articles 324–29) do not mention the electoral method at all. The earlier Article 81, which deals with the composition of the Lok Sabha, presents a slight obstacle to PR in that it prescribes that members be elected from 'territorial constituencies in the States,' and that 'each State shall be divided into territorial constituencies'; the use of the plural 'constituencies' implies that there have to be at least two election districts per state; therefore small states with only two representatives must have two single-member non-PR districts instead of one two-member PR district. On the other hand, Article 81 also stipulates that the districts be drawn 'in such a manner that the ratio between the population of each constituency and *the number of seats allotted to it* is, so far as practicable, the same throughout the State' (emphasis added)—which implies that multi-member districts are permissible. And, of course, two-member as well as a few three-member districts—but not PR districts—were in fact used in the 1951–2 and 1957 elections (Sridharan 2002b).

Although I have no serious doubts about the desirability of PR elections in India and the US, I do recognize that many people have strong objections to it, or are at least nervous about it. I also recognize that even a slight degree of risk is worth worrying about when fundamental changes are proposed for the democratic process in such very large countries as India and the US. Two specific features can be offered to meet the most serious objections. First, PR comes in many shapes and forms, and it would make sense for both India and the US to be cautious and not to adopt the most extreme—that is, the most highly proportional—form of PR. For instance, it would make sense to introduce PR in multi-member districts that are not overly large, such as using the smaller states as electoral districts and dividing the larger states into two or more districts, and certainly to avoid using the entire country as one large district (as Israel and the Netherlands do). Another useful rule in this respect would be to adopt an electoral threshold of say 3 or 4 per cent. Second, instead of introducing PR elections for the entire Lok Sabha in India and the entire US House of Representatives, why not follow the lead of the McKinney and Watt proposals and experiment with PR elections in just one or a few states as a first step?

Sir Arthur Lewis (1965: 55), whom I cited in the beginning of this chapter as the intellectual father of consociational theory and strong advocate of PR and coalition government for divided societies, aptly compares the effect of the British FPTP and two-party traditions to brainwashing. And he ruefully concludes that countries burdened with this heritage 'will need much un-brainwashing before they grasp their problems in true perspective'. Lewis was thinking mainly of the West African countries that he was familiar with, but his conclusion applies just as much to India and the US.

REFERENCES

Baar, Carl, 'Social Action Litigation in India: The Operation and Limits of the World's Most Active Judiciary', in Donald W. Jackson and C. Neal Tate, eds, *Comparative Judicial Review and Public Policy*, Westport, Conn.: Greenwood, 1992, pp. 77–87.

Bhargava, Rajeev, 'Do Muslims Have a Right to Their Personal Laws?', in Peter Ronald deSouza, ed., *Contemporary India—Transitions*, New Delhi: Sage Publications, 2000, pp. 182–202.

Crepaz, Markus M. L. 'Global, Constitutional, and Partisan Determinants of Redistribution in Fifteen OECD Countries', *Comparative Politics*, vol. 34 (2) January 2002, pp. 169–88.

Cukierman, Alex, Steven B. Webb, and Bilin Neyapti, 'Measuring the Independence of Central Banks and Its Effect on Policy Outcomes', *The World Bank Economic Review*, vol. 6 (3) September 1992, pp. 353–98.

Dershowitz, Alan M., *Supreme Injustice: How the High Court Hijacked Election 2000*, New York: Oxford University Press, 2001.

deSouza, Peter Ronald, 'Elections, Parties and Democracy in India', in Peter Ronald deSouza, ed., *Contemporary India–Transitions*, New Delhi: Sage Publications, 2000, pp. 203–19.

Diamond, Larry, *Developing Democracy: Toward Consolidation*, Baltimore: Johns Hopkins University Press, 1999.

Duchacek, Ivo D., *Comparative Federalism: The Territorial Dimension of Politics*, New York: Holt, Rinehart, and Winston, 1970.

Duverger, Maurice, *Political Parties: Their Organization and Activity in the Modern State*, 3rd edn, London: Methuen, 1964.

Elazar, Daniel J., 'Federalism', in David L. Sills ed., *International Encyclopedia of the Social Sciences*, vol. 5, New York: Macmillan and Free Press, 1968, pp. 353–67.

Engineer, Asghar Ali, ed., *The Shah Bano Controversy,* Hyderabad: Orient Longman, 1987.

Friedrich, Carl J., *Constitutional Government and Democracy*, revised edn., Boston: Ginn, 1950.

Fyzee, Asaf A.A., *Outlines of Muhammadan Law*, 3rd edn, London: Oxford University Press, 1964.

Gadbois, George H., Jr., 'The Institutionalization of the Supreme Court of India', in John R. Schmidhauser, ed., *Comparative Judicial Systems: Challenging Frontiers in Conceptual and Empirical Analysis*, London: Butterworths, 1987, pp. 111–42.

Gallagher, Michael, 'Proportionality, Disproportionality and Electoral Systems', *Electoral Studies*, vol. 10 (1) March 1991, pp. 33–51.

Goode, Erica, 'Group Backs Gays Who Seek to Adopt a Partner's Child', *New York Times,* 4 February 2002, A1, A19.

Grady, Denise, 'Few Risks Seen to the Children of 1st Cousins', *New York Times,* 4 April 2002, A1, A16.

Hasan, Zoya, 'Uniform Civil Code and Gender Justice in India', in Peter Ronald deSouza, ed., *Contemporary India—Transitions*, New Delhi: Sage Publications, 2000, pp. 282–301.

Horowitz, Donald L., *A Democratic South Africa? Constitutional Engineering in a Divided Society*, Berkeley: University of California Press, 1991.

Huntington, Samuel P., T*he Third Wave: Democratization in the Late Twentieth Century,* Norman: University of Oklahoma Press, 1991.

Huyse, Lucien, P*assiviteit, pacificatie en verzuiling in de Belgische politiek: Een sociologische studie*, Antwerp: Standaard Wetenschappelijke Uitgeverij, 1970.

Kashyap, Subhash C., ed., P*erspectives on the Constitution*, Delhi: Shipra, 1993.

Katzenstein, Peter J., *Small States in World Markets: Industrial Policy in Europe*, Ithaca: Cornell University Press, 1985.

Kothari, Rajni, *Politics in India,* Boston: Little Brown, 1970.

Landfried, Christine, 'Germany', in C. Neal Tate and Torbjörn Vallinder, eds, *The Global Expansion of Judicial Power,* New York: New York University Press, 1995, pp. 307–24.

Lawson, Kay, 'How State Laws Undermine Parties', in A. James Reichley, ed., *Elections American Style,* Washington DC: Brookings Institution, 1987, pp. 240–60.

Lehmbruch, Gerhard, *Proporzdemokratie: Politisches System und politische Kultur in der Schweiz und in Österreich,* Tübingen: Mohr, 1967.

Lewis, W. Arthur, *Politics in West Africa,* London: George Allen and Unwin, 1965.

Lijphart, Arend, *Democracy in Plural Societies: A Comparative Exploration,* New Haven: Yale University Press, 1977.

——, 'Proportionality by Non-PR Methods: Ethnic Representation in Belgium, Cyprus, Lebanon, New Zealand, West Germany, and Zimbabwe', in Bernard Grofman and Arend Lijphart, eds, *Electoral Laws and Their Political Consequences,* New York: Agathon Press, 1986, pp. 113–23.

——, 'Multiethnic Democracy', in Seymour Martin Lipset, ed., *The Encyclopedia of Democracy,* Washington DC: Congressional Quarterly, 1995, pp. 853–65.

——, 'The Puzzle of Indian Democracy: A Consociational Interpretation', *American Political Science Review,* vol. 90 (2) June 1996, pp. 258–68.

——, *Patterns of Democracy: Government Forms and Performance in Thirty-Six Countries,* New Haven: Yale University Press, 1999.

Linz, Juan J., 'The Perils of Presidentialism', *Journal of Democracy,* vol. 1 (1) Winter, 1990, pp. 51–69.

——, 'Presidential or Parliamentary Democracy: Does It Make a Difference?', in Juan J. Linz and Arturo Valenzuela, eds, *The Failure of Presidential Democracy,* Baltimore: Johns Hopkins University Press, 1994, pp. 3–87.

Lipset, Seymour Martin, *Political Man: The Social Bases of Politics,* Garden City, N.Y.: Doubleday, 1960.

Lowell, A. Lawrence, *Government and Parties in Continental Europe,* Boston: Houghton Mifflin, 1896.

Luthera, Ved Prakash, *The Concept of the Secular State and India,* London: Oxford University Press, 1964.

McRae, Kenneth D., ed., *Consociational Democracy: Political Accommodation in Segmented Societies,* Toronto: McClelland and Stewart, 1974.

Messarra, Antoine Nasri, *Le modèle politique libanais et sa survie: Essai sur la classification et l'aménagement d'un système consociatif*, Beirut: Librairie Orientale, 1983.

Mill, John Stuart, *Considerations on Representative Government*, London: Parker, Son, and Bourn, 1961.

Moosbrugger, Lorelei, 'Institutions with Environmental Consequences: The Politics of Agrochemical Policy-Making', Doctoral dissertation, University of California, San Diego, 2001.

Noorani, A.G., *The Presidential System: The Indian Debate*, New Delhi: Sage Publications, 1989.

Powell, G. Bingham, Jr., *Elections as Instruments of Democracy: Majoritarian and Proportional Visions,* New Haven: Yale University Press, 2000.

Reilly, Benjamin, *Democracy in Divided Societies: Electoral Engineering for Conflict Management*, Cambridge: Cambridge University Press, 2001.

Rudolph, Susanne Hoeber, and Lloyd I. Rudolph, 'New Dimensions of Indian Democracy', *Journal of Democracy*, vol. 13 (1) January 2002, pp. 52–66.

Sathe, Vasant, *National Government: Agenda for a New India*, New Delhi: UBS, 1991.

Sorabjee, Soli J., 'The Constitutional Order in India: A Framework for Transition', in Peter Ronald deSouza, ed., *Contemporary India— Transitions*, New Delhi: Sage Publications, 2000, pp. 173–82.

Sridharan, E., 'Does India Need to Switch to Proportional Representation? The Pros and Cons', in Paul Flather, ed., *Recasting Indian Politics: Essays on a Working Democracy*, London: Palgrave, 2002a.

——, 'The Origins of the Electoral System: Rules, Representation and Power-Sharing in India's Democracy', in Zoya Hasan, E. Sridharan, and R. Sudarshan, eds, *India's Living Constitution: Ideas, Practices, Controversies*, Delhi: Permanent Black, 2002b, pp. 344–69.

Steiner, Jürg, *Amicable Agreement versus Majority Rule: Conflict Resolution in Switzerland*, Chapel Hill: University of North Carolina Press, 1974.

Stepan, Alfred, *Arguing Comparative Politics*, Oxford: Oxford University Press, 2001.

Tummala, Krishna K., 'The Indian Union and Emergency Powers', *International Political Science Review*, vol. 17 (4) October 1996, pp. 373–84.

Vanhanen, Tatu, 'What Kind of Electoral System for Plural Societies? India as an Example', in Manfred J. Holler ed., *The Logic of Multiparty Systems*, Dordrecht: Kluwer, 1987, pp. 303–15.

——,*Politics of Ethnic Nepotism: India as an Example*, New Delhi: Sterling Publishers, 1991.

Verba, Sidney, 'Some Dilemmas in Comparative Research', *World Politics*, vol. 20 (1) October 1967, pp. 111–27.

Wheare, K. C., *Federal Government*, 4th edn., New York: Oxford University Press, 1964.

3

'Nation State' or 'State Nation'?
India in Comparative Perspective

Juan J. Linz, Alfred Stepan, and Yogendra Yadav

INTRODUCTION

One of the most urgent conceptual, normative, and political tasks
of our day is to think anew about how polities that aspire to be
political democracies can accommodate great socio-cultural
diversity within one state. The need to think anew arises from a
mismatch between the political realities of the world we live in
and an old political wisdom that we have inherited. The old wisdom
holds that the territorial boundaries of a state must coincide with
the perceived cultural boundaries of a nation. Thus, this understanding
requires that every state must contain within itself one and not
more than one culturally homogenous nation, that *every* state should
be a nation, and that *every* nation should be a state. Given the reality
of socio-cultural diversity in many of the polities of the world this
widespread belief seems to us to be misguided and indeed dangerous
since, as we shall argue, many states in the world, today do not
conform to this expectation. The present chapter is a preliminary
attempt to revise the received wisdom by placing the Indian
experience in comparative perspective.

The belief that every state should be a nation reflects perhaps
the most widely accepted normative vision of a modern democratic
state, that is, the 'nation state'. After the French Revolution, especially
in the nineteenth century, many policies were devoted to creating

a unitary nation state in France in which all French citizens had only one cultural and political identity. These policies included a package of incentives and disincentives to ensure that French increasingly became the only acceptable language in the state. Political mechanisms to allow the recognition and expression of regional cultural differences were so unacceptable to the French nation state builders that advocacy of federalism was at times a capital offence. Throughout France, state schools at any given hour were famously teaching the same curriculum with identical syllabi by teachers who had been trained and certified by the same Ministry of Education rules and tests. Numerous other state institutions, such as universal conscription, were designed to create a common French identity and to be robustly assimilative.[1]

Some very successful democracies, such as contemporary Sweden, the Netherlands, Japan, and Portugal are close to the ideal type of a unitary nation state. Some federal states such as Germany and Australia have also become nation states. In our view, if in a polity (at the historical moment when a state-directed political programme of 'nation state' building begins) socio-cultural differences have not acquired political salience, and most of its politicized citizens have a strong sense of shared history, the aspiration to create a nation state should not create problems for the achievement of an inclusive democracy. In fact, the creation of such a national identity and relative homogeneity in the nineteenth century was identified with democratization and was possible in consolidated states. In the twentieth century, however, attempts to create a nation state by state policies encountered growing difficulties, even in an old state like Spain. In our judgment, in the last century virtually no new nation states have been created except as the result of wars, violence, international

[1]   For a classic book on these policies see Eugen Weber, *Peasants into Frenchman: The Modernization of Rural France, 1870–1914* (Stanford: Stanford University Press, 1976). Most nineteenth-century progressives and democrats, particularly those associated with the French Revolution, were profoundly opposed to federalism. For the normative advocacy of a unified, homogeneous, nation state see the entries on 'Federalism', 'Federation', 'Nation', and 'Department' in the extremely illustrative but not well known, François Furet and Mora Ozouf, eds, *A Critical Dictionary of the French Revolution*, Cambridge: Belnap Press, 1989, pp. 54–64, 65–73, and 742–53.

decisions, oppression, and secession.[2] However, if a polity has significant politically salient cultural and/or linguistic diversity (and a large number of polities do) we will argue that political leaders in such a polity need to think about, and normatively legitimate, a type of polity with characteristics of a 'state nation'.

Linz and Stepan first introduced this concept in 1996, but only in a paragraph (and one figure):

We...believe some conceptual, political, and normative attention should be given to the possibility of state nations. The states we would like to call state nations are multicultural, and sometimes even have significant multinational components, which nonetheless still manage to engender strong identification and loyalty from their citizens, an identification and loyalty that proponents of homogeneous nation states perceive that only nation states can engender.

They went on to say that neither Switzerland nor India were [in the French sense]

strictly speaking a nation state, but we believe both can now be called state nations. Under Jawaharlal Nehru, India made significant gains in managing multinational tensions through skillful and consensual usage of numerous consociational practices. Through this process India became in the 1950s and the early 1960s a democratic state nation.[3]

In order to develop the concept of 'state nation' we think it necessary to clear some conceptual ground. In thinking about how 'socio-cultural diversities' are politically managed, there are two axes that need to be mapped, with the help of analytical distinctions. The first axis pertains to the nature of socio-cultural diversities that present themselves to political actors. Such diversities are of course a product of developments over a long historical period, but they appear as 'givens' to political actors.

[2]   See Juan J. Linz, 'State Building and Nation Building', *European Review* 1, 1993, pp. 355–69, and Juan J. Linz and Alfred Stepan, *Problems of Democratic Transition and Consolidation: Southern Europe, South America, and Post-Communist Europe*, Baltimore and London: Johns Hopkins University Press,1996, chapter 2.

[3]   See the chapter titled 'Stateness, Nationalism, and Democratization', in Linz and Stepan, Ibid., p. 34, as well as Figure 2.1.

Hence the temptation to see these diversities as essential, natural, or primordial. Nevertheless, what appear as essential divisions in any given society are no more than social cleavages that happen to be politically activated and mobilized at that moment. There is always a gap between the map of potential cleavages that underlie every society and the actual map of politically salient divisions.

All too often this axis is seen as ranging from 'homogenous societies' to 'diverse societies', as if homogeneity or its absence were a 'natural' condition or starting point. However, the division between so-called 'homogenous' and so-called 'diverse' societies is better captured as a distinction between societies in which socio-cultural divisions have not acquired political salience, on the one hand, and societies in which they have, on the other. A historical context is built into this distinction; and in our assessment, the crucial question is whether such potential cleavages have become activated by the time competitive politics is instituted.

Furthermore, we need to distinguish among societies with different types of politically activated socio-cultural divisions. At one extreme are societies where social divisions have a geographical concentration and are articulated in more than one 'nationalist' vocabulary throughout the territory of the state. Such a society may be called a 'multinational society'. At the other extreme are societies where socio-cultural divisions exist but are not geographically concentrated and are not articulated in a 'nationalist' vocabulary. Following the recent literature, we would call such a society a 'multicultural' society.

Between these two extremes are a range of societies, in which politically salient social divisions do permit varying degrees of geographical concentrations yet are not articulated in a 'national' vocabulary but of some other identity, such as class. We stress that the distinctions we are making here are between 'ideal types'. In reality, a society can be both 'multinational' and 'multicultural' at once, as well as class-divided.

The second axis that invites theoretical clarification is the one we will be principally concerned with in this chapter. It relates not to the nature and articulation of socio-cultural diversities, but to the models of *political strategies* and some *specific institutional responses* for dealing with such diversities. Two ideal types can be delineated along this axis, which we shall call (1) 'nation state', or (2) 'state nation'.

'Nation state' policies stand for a political–institutional approach that attempts to match the political boundaries of the state with the presumed cultural boundaries of the nation. Needless to say the cultural boundaries are far from obvious in most cases; thus the creation of a nation state involves privileging *one* socio-cultural identity over other potential or actual socio-cultural cleavages that can be politically mobilized. 'Nation state' policies have been pursued historically by following a variety of routes from relatively soft to downright brutal: (1) by creating or arousing a special kind of allegiance or common cultural identity among those living in a state; (2) by encouraging the voluntary assimilation of those who do not share that initial allegiance or cultural identity into the nation state's identity; (3) by various forms of social pressure and coercion to achieve this and to prevent or destroy alternative cultural identities; and (4) by coercion that might, in the extreme, even involve ethnic cleansing.

By contrast, 'state nation' policies stand for a political–institutional approach that respects and protects *multiple but complementary* socio-cultural identities. 'State nation' policies recognize the legitimate public and even political expression of active socio-cultural cleavages, and they evolve mechanisms to accommodate competing or conflicting claims made on behalf of those divisions without privileging or imposing any one claim. 'State nation' policies involve creating a sense of belonging (or 'we-feeling') with respect to the state-wide political community, while simultaneously creating institutional safeguards for respecting and protecting politically salient socio-cultural diversities. The 'we-feeling' may take the form of defining a tradition, history, and shared culture in an inclusive manner, with attachment to common symbols of the state and/or inculcating some form of 'constitutional patriotism'.

In democratic societies, the institutional safeguards constitutive of 'state nation' policies most likely take the form of federalism, and often specifically *asymmetrical* federalism, and/or consociational practices.[4] Virtually every long-standing and relatively peaceful contemporary democracy in the world whose polity has more

---

[4]   We accept Robert Dahl's definition of federalism as 'a system in which some matters are exclusively *within* the competence of certain local units—cantons, states, provinces—and are constitutionally *beyond* the scope of the authority of the national government; and where certain other matters are constitutionally

than one territorially concentrated, politically mobilized, linguistic-cultural group that is a majority in some significant part of the territory, is not only federal, but 'asymmetrically federal' (Belgium, Spain, Canada, and India).[5] This means that, by a certain point, these polities, in order to 'hold together' their great diversity in one democratic system, had to constitutionally embed special cultural and historical prerogatives for some of the member units, prerogatives that respond to their somewhat different linguistic/cultural aspirations, demands, and/or historical identities.[6] We believe that had political leaders in India, Belgium, Spain, and Canada insisted upon attempting to impose one language and culture on the country and insisted upon a homogenizing nineteenth-century French-style unitary nation state, the cause of social peace, inclusionary democracy, and individual rights would not have been served in any of these four, long-standing democratic states. This was so because more than one territorially based, linguistic, cultural cleavage had already been activated in each of these four countries. The strategic question therefore was whether to attempt to *reject* or *accommodate* this pre-existing, politically activated diversity.

Asymmetrical federalism historically emerged in Belgium, Spain, Canada, and India as a policy response aimed at accommodation. We therefore think that, as a normative concept, an institutional framework, and a set of historical experiences, 'asymmetrical federalism' should be strongly considered, by theoreticians and political leaders alike, as a possible approach to democracy in polities such as Sri Lanka and Myanmar that

---

outside the scope of the authority of the smaller units.' See his 'Federalism and the Democratic Process', in *Democracy, Liberty and Equality*, Oslo: Norwegian University Press, 1986, pp. 114–26. Quote from p. 114.

5 A borderline case might be Sri Lanka, but while it may be a marginal democracy, it certainly is not peaceful. Also, the United Kingdom is a multinational society with Scottish, Irish, and Welsh assemblies but English is spoken by the overwhelmingly majority of the population in all three areas.

6 The concepts of 'asymmetrical federalism' and 'holding together federalism' are developed with greater detail and documentation in Stepan's chapter in this volume, and in his article cited in footnote 11.

have at least one territorially based, already politically activated, linguistic-cultural cleavage within the existing state.[7] At the same time it needs to be clarified that federalism is neither sufficient nor necessary for the establishment of a state nation.[8] The creation and maintenance of a state nation requires a number of diversity sustaining measures that are not exhausted by federal instruments. For the same reason, it is possible for a unitary state, where diversities are not geographically concentrated, to institute many multicultural practices towards establishing a state nation.

In sum, then, the idea of the nation associated with the 'nation state' approach implies creating one common culture within the state, while the idea of the nation associated with the 'state nation' approach can contain more than one politically salient culture, but nonetheless encourages and requires respect for the common institutions of the state, as well as respecting existing socio-cultural diversities.[9]

Thus, 'state nation' is a term introduced to distinguish democratic states that do not, and cannot, fit well into the classic French-style 'nation state' model based on a 'we feeling' resulting

[7]   For a thoughtful examination of the problems and promises associated with asymmetrical federalism, see Rainer Bauböck, 'United in Misunderstanding? Asymmetry in Multinational Federations', (unpublished paper presented at the International Workshop on European Identities: Constructs and Conflicts, Austrian Academy of Sciences, 13–15 December 2001).

[8]   For example, Luxembourg, is a unitary state but a 'state nation'. Ukraine, even though it is a unitary state is following many 'state-nation' policies because most political elites, both ethnic Ukrainian and ethnic Russian, were worried that strong ethnic Ukrainian 'nation state' policies would generate conflicts with the Russophone population, especially in the eastern regions bordering Russia, where 90 per cent of the Ukrainian citizens speak Russian. Also, given the above, and irredentist sentiments in Russia, a policy of decentralization, but not necessarily, federalization might be prudent. See Alfred Stepan, 'Ukraine: Improbable Democratic "Nation-State" but Possible Democratic "State Nation"?', *Post-Soviet Affairs*, vol. 21, (4), October–December 2005, pp. 279–308.

[9]   The analytical distinction between 'nation state' and 'state nation', as the terms imply, involves an affinity—since both include the term 'nation', and certainly, for some theorists of nationalism, both terms would fit under their conception of a nation.

from an existing or forged homogeneity. For the difference between 'nation state' and 'state nation' as ideal types see Table 3.1

Table 3.1: Two Contrasting Ideal Types of Democratic States and Cultural Nation(s): 'Nation State' and 'State Nation'

	Nation State	State Nation
Pre-Existing Conditions		
Sense of belonging/ we-ness	Awareness of, and attachment to, one major cultural civilizational tradition. This cultural identity corresponds to existing state boundaries with minor exceptions.	Awareness of, and attachment to, more than one cultural civilizational tradition within the existing boundaries. These attachments do not preclude identification with a common state.
State Policy		
Cultural policies	Homogenizing attempts to foster one core cultural identity; non-recognition of multiplicity of cultures. Unity in oneness.	Recognition of, and support to, more than one cultural identity, even more than one cultural nation. All within a frame of some common polity-wide symbols. Unity in diversity.
Institutions		
Territorial division of power	Unitary states or mono-national federations. Federacies possible.	Federal system. Often de jure, or de facto, asymmetrical. Can even be a unitary state if aggressive nation state policies not pursued. Federacies possible.
Politics		
Ethno-cultural-territorial cleavages	Not too salient.	Salient and are recognized and democratically managed.
Autonomist and/or secessionist parties	Autonomist parties are normally not 'coalitionable'. Secessionist parties are outlawed or marginalized in democratic electoral politics.	Autonomist parties can govern in federal units and are 'coalitionable' at the centre. Non-violent secessionist parties can sometimes participate in democratic politics.

Contd.

Citizen Orientation		
Political identity	Single identity as citizens of the state and overwhelmingly as members of the nation.	Multiple but complementary identities.
Obedience/loyalty	Obedience to the state and loyalty to the nation.	Obedience to the state and identification with institutions, neither based on a single national identity.

Our conception of 'state nation' derives from our belief, based on historical case studies and analysis, that democracy is possible in polities that are sociologically and politically multicultural and even partly (but not exclusively) multinational, *if* an effort is made to legitimate the state by those minorities and majorities who could conceivably aim at its de-legitimation. Our advocacy of the term 'state nation' is also based on our recognition that in some countries, cultural groups are not territorially concentrated but instead are so diffusely located that even 'asymmetrical federalism' is not an option. However, given the robustness of these different politically salient cultural groups, a classic French-style 'nation state' may also not be an option for a peaceful democracy without a costly, and most likely non-democratic, period of state imposed assimilation efforts, and possibly even ethnic cleansing. Nonetheless, in the same cultural context, a state nation may be a possibility, and probably the most possible, democratic model to pursue.

Our introduction of the term 'state nation' is intended both to introduce a normative standard to which democracies in polities that appear highly diverse can aspire to, and to introduce a set of at least four observable empirical socio-political realities that a polity, if it is a state nation, will manifest.

Although 'nation state' and 'state nation' at one level are analytic ideal type distinctions they can be operationalized using a range of indicators. 'State nations' can, and have, managed to create powerful and positive citizens' identification with the institutions and symbols of the state, such as the constitution, inclusive democratic institutions and procedures, and guarantees of basic freedoms. A diverse polity, if it has become a state nation, will have the four following, empirically demonstrable patterns: (1) Despite multiple cultural identities among the citizens of the polity there will be at the same time a high degree of *positive identification* with the state, and pride in being citizens of that state. (2) Citizens of the state will have *multiple but complementary* political identities and loyalties. (3) There will be a high degree of *trust* in the most important constitutional, legal, and administrative components of the state. (4) By world democratic standards, there will be a comparatively high degree of positive *support for democracy*, among all the diverse groups of citizens in the country, for the specific state-wide democratic institutions through which the multicultural and possibly multinational polity is governed.

At this point, we need to address a potentially powerful, but in our view, misguided, argument about socio-cultural diversity. After the bloody disintegration of Yugoslavia and parts of the Soviet Union, many analysts have begun to reject wholesale all political and institutional frameworks that grant any form of prerogatives to territorially concentrated, socio-cultural groups—arrangements which they refer to as 'ethno-federal' and/or 'national federal'. These scholars criticize 'ethno-federal' arrangements because they believe that such arrangements privilege 'sub-national' socio-cultural identities at the expense of identification with common symbols, institutions, and individual rights. This privileging, they claim, is likely to foster, at least, the activation of conflictual, *as opposed to complementary*, identities, and perhaps violence and fragmentation.[10]

These critics ignore, however, the fact that nearly all successful democratic states with at least one politically activated, territorially concentrated, linguistic–cultural cleavage, have institutional frameworks that include a substantial (but absolutely *not*, as in Yugoslavia by the late 1980s, a virtually exclusive) 'ethno-federal' dimension. In successful state nations, group rights do not, and should not ever, violate the individual's rights that come to them as individual members of the state. Witness the institutional frameworks of the states that we consider to be exemplary state nations—namely, Switzerland, Belgium, Canada, Spain, and India. The institutional frameworks of all of these contain an element of 'ethno-federalism'. Nevertheless, none of these states can be classified as

---

10   See for example Valerie Bunce, *Subversive Institutions: The Design and Destruction of Socialism and the State*, New York: Cambridge University Press, 1999.

purely 'ethno-federal' either, since in these states recognition of the legitimate public and political expression of active socio-cultural 'national' cleavages is balanced with constitutionally sanctioned respect for common symbols, institutions, and individual rights, thus facilitating the maintenance and nurturing of *multiple and complementary*, as opposed to *exclusive and conflictual*, identities.

We believe that it would be a grave error to discard the state-nation approach simply because the institutional framework associated with it tends to contain a significant ethno-federal dimension. In our analysis for a variety of states (such as Sri Lanka or Myanmar) that are not now peaceful and/or democratic to achieve a consolidated democracy, they would have to strive to become state nations. This means, quite simply, that for consolidated democracy to be possible, these states would have to craft institutional frameworks that contain both (1) a substantial 'ethno-federal dimension' and (2) mechanisms facilitating identification with common symbols and institutions. If, in the process of democratization, leaders of these states were to pursue either a pure nation state model, or a pure ethno-federal model, the result would almost certainly be continued armed struggle and failure to achieve democratic consolidation (see Figure 3.1).

Let us now attempt to develop our analytic argument in more empirical detail to see if, and if so how, culturally diverse countries such as Spain, Belgium and, especially India, approximate our ideal-typical model of 'state nations'. We shall first examine the key role of the *origin*s of federalism in state nations (which tend to grow out of an effort to 'hold together', rather than an effort to 'come together'). The traditional theory of federalism relies heavily on the US experience in which a group of political entities with great political autonomy make a decision to pool some of their sovereignty to create a new state which is federal in form. We call this process 'coming together' federalism. Many observers think this is the only model of federation formation.

However, federations can also be formed by political groups in existing unitary states that come to the conclusion that, in order to hold together peacefully and democratically, it is necessary to devolve substantial power to territorially based cultural groups, and in the process shift from being a unitary state to becoming a federal state. Two major examples are Spain after Franco and Belgium from the mid-1970s to 1993. We call the origins of this

Figure 3.1: Democratically Probable and Improbable Relationships between Activated, Territorially Concentrated, Socio-Cultural Identities and Political-Institutional Strategies

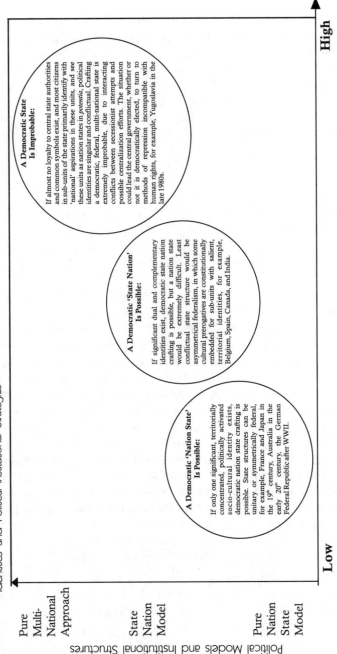

Political Models and Institutional Structures

Pure Multi-National Approach

State Nation Model

Pure Nation State Model

A Democratic State Is Improbable:

If almost no loyalty to central state authorities and common symbols exist, and most citizens in sub-units of the state primarily identify with 'national' aspirations in these units, and see these units as nation states in *potentia*, political identities are singular and conflictual. Crafting a democratic, federal, multi-national state is extremely improbable, due to interacting conflicts between secessionist attempts and possible centralization efforts. The situation could lead the central government, whether or not it is democratically elected, to turn to methods of repression incompatible with human rights, for example, Yugoslavia in the late 1980s.

A Democratic 'State Nation' Is Possible:

If significant dual and complementary identities exist, democratic state nation crafting is possible, but a nation state would be extremely difficult. Least conflictual state structure would be asymmetrical federalism, in which some cultural prerogatives are constitutionally embedded for sub-units with salient, territorial identities, for example, Belgium, Spain, Canada, and India.

A Democratic 'Nation State' Is Possible:

If only one significant, territorially concentrated, politically activated socio-cultural identity exists, democratic nation state crafting is possible. State structures can be unitary or symmetrically federal, for example, France and Japan in the 19th century, Australia in the early 20th century, the German Federal Republic after WWII.

Low   High

Intensity of Political Activation of Multiple, Territorially Concentrated, Socio-Cultural 'National' Identities

type of polity 'holding together' federalism. Because of their quite dissimilar origins, the prerogatives and powers of the member units of these two types of federations also tend to differ. Coming together federations tend to arrive at constitutional agreements whereby all full constituent members have exactly the same rights and obligations. They are thus called 'symmetrical' federations. However, holding together federations, in order to accommodate some of the most politically salient cultural differences (such as language or religion) that were threatening the unitary state, might constitutionally embed somewhat different prerogatives for different constituent members, such as the status of the French language, Napoleonic Code, and the Catholic Church in Quebec when the Canadian Federation was first formed in 1867, or the status of non-Spanish languages in Spain in Catalonia and the Basque Country when the Spanish federation was created after the death of Franco. Such federations are called 'asymmetrical' federations.[11]

Some federal states are based on a strong national identity shared by practically all its citizens. They are relatively homogeneous in their culture, language, and sense of history and can be seen as nation states as the state and the nation are one. Germany, after giving up claims to Alsace-Lorraine and losing the eastern territories inhabited by large numbers of Poles, is now a nation state with tiny minorities enjoying a special status like the Danes on the northern border and the Sorbs. However, with the Cold War division between the *Bundesrepublik* and the German Democratic Republic, there were two states and one nation. The two states each sought to legitimize their rule, in West Germany by what was called the *Verfassungspatriotismus* (constitutional patriotism), the loyalty to the democratic liberal state and its market institutions, and in East Germany by the construction of a socialist state.[12]

[11]   For a more extensive discussion of these distinctions, see Alfred Stepan, 'Toward a New Comparative Politics of Federalism, (Multi) Nationalism, and Democracy: Beyond Rikerian Federalism' in his *Arguing Comparative Politics* (Oxford: Oxford University Press, 2001), pp. 315–62, esp. pp. 320-8. Also see his chapter in this volume.

[12]   For the original formulation of the concept of 'constitutional patriotism', see Dolf Sternberger, *Verfassungspatriotismus*, Frankfurt am Main: Insel-Verlag, 1990. For a recent elaboration on the theme

The first Austrian republic was founded in 1918 and in its Constitution defined itself as part of the German nation and was committed to joining the German Federal Republic. Only after the Second World War did Austria acquire an identity of its own as a state, though not for a long time as a nation.[13]

Most of those writing about Switzerland do not see it as a nation state, but as a voluntary state that we would characterize as a state nation. With its linguistic heterogeneity of largely monolingual German, French, Italian, and Raeto-romansch speaking cantons, Switzerland is a unique federation. Given the fact that none of its linguistic regions, nor its religious communities, or its cantons consider themselves nations, as many Basques and Catalans consider their Autonomous Communities in Spain, it would be wrong to consider Switzerland a multinational state. The Swiss confederation enjoys a legitimacy, felt by all its multicultural and largely cantonal-focused citizens, which is unique, and provides the ideal type of what we call a state nation, where the institutions of the state with its distinctive political culture is the basis of a particular type of identification of its citizens.[14]

In contrast to the ideal-typical state nation of Switzerland, in state nations with important multinational components, such as Spain, Belgium, or Canada, many citizens, who may constitute a significant proportion of the population of federal units, identify with a distinctive nation with its own language, culture, history, rights, and grievances against the state in which they live. The federal state nation is a nightmare to those who originally conceived of the state as a nation state, a nightmare to those who want to nationalize the whole population in the process of nation-building, of which the French Republic would be historically the most

---

(in English) and adaptation of it to contexts outside of Germany, see Jürgen Habermas, 'Citizenship and National Identity', in *Facts and Norms*, Cambridge, Mass: MIT Press, 1998, pp. 491–515.

13   On the very recent emergence of national consciousness in Austria, see T. Bluhm, *Building an Austrian Nation: The Political Integration of a Western State*, New Haven: Yale University Press, 1973, see especially pp. 220–41.

14   A fine overview of the Swiss case can be found in Lidija Basta, 'Minority and Legitimacy of a Federal State', in L. Basta and Thomas

successful model; a nightmare for those nation-builders for whom federalism would be conceived, at the most, as a form of decentralization for the purposes of administrative efficiency.

Multinational Societies: Multiple and Complementary Identities? Possible State Nations? Spain and Belgium

There are those who think that the multinational federal state is inevitably condemned to break up, who see federalism in those states as only a step towards disintegration, and who therefore want to limit the federal constitution and engage in a process of more or less aggressive nation-building. For complex reasons into which we cannot enter here, such efforts are likely to fail, producing a backlash that will lead to the opposite result from the one that their proponents pursue.[15] However, intelligent political engineering, constructive political leadership, and some favourable contextual factors can help to overcome some, but of course not all, the tension inherent in multinational societies. A federal state in a multinational society can become a successful state nation. Unfortunately, we have few systematic studies of how this has been achieved.

A study of the Indian Republic and its history and institutions could make an important contribution to this important task for social scientists and policy-makers—as can a closer study of Spain and Belgium. Unfortunately, some of the brilliant theorizing about multiculturalism, particularly in the US and, to a lesser extent, in Europe, in recent years, is only in part relevant to this task. Multiculturalism in the way that we find it discussed in that literature is not distinctive to federal states. The literature is equally relevant to unitary states like France, with its increasingly important Muslim immigrant population. The literature on multiculturalism is

---

Fleiner, eds, *Federalism and Multiethnic States: The Case of Switzerland*, Fribourg, Switzerland: The Institute of Federalism, 1996, pp. 41–69. For another treatment that deals extensively with language policy in Switzerland, see Kenneth D. McRae, *Conflict and Compromise in Multilingual Societies*, vol. 1, Ontario, Canada: Wilfred Laurier University Press, 1986.

[15] See Linz, 'State Building and Nation Building', *European Review* 1, 1993, pp. 355–69.

especially relevant to cultural minorities, particularly immigrants claiming a range of rights as individuals and communities, but who are not the same as territorially based autochthonous communities with an articulated or latent national identity. Most of the literature on nationalism treats national identities as if they were mutually exclusive. The literature is plagued with the use of expressions like 'the Catalans', or 'the Flemish', and their opposites, 'the Spanish', or 'the Belgians'. However, such expressions represent a gross over-simplification. Though nationalists on both sides reject the idea of dual identities as a form of bigamy, in fact, in all more or less multinational societies, most citizens tend to have dual, and often complementary, or at least not exclusive, identities.

Spain provides a case in point. Since the late-nineteenth century and particularly in the twentieth century, there has been a growing sense of cultural and, increasingly, *national* identities among people in bilingual regions in certain parts of Spain— most acutely, in Catalonia and the Basque Country.[16] At the turn of the century, nationalist parties emerged in both of these regions and began to articulate these identities. With the transition to democracy, such identities gained additional strength as a reaction to the Franco regime, since that regime had pursued an aggressive policy against peripheral nationalist movements, including discriminatory language policies. By the end of the Franco era, the democratic opposition had come to sympathize with the peripheral nationalist movements and to demand that their aspirations be at least partly recognized. In the transition to democracy, the drafters of the 1978 Constitution did just that; they agreed to accommodate linguistic, cultural, and national differences by organizing the state as an '*Estado de autonomías*', a type of federal political system.[17]

16 For the historiographical debates about the rise of peripheral nationalisms in Spain, see Juan Linz, 'Early State-Building and Late Peripheral Nationalisms against the State: the Case of Spain', in S.N. Eisenstadt and Stein Rokkan, eds, *Building States and Nations: Analyses by Region*, vol. II, Beverly Hills: Sage, 1973, pp. 32–116.

17 On the process of devolution to a federal state in Spain, see Juan Linz, 'Spanish Democracy and the Estado de las Autonomías,' in Robert A. Goldwin, Art Kaufman, and William A. Schambra, eds,

Since the transition to democracy in Spain, a number of questions about national identity have been asked in opinion polls —all of which reveal the predominance of multiple and complementary identities. Exclusive and competing identities turn out to be the exception, not the rule. For example, when asked, 'Which of the following sentences would you identify with most: I feel only Spanish, I feel more Spanish than Basque/Catalan/etc., I feel as Spanish as Basque/Catalan/etc., 'as Spanish as Basque/ Catalan/etc.', only a small minority of the population registers an exclusive identity.[18] To be exact, in Catalonia a mere 16 per cent of the population identify themselves as exclusively Catalan, while another 9 per cent identify themselves as exclusively Spanish. The rest—approximately three-quarters of the population there— report some kind of dual identification. They feel as Catalan as Spanish (41 per cent), or more Spanish than Catalan (4 per cent), or more Catalan than Spanish (27 per cent); but they do not exclude one or the other identity. The same can be said for the Basque Country, the region in which identification with the Spanish nation is weakest: even there, those who identify themselves as exclusively Basque barely reach one quarter of the population (see Table 3.2).

Nor is Spain an exception in this regard, for the same is true in the case of Belgium. Belgium was founded in 1830 as an independent unitary parliamentary monarchy. In the course of a complex process marked by considerable conflict, it has evolved in the twentieth century into a basically binational and bilingual federal democracy.[19]

Forging Unity Out of Diversity, Washington D.C.: American Enterprise Institute for Public Policy Research, 1989, pp. 260–303. On electoral results in and public opinion about the Estado de las Autonomías during the first decade-and-a-half of democracy, see Juan Linz, 'De la crisis de un estado unitario al Estado de las Autonomías', in Fernando Fernández Rodríguez, ed., *La España de las Autonomías,* Madrid: Instituto de Estudios de Administración Local, 1985, pp. 527–672.

[18]   All the data we cite from Spain is based on the *Sondeo de opinión del Observatoria Político Autonómico: 2003,* Barcelona: ICPS, 2004.

[19]   For a good synthesis of this historical process and an extended discussion of language policy there, see chapter one of Kenneth D. McRae's *Conflict and Compromise in Multilingual Societies: Belgium,*

Table 3.2: Subjective National Identity in Spain

	Basque Country	Catalonia	Galicia	Rest of Spain	All of Spain
Only Spanish	6	9	3	14	13
More Spanish than Cat/Basque/Gal	6	4	6	9	8
As Spanish as Cat/Basque/Gal	34	41	58	59	56
More Cat/Basque/ Gal than Spanish	23	27	27	12	14
Only Cat/Basque/Gal	27	16	5	3	6
Don't know/ Don't answer	4	3	1	4	4
	100	100	100	101	101
N	1800	1200	1200	7874	10476

Note: All figures except N are in percentages rounded off to the nearest integral.

Source: For the Basque Country, Catalonia, and Galicia, *Sondeo de opinión del Observatorio Político Autonómico: 2003*, Barcelona: ICPS, 2004; for the rest of Spain and all of Spain, *CIS study* #2455 2002.

In Belgium, a number of relevant questions about national identity have been asked in opinion polls too, distinguishing between those who speak Dutch, those who speak French, and the inhabitants of Brussels. All of these again reveal the predominance of multiple and complementary identities. For example, when asked, 'Which of the following statements applies most to you: I consider myself only as a Belgian, I feel more Belgian than Flemish or Walloon, I feel as Belgian as Flemish or Walloon, I feel more Flemish or Walloon than Belgian, or I feel only Flemish or Walloon?,' only 3 per cent of the Belgian population choose an exclusive Flemish or Walloon identity. Thus, despite all the talk about the polarization

Ontario, Canada: Wilfrid Laurier University Press, 1986. For a study that focuses on linguistic conflict in the metropolitan region of Brussels, the only place where significant numbers of French-speakers and Flemish-speakers live side by side, see Jan de Volder 'Le FN Brade Brussels', in *Revue Française de Geopolitique*, no. 6, May 1998.

of identities in Belgium, only a tiny fraction of Belgian citizens reject outright any kind of affective identification with the state. Though another 14 per cent choose an exclusive Belgian identity, the overwhelming majority choose a dual identity of one kind or another—in descending order, 'as Belgian as Flemish or Walloon' (43 per cent); then 'more Belgian than Flemish or Walloon' (21 per cent); and finally 'more Flemish or Walloon than Belgian' (17 per cent).[20]

Among the French-speaking Walloons, who at the time of the founding of the state lived in the more prosperous and state-building communities, identification with the Belgian nation is somewhat stronger than it is for the whole of the population: 18 per cent of them identify themselves as only Belgian and a miniscule 2 per cent feel only Walloon. In the capital city of Brussels, the only place in the country where significant numbers of French-speakers and Dutch-speakers live side by side, 24 per cent identify themselves as only Belgian; and only 3 per cent fail to mention the Belgian identity. But despite the fact that identification with the region is stronger in Flanders than for the population as a whole, perhaps what is most surprising about the Belgian case is the strength of the Belgian identity among the Flemish people. In Flanders, which some analysts see as moving towards separation, those who identify themselves as exclusively Flemish amount to a mere 4 per cent of the population. Over 95 per cent of 'the Flemish' identify to some degree with the Belgian state (see Table 3.3).

What's more, not only do the overwhelming majority of citizens in Belgium, regardless of the territory from which they hail, identify themselves at least sometimes as Belgians, but also register a very high degree of affective attachment to an important common state institution—specifically, the monarchy. Such attachment is evident in the responses of Belgian citizens to a question about how much they trust their king. As many as 54 per cent of them claim to trust him either very much or a lot (13 per cent and 41 per cent, respectively); while a mere 11 per cent claim to trust him only a little or very little (6 per cent and 5 per cent, respectively). Now, it needs to be noted that among Walloons, the level of trust in

[20]   The data we use for Belgium is based on the 1995 *General Election Study*, conducted by the Interuniversitair Steunpunt Politieke-Opinieonderzoek, K.U. Leuven, and the Point d'appui Interuniversitaire sur l'Opinion publique et la Politique, U.C. Louvain. Results published in 1998.

Table 3.3: Subjective National Identity in Belgium, 1995

	All of Belgium	Flanders	Wallonia	Brussels
Only Belgian	14	11	18	24
More Belgian than Flemish/Walloon	21	17	25	27
As Belgian as Flemish/Walloon	43	45	44	32
More Flemish/Walloon than Belgian	17	23	10	11
Only Flemish/Walloon	3	4	2	3
Don't know/Don't answer	2	1	2	5
	100	101	101	101
N	3651	2099	1258	311

Note: All figures except N are in percentages rounded off to the nearest integral.

Source: *1995 Belgian General Election Study.* See footnote 20.

the king is moderately higher than it is among the Flemish. Whereas 59 per cent of the former claim to trust their king at least a lot, 51 per cent of the latter do so. Nevertheless, despite this difference, the fact remains that *both* communities share a very strong sense of attachment to the king, and by extension to the institution of the monarchy (see Table 3.4).

We understand this kind of affective attachment to a set of common institutions and symbols to be indispensable for the legitimacy, and therefore stability, of any state in contexts with a high level of cultural, linguistic, and even national heterogeneity. This is why we stress the importance of not only *multiple* but also *complementary* identities within a multinational, federal, democratic framework. Of course, as we have already suggested, there are two intimately related difficulties with this framework: (1) that centralists often dream of doing away with the fact of *multiple* identities; and (2) that peripheral nationalists often seek to undermine the fact of *complementary* identities. But, at least in the Belgian case, neither of these difficulties seem to be unmanageable. We do not share the skepticism of some other commentators, who feel that Belgium is falling apart. Both the overwhelming preponderance of dual identities and, especially, the high level of

Table 3.4: Trust in the King in Belgium, 1995

	Trust very much	Trust a lot	No trust, no distrust	Little trust	Very little trust	Don't Know / Don't answer	N
All of Belgium	13	41	33	6	5	3	3668
Flanders	11	40	35	7	4	3	2099
Wallonia	16	43	30	3	5	2	1258
Brussels	19	41	27	6	6	1	311

Note: All figures except N are in percentages rounded off to the nearest integral.

Source: 1995 Belgium General Election Study.

affective attachment to common symbols and institutions there justify our sense of optimism. Were such affective attachment to common symbols and institutions lacking, there would be reason for pessimism. In Yugoslavia, for example, it is highly doubtful that any Yugoslavian institution commanded a high level of trust by all the citizens of the country. Fortunately, however, the Belgian case is quite different from that of Yugoslavia.

By all means, nationalists would like the question formulated not as, 'Are you *more* Flemish *than* Belgian?' or 'Are you *more* Catalan *than* Spanish?' but rather as, 'Are you *either* Flemish *or* Belgian?' or 'Are you *either* Catalan *or* Spanish?'—despite the ubiquity of multiple and complementary identities in settings that are more or less multinational. And inevitably, both those who speak of self-determination, that is, the right of every nation to become an independent state, and those who favour a total national integration into a single cultural or linguistic community, reject the very idea of dual identities.

This is the main reason (and there are many) why democratic plebiscites are normally such an undesirable solution. People have to make one or another choice, like the one of defining the territorial units for which the decision should be binding. The quorum necessary to reverse such a decision is totally different from a normal election since it cannot be reversed four years hence. A plebiscite might be the only solution in certain extreme situations where the polarization created by violent conflict has destroyed any dual identity. But in those cases it will mean a loss of rights and equal citizenship for those not supporting the majoritarian choice.

India as a State Nation: Where Does the Indian Polity Fit Comparatively?

For the rest of this chapter, we will focus largely on the world's most diverse democracy, India, which we argue has created a state nation but cannot, in the foreseeable future, create a nation state in the French sense of the term. India, perhaps more than any country in the world, has rich lessons to offer about democracy and diversity.

Before we turn to some of these lessons, it is necessary to delimit the scope of this analysis. We are very aware of India's continuing problems with poverty and with low levels of literacy, nutrition, basic sanitation, as well as periodic communal riots. Some of these comparative problems are made abundantly clear in Table 3.5.

However, the focus of this chapter is not on democracy and its linkage to development; we focus here only on how democratic political arrangements of the kind that we analyse below serve as mechanisms for handling societal diversity and potential conflict. It is quite clear to any student of democracy and democratization in the world, or of nationalism, multinationalism, and diversity and extreme crises of 'stateness' such as in the former USSR and Yugoslavia, that India began its democratic experiment with greater politicized diversity than any other long-standing democracy in the world. It is also evident to any analyst of survey data about contemporary India that democracy is increasingly supported by the overwhelming majority of these diverse groups in India. This pattern is not sufficiently recognized, or analysed, by general readers or even by most specialist scholars, so one of our major tasks in this chapter is to attempt to document, and explain, these phenomena.

We believe that this task requires placing India's experience in comparative perspective. However, this does not mean a simple-minded comparison between India and the US; we believe that the terms of comparison need to be expanded for us to gain insights into the Indian experience of dealing with diversity. Since some basic characteristics of Indian society and polity are clearly distinct

Table 3.5: Comparative Indicators of India's Human and Income Poverty

Average GDP per Capita in Purchasing Power Parity (PPP) in 2000 (US Dollars) among Arend Lijphart's universe of the thirty-six continuous democracies of the world from 1977 to 1996	$20,252
India's GDP per Capita in PPP in 2000 (US Dollars)	$2,358
India's Human Development Index (HDI) Ranking among the 173 countries of the world ranked by the United Nations Development Programme (UNDP)	124/173
India's HDI Ranking among Arend Lijphart's thirty -six continuous democracies	34/36
India's Human Poverty Index (HPI-1) among the 88 developing countries ranked by the UNDP	55/88
Adult Female Literacy Rate in India	45.4%
Percentage of Underweight Children in India at age 5	47.0%

Sources: UNDP, *Human Development Report 2002: Deepening Democracy in a Frag-mented World*, New York and Oxford: Oxford University Press, 2002, pp. 149–52, 157–9, 172, 190–3, and 224. Arend Lijphart, *Patterns of Democracy: Government Forms and Performance in Thirty-Six Countries*, New Haven and London: Yale University Press, 1999.

from the US the experience of the American democracy is not always relevant; indeed at times can be quite misleading, for our understanding of India. Comparisons should not be limited to the federalism of the US (or, for that matter, to the party system of the UK, as is often done), but should extend to other long-standing democracies as well. India shares some institutional characteristics with a number of other federal democracies, which should allow us to understand better its problems, successes, and failures. This facilitates some comparisons with the US but also makes it necessary to think of India in the wider context of federal democracies. The US and India are both among the eleven long-standing federal democracies of the world but their federal structures have different historical origins and different functions.[21]

[21]   The eleven federal countries that have been functioning democracies for at least the last fifteen years are India, the US, Switzerland, Germany, Austria, Belgium, Spain, Australia, Brazil, Argentina, and Canada. Belgium's long transformation from a unitary to a federal state was only completed in 1993 but it had increasingly functioned as a federal system since the 1970s.

India houses substantially greater and more intense politicized diversity involving culture, language, and religion than the US. There is no numerically preponderant 'ethnos' that might dominate democratic politics to the exclusion of the rest. Looked at in pure religious terms, it might appear that there is a dominant community, for the Hindus constituted 82.4 per cent of the population according to the 1991 census. But this apparent homogeneity breaks down if one looks at the regional and the linguistic diversity. According to the same 1991 census, the speakers of the largest language, Hindi, comprised only 40.2 per cent of India's total population. Even this 40.2 per cent included a large proportion of persons who speak the various 'dialects' of Hindi that are often mutually incomprehensible. In regional terms, the dominant 'Hindi heartland', a broad strip comprising nine states of the union and two 'union territories' from west to east of north India, had 43.8 per cent of the country's population. But if one looks for the signs of a dominant 'ethnos' that shares religion, language, and region—those who are Hindus, Hindi speakers, and reside in the Hindi heartland states—the proportion is only a little over one-third, 34.7 per cent to be precise.[22] A group of this size is not in a position to dominate the country's politics. Besides, these 34.7 per cent of the Indian population articulate their political identities in many other ways, such as caste differences, that serve to fragment this group.

Furthermore, longstanding 'separatist' struggles for national independence in some parts of the Indian republic, particularly in Kashmir and in Nagaland, introduce a multinational dimension

[22] All the above calculations are based on the population figures of the Census of India 1991. It should be noted that while the census provides the exact break-up of language and religion for each state, it does not provide religious break-up by language speakers. This has been estimated here by assuming that all the Urdu speakers in the Hindi heartland states are Muslims and that the rest of the language speakers are evenly distributed across religions. The total population of the country in 1991 was 838 million. Of these, 367 million were citizens of the Hindi states. The number of Hindi speakers in these states stood at 319 million. We estimate the number of non-Hindus among this group to be 27.5 million, thus leaving 291 million of Hindu, Hindi-speaking persons, living in the Hindi heartland. This works out to be 34.7 per cent of the population of India (*Source: Census of India 1991, Statement 3, Paper 1 of 1997—Language: Registrar General of India, New Delhi.*)

into the Indian polity. India's federal structures, to a certain extent, reflect a territorially-based pluralism. In contrast, the US, in spite of its multicultural society, is more homogeneous than India, its pluralism has little territorial basis, and federalism does not reflect that pluralism directly partly because, unlike India, Canada, Spain, and Belgium, the US does not have a politically salient multinational dimension. The distinct nature of India's diversity also means that the large body of theorizing and analysis of multiculturalism in the US and in Europe as the result of large-scale immigration from other societies in recent decades, is only in part relevant to India. This is so because in India the multicultural characteristics are the result of a long history and have a distinctive territorial basis to which Indian federalism has been a response. Witness the creation of the new linguistic states in the 1950s and the process of the creation of new states that continues to this day. It should be noted that although the latest creation of three states (Uttaranchal, Jharkhand, and Chhattisgarh) in 2000 was not on the basis of languages, it did reflect the logic of political representation of diversities, for these states gave better representation to tribal populations (as in Jharkhand and Chhattisgarh) or otherwise socio-culturally different groups (as in Uttaranchal).

Before turning to the Indian experience of dealing with diversities, it is worth noting some of the institutional features of the Indian state. India, in contrast to many countries in the developing world, has a relatively strong and usable state with a government, a bureaucracy, an army, a judiciary, and above all, democratic institutions which enjoy considerable legitimacy and are able to exercise their authority over most of its population and territory. As we shall document, the overwhelming majority of Indian citizens respect the Indian state and generally expect it to serve the collective interests of its citizens.

In analysing the Indian experience, one cannot overlook the external aspects, specifically the fact that the exit options were effectively closed. It is true that the struggle for independence and the democratic institutions created at that time legitimated a sense of Indian nationhood and a conception of the nation open to its pluralism. This makes it unlikely that major political forces, parties, and intellectuals would favour whatever secessionist demands may appear in the periphery (with perhaps the exception of Kashmir). Even the two main communist parties, the Communist Party of India (CPI) and the Communist Party of India (Marxist)

(CPI[M]), have on balance sided with the project of preserving the boundaries of the Indian state, even if by selective use of coercive state apparatus.[23] This consensus on the importance of the Indian nation, *and* on the Indian state nation, give support to the institutional rules in the Constitution that allow the government to act in defence of the Indian Republic. At the same time, we must remember that, as in many other federal constitutions, there are provisions to defend the Constitution and the unity of the state, if necessary by coercive means. The awareness of that possibility, and the actual record of using those resources in Nagaland, Mizoram, and the Punjab has left those who might question the state in a 'no-exit' position, one that forces the search for negotiated compromise within the context of the federal institutions of the state.[24]

[23]   A case in point was the support by the communist parties for the suppression of Khalistani secessionism in the Punjab. The Indian communists did not extend any support in this instance to the demand of separation from the Indian state. The communist workers were among the prime targets of the pro-Khalistan militants. A veteran leader of the CPI, Satyapal Dang, offers a defence of this stance in his *Genesis of Terrorism: Analytical Study of Punjab Terrorists*, New Delhi: Patriot Publishers, 1988. A statement by the Punjab state committee of the CPI(M) 'expressed deep concern over the increasing activities of Sikh fundamentalists and extremists in the state and felt that they posed a threat to the hard-earned peace in the state and also to the unity and integrity of the country.' *People's Democracy*, vol. XXIX (35), 28 August 2005.

[24]   Various human rights groups within and outside India have documented the denial of basic civil rights guaranteed by the Indian constitution and law and the use of brutal repressive measures by security forces in the conflicts mentioned above. See the various annual reports and other India related material of Amnesty International at *http:// web.amnesty.org/library/eng-ind/index*. Various human rights groups within the country have also extensively documented these violations. See the various publications of the reputed and independent Peoples' Union for Civil Liberties (PUCL) at *www.pucl.org*, especially its report *Kashmir: A Report to the Nation*, published by PUCL and CFD, 1993. An academic compilation of these reports can be found in, A.R. Desai, ed., *Violation of Democratic Rights in India*, Bombay: Popular Prakashan, 1986. For some recent reports, see Ram Narayan Kumar, Amrik Singh, Ashok Agarwal and Jaskaran Kaur, *Reduced To Ashes: The Insurgency and Human Rights in Punjab*, New Delhi: South Asia Forum for Human Rights, 2003, (copy available at *www.punjabjustice.org*), and *Touch Kashmir: An Enquiry into the Healing*, a report by AFDR, HRF and OPDR, Hyderabad, 2003.

Besides, India is not very vulnerable to 'international' opinion when confronting secessionist threats, due to its longstanding democracy, its demonstrated atomic capability and large mobile ground forces, and its geo-political location in the world. Also, it so happens that most of the states (with the exception of the Punjab) where secessionist tendencies have been strong, or might arise, are numerically too small, geographically peripheral, and weak in terms of resources to sustain aspirations to independent statehood without external support.[25] This again is not the case in some other federal multinational states, like Spain, or the case of Quebec in Canada. Geography is also a favourable factor since there is a continuity of territory that, for example, does not exist in an island state such as Indonesia. The fact that India has a strong state with, as we shall show, longstanding and legitimate democratic institutions, a functioning legal system, and loyal armed forces, makes it very different from other federal states in the developing world. Federalism and the processing of new member states, the asymmetrical status of different states, and the multi-tier federalism in some of the states, are essential elements of the building of India as a state nation.

In India, as in other federal democracies like Spain or Canada, the institutionalization of an asymmetrical federalism creates tension and hostility. Many think that only a constitutionally symmetrical federalism, like the one we find in the US, Australia, Switzerland, and Germany, is the ideal form of federalism. However, we want to argue, again, that a comparison of Indian institutions with those of the US, or for that matter Germany, is not the most fruitful approach. Once we enlarge our scope of analysis, we will see that many of the problems that scholars

[25]   According to the Census of India 2001, the population of Nagaland was 1.9 million, just about 0.19 per cent of the Indian population. Manipur's population was 2.1 million and accounted for about 0.21 per cent. Jammu and Kashmir's population was 10.1 million. With this absolute number, Jammu and Kashmir had about 0.99 per cent of the total population of the country (of this 5.7 million or 0.56 per cent of the Indian population lived in the Kashmir Valley, the heart of political alienation). Of these states, only Punjab has a national population share of more than one per cent. (*Source*: *Census of India— 2001*, Primary Census Abstract, Series 1 and 2: Registrar General of India, New Delhi.)

working on India see as unique and threatening may be found in one way or another in other federal multicultural, multilingual, and/or multinational societies in which there is no shared conception of the nation or a nation state. At the same time, the comparison will show that India and its democratic institutions enjoy legitimacy among the citizens equal to, if not greater than, the institutions in other longstanding democratic federal pluralistic societies. It should be noted that in no political system do all the citizens grant to the state, its institutions and democratic processes, a unanimous legitimacy or allegiance. It is only the size of India and the number of its people, that makes these problems somewhat more significant than in some other countries, once we translate the proportions into absolute numbers of citizens.

The building of a state nation in India was not an accident. The idea of India, closer to state nation than to nation state, was nurtured by the national independence movement and would eventually be enshrined in the Indian constitution, sustained by the first generation of post-Independence leadership and institutionalized in competitive politics thereafter. Right from its early stages, much before it became a mass movement in the 1920s, the leaders of the nationalist movement were keen to present themselves as representing different regional identities while representing the Indian nation. The mass phase of the national movement under the leadership of Mahatma Gandhi took this one step further. Rather than deny linguistic and cultural heterogeneity within India, the national movement took pains to recognize and protect it. As early as 1921, the Indian National Congress reorganized its provincial units on the basis of language spoken in that region and thus laid down the basis of regional autonomy based on language.

Recognition of and respect for diversity was at the heart of the various proposals for the Constitution for independent India. Thus, when the Constituent Assembly formally set about its task in 1946, there was little doubt about the provisions for protection of linguistic, cultural, and religious diversity. The makers of the Indian constitution did not use a phrase like 'state nation'. After the partition of India took effect in the middle of the deliberations of the Constituent Assembly, the constitution makers were reluctant to use an expression like 'federalism', opting to use 'union of states' instead. Yet the institutional structures they set up provided for a robust state nation.

In this sense the Constitution of India inherited the intellectual legacy of modern Indian political thought.

The first generation of leaders of independent India, most notably Nehru, were very conscious of the need to accommodate diversity in what they saw as the uniquely Indian model of 'nation-building'. One of the most oft repeated clichés of independent India, 'Unity in Diversity', expresses the spirit of the Indian acceptance of what we call state nation. This ensured that the demand for reorganization of all the remaining states on the basis of language was conceded, even though Nehru was personally disinclined to do so. It is this spirit that has made for a smooth transition from the national dominance of one-dominant party in the 1980s to a regionalized polity in the 1990s. The acceptance of this model is not confined to the centrist parties like the Congress; it cuts across the left-right divide. Even the right wing Bharatiya Janata Party (BJP), which has questioned the consensus on secular character of the Indian state, has accepted the regional and linguistic diversity as one of the basics of Indian nationhood.

SOME INDICATORS CHARACTERIZING THE INDIAN POLITY AS A STATE NATION: PRIDE IN INDIA AND MULTIPLE BUT COMPLEMENTARY IDENTITIES

After this broad comparative introduction we can turn to some of the relevant empirical evidence in the hope that it will contribute to stimulate Indian and foreign scholars to further research using broader and even better sets of indicators than the ones we now have.

One important indicator of identification of a citizen with the society and the state is the sense of pride, in this case the pride of being Indian. Fortunately, a similar question has been asked in the federal democracies we are comparing and is continuously asked in the member states of the EU by the Eurobarometer surveys.

The question of pride has been asked in the widely used comparative public opinion survey *World Values Survey* under the direction of Ronald Inglehart *et al.*, based at the University of Michigan. To date there are four rounds of these surveys available for our comparative analysis, 1981–4, 1990–3, 1995–7, and 1999–2001. The first round covered twenty-two independent countries, the second forty-two, the third fifty-three, and the fourth seventy-five. India has been included in all four rounds. This set of surveys is particularly interesting for comparativists, because each country asks most of the same questions and many of the questions have been used in all the rounds. We have from the *World Values Survey* (WVS) three fairly similar readings on the pride question. In all the three waves about two-thirds of the respondents said they were 'very proud' to be an Indian. About 20 to 25 per cent said they were 'proud', thus pushing the proportion of 'very proud' and 'proud' to between 85 to 90 per cent. In each of these waves, the proportion of those who said they were 'not proud' or 'not at all proud' was recorded as less than 10 per cent. This can be confirmed with the State of Democracy in South Asia (SDSA) survey of the Centre for the Study of Developing Societies (CSDS) that has a larger and more representative sample. Better representation of rural and uneducated voters in the CSDS survey has led to a little higher proportion of 'Don't Know' responses, but the basic pattern is the same as that reported by the WVS (see Table 3.6).

A sense of pride can be based on many different things—from political institutions, cultural and the artistic heritage, the landscape, and last but not least, cuisine. Indians, more than people in many countries of the world, have reasons to be proud of many aspects of Indian society, culture, and history, while the more recent history of some other countries makes it more difficult for its citizens to feel fully proud of their nation. One such case is Germany, for which

Table 3.6: Pride in India, 1990–2005

	WVS 1990	WVS 1995	WVS 2001	SDSA 2005
Very proud	67	66	67	61
Quite proud	25	19	21	28
Not proud	5	8	5	2
Not at all proud	3	1	2	1
Don't know/ No answer	0	6	5	8
N	2466	2040	2002	5387

Note: All figures except N are in percentages rounded off to the nearest integral.

Source: WVS stands for different waves of the *World Values Survey*, while the SDSA stands for the *State of Democracy in South Asia* survey conducted by the CSDS.

the Nazi period and the holocaust legacy represent a heavy burden.[26] Those who feel an exclusive identity with another nation and reject the state in which they live are also not likely to feel proud of the state or the nation and its heritage. Some of the variations between countries reflect these different attitudes.

When asked 'How proud are you to be an Indian?' 67 per cent say 'very proud'. Among the world's eleven longstanding federal democracies, only in the US (71 per cent) and Australia (70 per cent) was the number larger, but the percentage was less in Argentina (65 per cent) and Brazil (64 per cent), lower still in Spain (51 per cent), surprisingly low in Switzerland (23 per cent), and lower yet in Germany (14 per cent).[27] Those saying 'not very' or 'not at all' add up to 8.3 per cent in India, certainly more than the US (1.8 per cent) and Australia (2.5 per cent), but less than in the other federal democracies, particularly Germany (31.6 per cent), and surprisingly again, Switzerland. Perhaps these figures would be different with a more representative sample of the Indian population than the *World Values Survey*, 1995–7, but they are certainly impressive (see table 3.7).

The findings of the *World Values Survey* can be largely confirmed with the *State of Democracy in South Asia Study 2005*. When asked this question in the SDSA 2005, as many as 61 per cent of Indians said they were very proud of being an Indian. Surprisingly, citizens from the once conflictual context of Tamil Nadu register a slightly higher percentage of 'very proud' responses (68 per cent) than India as a whole, and in the once secession-torn Punjab, the total percentage of 'very proud' and 'quite proud' responses (92 per cent) is three points higher than the all-India average. However, citizens belonging to some of

---

[26]   On the complex issue of pride (or lack thereof) in the German nation, see Elisabeth Noelle-Neumann, 'Nationalgefühl und Glück', in Noelle-Neumann and Renate Köcher, *Die verletzte Nation*, Stuttgart: Deutsche Verlags-Anstalt, 1987, pp. 17–74.

[27]   Concerning Switzerland, as the reader will see later (in Table 3.14), consistent with our idea of the state nation, of the eleven longstanding federal democracies, Switzerland has the highest percentage of people with confidence in the government and the second highest percentage of people with confidence in the legal system. So while they may not have pride in being Swiss *as such*, they nevertheless have great pride in their Swiss institutions.

Table 3.7: Pride in Nationality in the Eleven Longstanding Federal Democracies

	Very proud	Quite proud	Not very	Not at all	Don't know / Not applicable	Total
United States	71	23	4	0	2	99
Australia	70	23	2	0	5	100
India	67	21	5	2	5	100
Canada	65	28	3	2	2	100
Argentina	65	24	4	3	5	101
Brazil	64	19	14	2	1	100
Spain	51	36	6	3	4	100
Austria	50	37	6	2	5	100
Belgium	20	46	15	7	11	99
Switzerland	23	47	16	7	7	100
Germany	15	46	22	7	9	99

Note: All figures are in percentages rounded off to the nearest integral.

Source: The data for all countries is from responses to the question 'How proud are you to be (nationality)?' *Human Beliefs and Values: A Cross-Cultural Sourcebook Based on the 1999–2002 Values Survey*, eds, Ronald Inglehart *et al.*, Mexico D.F.: Siglo XXI Editores, 2004

the country's other significant marginal groups do register 'very proud' responses in lower proportions; even so, among the seven marginal groups or states listed in Table 3.8, only in Mizoram does the proportion of those who feel very proud or proud dip below three quarters of the population (see Table 3.8).

Table 3.8: Pride in India for all Citizens and for Marginal Groups and States, 2005

	All India	Tamil Nadu	Mus-lim	Sched-uled Caste	Punjab	Sched-uled Tribe	Non liter-ate	Mizo-ram
Very proud	61	68	58	57	55	44	44	36
Quite proud	28	24	31	31	37	38	34	38
Not proud	2	1	1	3	3	2	3	11
Not at all proud	1	0	2	2	1	1	2	2
Don't know/ No answer	8	7	8	7	4	15	17	13
Total	100	100	100	100	100	100	100	100
N	5387	345	635	1023	73	443	1964	121

Note: All figures except N are in percentages rounded off to the nearest integral.

Source: *State of Democracy in South Asia Survey, 2005*, CSDS, provisional figures.

There are certainly citizens of India who do not question the Indian state, but feel very strongly a part of another identity, which potentially can serve as a basis for a nationalist sentiment and political movement, as has been the case with a minority among Sikhs identifying with the project of Khalistan, as an independent Sikh state. There are finally some groups in the North-East who share very little of the Indian national identity, who feel a distinctive national, or at least tribal, identity, and who at one point or another have questioned the authority of the Indian state and fought for an independent status. Some of these, most notably in Mizoram, have been reintegrated into the Indian state and participate, thanks to federalism, in the Indian political process.[28] However, for some

[28] Mizoram's population is predominantly Christian: as per the latest census of 2001, 87 per cent of the population is Christian while less than 4 per cent are Hindus, *Source: Census of India 2001, The First Report on Religion Data: Registrar General of India, New Delhi*. In terms of language too, Mizoram is radically different from the rest of the country: in 1991 less than 2 per cent spoke Hindi, the national language, while 75 per cent of the population spoke Lushai/Mizo, a local language. (*Source: Census of India 1991, statement 3, paper 1 of 1997 Language: Registrar General of India, New Delhi*; also see website of Census of India: *www.censusindia.net/religiondata* and *www.censusindia.net/data/ 15_miz.pdf*). Mizoram was on the fringes of British India and did not have much of a nationalist movement against the British rule. India's independence was followed by a refusal on the part of the Mizo leadership to accept India's sovereignty. The Mizo leaders waged a thirty-year-long, bloody, and ultimately unsuccessful armed struggle for independence from India. The long history of armed insurgency and state repression was brought to an end in the Mizoram Accord between the insurgents and the Government of India in 1987. This was followed by the institutionalization of the routines of democratic politics with surprising success. The CSDS, Delhi, carried out a post-poll survey with a sample of 1,116 following the state assembly elections in Mizoram in 2003. The survey findings indicate a surprisingly high level of integration into India's federal democracy: as many as 84 per cent expressed a preference for democracy. A majority of the respondents included India as constitutive of their identity: only 32 per cent of the respondents identified themselves as 'only Mizo'. Two-thirds of those who had an opinion supported the Mizo accord of 1987. (*Source*: Mizoram Assembly Election Study 2003, CSDS Data Unit.) Stepan also carried out interviews with political leaders in Mizoram in January 2003 and arrived at similar conclusions.

people, India is just a state nation, and for a few of them probably something like a multinational state from whose authority they cannot escape under normal circumstances. Fortunately for India's federal democracy there are not many such states and most can be found in the periphery in the North-East. The Nagas (inside Nagaland and to a lesser extent in surrounding states such as Manipur) are the prime example[29] as are the people of the Kashmir Valley.[30]

[29]   Nagaland is home to at least sixteen major tribes that speak different languages but accept a broad modern political identity of being a 'Naga'. Thus defined, the territory inhabited by the Nagas spills over to the state of Manipur and a bit of Assam and Arunachal Pradesh within the Indian Union and Myanmar across the international border. Disaffection with the Indian state dates back to the very foundation of independent India when Angami Phizo, the charismatic leader of the Nagas, refused to accept the authority of the Indian state. Thus followed decades of civil war and insurgency that severely limited the writ of the Indian state, the formal state control being maintained only with the presence of the Indian army. Formally, the insurgency still continues and is led by the Nationalist Socialist Council of Nagalim (Isaac–Muivah)[NSCN(I–M)]. But on the ground the situation has eased considerably since August 1997 when a ceasefire was announced between the Government of India and the NSCN(I–M). A series of informal dialogues outside the country paved the way for an official dialogue on Indian soil in January 2003. The peace talks have proceeded slowly since then but the ceasefire has continued. The National Election Study (NES) 2004 by the CSDS included a sample of 522 randomly-chosen respondents from Nagaland and was perhaps the first ever survey of political opinions and attitudes in the state. The survey brought out an unwillingness to accept the Indian identity: about 57 per cent respondents identified themselves as 'only Nagas' as against 9 per cent 'only Indian', and 34 per cent 'Indian and Naga'. However, the alienation did not affect attitudes to the peace process: 85 per cent had heard about the negotiations and two-thirds of those who had an opinion were optimistic of a positive outcome. The survey also revealed a lack of strong support for the hardline agenda of 'greater Nagaland' that has blocked the negotiations.

[30]   The limited survey evidence at our disposal does indicate a deep political alienation from India in the Kashmir Valley (which itself is a little over half of the population of the Indian state of Jammu and Kashmir) but it does not prove that there is widespread support

Survey evidence gathered by the CSDS allows us to examine the question of political identities in contemporary India in an empirical manner. A question about subjective national identity was asked in two of its recent surveys based on a probability sample of the national electorate. The first survey, the NES 1998, provided for three answer categories, while the most recent survey, the Indian component of the *State of Democracy in South Asia Survey, 2005*, also provided for the two in-between categories ('more Indian than state identity' and 'more state identity than Indian'). Notwithstanding the minor differences in question wording, the pattern of responses is quite similar. Unlike both Spain and

---

for Pakistan in the Valley. In 2002, the CSDS (in collaboration with the Department of Political Science, University of Jammu) carried out a post-poll survey among a sample of 2,195 adult persons, including 1,118 respondents in the Kashmir Valley. Unlike other surveys of the CSDS, this survey was not based on a strict probability sample. But the profile of the sampled respondents was a fair representation of the state's demographic profile except in terms of gender. In this first survey of its kind, the respondents were asked to choose from various options for Kashmir: as many as 79 per cent of the respondents from the Kashmir Valley opted for Kashmir on both sides of the border to be merged to form an independent country with the remaining respondents about equally divided between India and Pakistan. The situation in the Kashmir Valley has no doubt improved somewhat since this survey in 2002, given the reasonably free and fair elections in the state that led to the defeat of the National Conference government that was seen as an imposition of the central government. The NES 2004 records some of these changes. While nearly half of the sample of 954 respondents kept quiet on sensitive questions dealing with the fairness of the electoral process, an overwhelming majority of those who gave any response acknowledged marked improvement: 76 per cent said that the 2004 parliamentary polls saw virtually no rigging, 71 per cent thought the level of electoral malpractice had gone down, and 90 per cent felt either no fear or said the fear had come down. These responses are for the entire state of Jammu and Kashmir, and not just the Kashmir Valley. The public opinion in the other regions of the state was sharply different. Only 7 per cent of the respondents in Jammu region and 2 per cent of the respondents in Ladakh supported the demand for independence and none supported merger with Pakistan.

Belgium, the modal response category in India is 'only Indian'. Nearly half the respondents privilege their Indian identity over identities of their respective states, which also happen to be linguistic identities in most cases.[31] Even when the in-between category of 'more Indian than state identity' was introduced in the 2005 survey, as many as 35 per cent of all respondents chose 'only Indian' to describe their identity with 12 per cent opting for the new category. To recall, only 13 per cent Belgians and 14 per cent Spanish respondents opted for only national identity in response to the same question. This reflects the depth of nationalist sentiment in a country where nationalism emerged from intense anti-colonial struggle. At the same time this response does not rule out significant reservations: about a fifth of the respondents privileged their state identity over their Indian identity. Even after providing the in-between option of 'more state identity than Indian' the proportion of those who opted for 'only state' identity was a little higher than in Belgium or Spain. Less than one-fifth Indians opted for the middle category of equally Indian and state identity, compared to about half of the respondents in Spain and Belgium (see Table 3.9).

Table 3.9: Subjective National Identity in India, 1998–2005

	NES 1998	SDSA 2005
Only Indian	50	35
More Indian than state identity	NA	12
As Indian as state identity	16	19
More state identity than Indian	NA	10
Only state identity	20	12
Don't know/don't answer	14	12
	100	100
N	8140	5385

Note: All figures except N are in percentages rounded off to the nearest integral.

Source: National Election Study 1998 and State of Democracy in South Asia Survey 2005.

31   While there is a great deal of overlap between the linguistic divisions of India and the boundaries of the various states of the Indian Union, there is no perfect match here. Most of the states have significant linguistic

DEMOCRATIC STATE NATIONS: WHO SUPPORTS DEMOCRACY IN INDIA?

We argue that democratic political institutions and processes are essential components of the viability and stability of multicultural, multilingual, multinational state nations. Democracy makes possible the identification with the state of many of its citizens who might have different identities, who might question their nation state, but are ready to be loyal citizens of the state. Authoritarianism might serve to impose a nation state model on the society, as was the case of Spain under the authoritarian regime of Franco. But, as the data for Spain show, the result ultimately was a backlash of resurgence and, in the Basque Country, violent extreme nationalism.

Democracy, and more concretely federal democracy, can serve to integrate such a society. The *Verfassungspatriotismus* of Dolf Sternberger, developed by Jürgen Habermas in the German Federal Republic, might not have been important in Germany after the unification of the Bundesrepublik Deutschland (BDR or West Germany) and the Deutsche Demokratische Republik (DDR or East Germany), but it certainly is an important component for more heterogeneous societies. It is not the only component of support for a state nation but is certainly one of the most important ones. It is for that reason that a more detailed discussion of the attitude of Indians and of different groups in Indian society towards democracy and democratic institutions is so vital to our interpretation of the politics of diversity.

In analysing the attitudes of citizens towards democracy and democratic institutions, there are some necessary distinctions that are not always made. For example, there is strong evidence from many countries that we need to distinguish the belief in the need for certain institutions and their desirability and legitimacy, from the attitudes about the way those institutions actually perform. People in principle might support democracy, but they may often have serious misgivings about how their particular democracy is actually functioning. A distinction between the 'legitimacy of

---

minorities. The language spoken by the largest number of people, Hindi, is the official language of eight states of the Indian Union. Most of the dominant languages are internally divided among various 'dialects' that vary considerably.

institutions' and the 'efficacy of institutions' is therefore crucial.[32] Citizens may believe that democracy is the best form of government for a country like theirs, but when asked if democracy is able to solve the problems of their society, they might be less enthusiastic. When that question is followed by, 'How is democracy working in our country?,' the answers might be quiet negative in many circumstances. The negative response to the actual performance of democratic institutions in the long run is likely to erode the belief in the need for those institutions, but there is also evidence from many studies that these are different dimensions. The same is true, even more so, with political parties. In many democratic countries people agree on the need for parties to articulate their interests and demands but, at the same time, a large number of people have little trust in actual political parties. There are many and complex reasons for this distrust in practically all democracies, a distrust which is not translated into rejection of political parties in principle as necessary institutions in a democracy, and even less of democracy itself.[33] Nor does it necessarily translate in declining levels of identification with actual political parties. The same is true to an even greater extent in attitudes towards the incumbents of many offices in democratic systems. The use of one or another indicator alone may capture different dimensions and sometimes leads to pessimistic perceptions about the stability of democracy.

A classic question that has been asked in many countries that we find quite useful because it gives the respondent four alternatives is: 'With which of the following phrases are you most in agreement?,' (1) 'Democracy is preferable to any other form of government'. (2) 'In some circumstances an authoritarian government can be preferable to a democratic government,' (3) 'For someone like me a democratic or non-democratic regime

---

[32] This is a theme developed in Juan Linz, 'Crisis, Breakdown, and Reequilibration', in Linz and Stepan, eds, *The Breakdown of Democratic Regimes*, Baltimore: The Johns Hopkins University Press, 1978.

[33] For an elaboration on this theme, see Juan Linz, 'Parties in Contemporary Democracies: Problems and Paradoxes', in Richard Gunther, José Ramón Montero, and Juan J. Linz, eds, *Political Parties. Old Concepts and New Challenges*, New York: Oxford University Press, 2002, pp. 291–317.

makes no difference.', (4) 'Do not know' or no answer. Our studies document that in India the 'do not know' response is more likely among poor and uneducated segments of the population and therefore it should not be surprising that in the NES, 1999, this is 27 per cent, the largest proportion ever recorded in the list of countries where this question has been asked (though it had dropped to 20 per cent by 2004).

When we turn to the first alternative, agreement with the statement that democracy is better than any other form of government, the results vary considerably between countries, but nowhere is the proportion unanimous. In India, according to the NES, 2004, it is 70 per cent of all those interviewed, which means that 88 per cent of those expressing an opinion, agree that democracy is preferable. The second alternative, that in some circumstances an authoritarian government may be preferable, is the choice of 4 per cent of the population. Those who say that for someone like themselves a democratic or non-democratic regime makes no difference are only 6 per cent of the population.

Let us look at the answers in a few other countries. In Brazil, the number with no opinion is 15 per cent, a large one in comparison to other democracies, but those clearly preferring democracy are only 41 per cent, those expressing the potential support for an authoritarian alternative 21 per cent, and those indifferent 23 per cent, a much less favourable response than we find in India. If we turn to a relatively new democracy, Spain, the number of 'no answer' is quite small, 6 per cent, and those preferring democracy 78 per cent, those potentially supporting an authoritarian alternative 9 per cent, and those indifferent 7 per cent—figures that are very similar to those we find in India. The Spanish data have been consistently within this range over a long period of time. In Latin America, only Uruguay, with 80 per cent democratic, 8 per cent authoritarian, and 6 per cent indifferent, is regularly more supportive of democracy than India.[34] Even in Chile after the painful experience of authoritarianism, democracy is endorsed by only 52 per cent, 19 per cent do not exclude the authoritarian alternative, and 25 per cent are indifferent, though

---

[34]   Among the other Latin American countries, Costa Rica sometimes, but not always, has a higher support for democracy than does India.

those without opinion are only 4 per cent. In summary, in an international comparative perspective the support for democracy in India is very high (see Table 3.10).

Table 3.10: Attitudes towards Democracy and Authoritarianism in India and Five Important 'Third Wave' Democracies

	India 2004	Uruguay	Spain	India 1999	Korea	Chile	Brazil
Democracy is preferable to any other form of government	70	80	78	60	58	52	41
(Per cent of valid responses excluding DK)	(88)	(85)	(83)	(82)	(62)	(54)	(48)
In some circumstances an authoritarian government can be preferable to a democratic government.	4	8	9	6	27	18	21
For someone like me, a democratic or a non-democratic regime makes no difference.	6	6	7	7	8	25	23
Don't know/ No answer	20	6	6	27	7	4	15
N	27148	1213	1000	8133	1037	1200	1240

Note: All figures except N are in column percentages, rounded off to the nearest integral. Figures in parentheses in the second row are for percentage of valid responses if the DKs, and no answer, are treated as missing data.

Source: The data for India are from the *National Election Study, 1999 and 2004*, of the CSDS, Delhi. Data for Uruguay, Brazil, and Chile are from the *Latino Barometer 1996*, directed by Marta Lagos. The Spanish data are from the *Eurobarometer 37*, 1992. The Korean data is from the *Korea Democracy Barometer*, 2004, directed by Doh Chull Shin.

Despite India's high approval of democracy at the aggregate level, we immediately have to ask ourselves whether in the heterogeneous Indian population there are some segments of society that are much less supportive of democracy than the all-India average. A very important finding is that in India, *all* religious groups are strongly supportive of democracy. Indeed, statistically, the responses are virtually identical across all religious groups. From a comparative perspective, it is also interesting to note that the 71 per cent of Indian Muslims saying 'democracy is always preferable' is higher than that recorded by any Latin American country ever, with the exceptions of Costa Rica and Uruguay (in some years). Evidently, whatever deep cleavages and differences might exist along religious or communal lines, they are not reflected in attitudes towards democracy. Democracy can be a key unifying element among all Indians (see Table 3.11).

Table 3.11: Support for Democracy in India as a Whole and for Marginal Groups and Minorities

	All India	Muslim	Christian	Sikh	Sched-uled Caste	Sched-uled Tribe	Very poor	Poor
Democracy is always preferable	70	71	74	71	65	61	61	71
(Percen-tage of valid responses)	(88)	(87)	(91)	(88)	(87)	(81)	(87)	(88)
Sometimes authoritari-anism is preferable	4	4	3	4	3	5	3	4
No difference	6	7	5	6	6	8	6	6
Don't know/ No answer	20	18	19	19	25	26	30	19
Total	100	100	101	100	100	100	100	100
N	27145	3103	838	687	4967	2356	8117	9409

Note: All figures except N are in column percentages, rounded off to the nearest integral. Figures in parentheses in the second row are for percentage of valid responses if the DKs, and no answer, are treated as missing data.

Source: *National Election Study India, 2004.*

Not unexpectedly, among the 'very poor' the number of those who do not know or have no answer is particularly large. Even so, a majority of them, 61 per cent, opt for democracy, and 9 per cent opt for a non-democratic alternative. Among the 'poor' the proportions are 71 per cent and 10 per cent respectively. Indeed, among those who expressed their opinions, the proportions were virtually identical across all income groups. What's more, a very similar pattern of convergence is apparent across the different castes. As such, it is clear that democracy is not the preference of either the more privileged or the more underprivileged, or of any given caste among Indians but is a shared preference.

In view of the historic tensions between Tamil Nadu and the Republic in the early years, and the more recent conflict in Punjab, it is noteworthy that a commitment to democracy is above the Indian average in both states. In Tamil Nadu, 81 per cent prefer democracy, 4 per cent authoritarianism, 5 per cent see no difference, and 11 per cent have no opinion. In Punjab, 70 per cent prefer democracy, 4 per cent prefer an authoritarian alternative, and 7 per cent see no difference for themselves. Similar patterns can be observed in two other conflictual contexts, namely, Gujarat and Mizoram. In Gujarat, 82 per cent prefer democracy, 6 per cent authoritarianism, 5 per cent see no difference, and 7 per cent have no opinion; while in Mizoram 89 per cent prefer democracy, 3 per cent authoritarianism, 3 per cent see no difference, and 5 per cent have no opinion (see Table 3.12).

In summary, whatever deep cleavages and differences might exist along religious, social, or regional lines, these are not reflected in the attitudes towards democracy.

Although we will turn later to the problem of the distrust of different institutions and particularly political parties, it is important to note how much the Indians agree with the need for parties in answering the question, 'Suppose there were no parties or assemblies, and elections were not held, do you think that the government in this country can be run better?', only 19.8 per cent of the population has no opinion, and 68.8 per cent reject a system of government without parties, assemblies, and elections, and only 11.4 per cent agree with that possibility. These answers are obviously quite consistent with the commitment to democracy we have just noted.

Table 3.12: Support for Democracy in India as a Whole and in Some States

	All India	Tamil Nadu	Punjab	Gujarat	Mizoram
Democracy is preferable (percentage of valid responses)	70 (88)	81 (91)	70 (88)	82 (88)	89 (94)
Sometimes authoritarianism is preferable	4	4	4	6	3
No difference	6	5	7	5	3
Don't know/ No answer	20	11	20	7	5
Total	100	100	100	100	100
N	27145	843	814	1106	505

Note: All figures except N are in column percentages, rounded off to the nearest integral. Figures in parentheses in the second row are for percentage of valid responses if the DKs, and no answer, are treated as missing data.

Source: *National Election Study India 2004*

INDIA AS A STATE NATION: ASSESSING TRUST IN INSTITUTIONS

Let us try to go beyond the overall question of support for democracy to trust in the major institutions of the Indian state. The study of trust has been a major research area in policy analysis and social science research for the last three decades or so. Recently, Pippa Norris from Harvard, attempted to bring this research together so as to be able to make comparative judgments about trust in institutions.[35] Using the *World Values Survey* 1990–3, she constructed a composite index of trust by measuring expressed trust in five major institutions she felt were important for a democratic state: parliament, civil service, the judiciary, police, and the military. She did this for twenty-three democracies, one of which was India. India's composite score for citizen's institutional trust was the highest among these twenty-three

[35]   Pippa Norris, *Critical Citizens: Global Support for Democratic Governance,* Oxford: Oxford University Press, 1999.

democracies, clearly ahead of its closest competitor, Norway
(see Table 3.13).

Table 3.13: Institutions and Political Trust in India and Twenty Other Democracies: 1990–1993

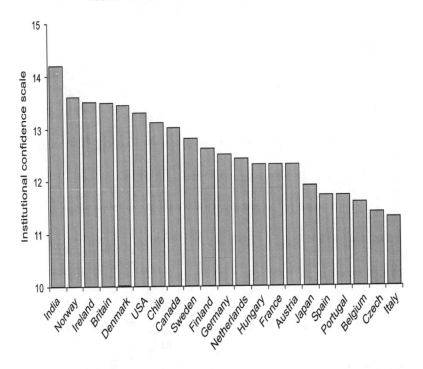

Source: Pippa Norris, *Critical Citizens: Global Support for Democratic Governance*, Oxford: Oxford University Press, 1999, Figure 11. 2, p. 229.

In order to see if India's very high comparative standing
concerning trust in institutions held up in a later survey, we ran
the data on trust in institutions for the eleven longstanding federal
democracies based on the 1995–7 round of the *World Values Survey*.
If we combine the total percentages of respondents who answered
that they had a 'Great Deal of Trust' or 'Quite a Lot of Trust' in
an institution, India ranks first or second out of the eleven
longstanding federal democracies in five of the six categories.
No other country scores in the top two more than twice. At the
opposite end of the scale Argentina ranks last in four of the six
categories (see table 3.14).

Table 3.14: Citizen Trust in Six Major Institutions in Eleven Longstanding Federal Democracies

Institution	India	India's rank	Switzer-land	Canada	Brazil	Austria	USA	Belgium	Spain	Germany	Australia	Argen-tina
Legal system	67	1st	65	54	55	58	36	45	45	54	35	27
Parliament	53	1st	41	38	33	41	30	43	35	28	31	16
Political parties	39	1st	25	n.a.	32	n.a.	21	n.a.	18	14	16	8
Central government	48	2nd	50	38	48	n.a.	31	n.a.	30	24	26	27
Civil service	53	2nd	43	50	59	42	52	43	40	47	38	8
Police	36	10th	67	84	45	68	71	51	61	70	76	23

Note: All figures in percentages, rounded off to the nearest integral. Table entries refer to the sum total of those who respond 'Great deal' or 'Quite' to the question 'How much confidence you have in ....? Great Deal, Quite, Not very much, None'.

Source: The data for all countries except Austria, Belgium, and Canada is from *World Values Survey: 1995–7*, Ronald Inglehart *et al.*, Inter University Consortium for Political and Social Research, University of Michigan. The data for Germany is from the Lander of the former West Germany. Canada, Belgium, and Austria were not included in the 1995–7 survey. The data for these countries is from *World Values Survey: 1990–3*. For both the 1990–3 and 1995–7 surveys the question numbers were, from top to bottom, 142, 144, 137, 141, 143, and 145. Question 143, was not asked in Canada. Questions 142 and 143 were not asked in Belgium and Austria.

What's more, when we calculate the average ranking in trust for all of the major institutions indicated above, we find that of the eleven longstanding federal democracies, India is the country that ranks the highest on trust, followed by Switzerland, and then Canada. This finding is of major theoretical import, because none of these countries approximate the 'nation state' model. Rather, they are all closer to the ideal type of the 'state nation'. Nor does such a finding appear to be a fluke; for when we examine the entire universe of the eleven longstanding federal democracies and calculate and compare the mean trust score and average ranking of the five federal states closest to the 'state nation' model with that of the six states closest to the 'nation state' model, we find that on the whole, the state nation set scores significantly better than the nation state set. The mean trust score for all the five state nations in this set is 46.8, while the score for the nation states is only 38.2. In terms of the rank, the average rank of state nations is 4.8, compared to 7.0 for the state nation. Prima facie, thus, it does not appear that the 'state nation' model produces any deficit in political trust, as many analysts fear. To the contrary, there is strong evidence that shows a higher level of citizen trust in longstanding federal democracies approximating the model of the 'state nation', than in the longstanding federal democracies that approximate the model of the 'nation state' (see Table 3.15).

While very impressive, Tables 3.14 and 3.15, are based, as we discussed previously, on a sample in India that under-represents illiterates and rural dwellers and was only given in eight of the country's fifteen official languages, so we must look at other surveys to measure trust with greater confidence. Table 3.16 presents a comparison of the responses on trust in institutions from the latest round of the *World Values Survey* of 2001 with the SDSA survey carried out by the CSDS in 2005. While the level of trust recorded in the latter is a little higher than the WVS, the internal order of the five institutions is more or less the same: the police and political parties finish at the bottom of the heap. The data from the survey carried out by the CSDS has the advantage of expanding the range of institutions about which we have information. It shows that two of the most trusted institutions in India are the judiciary and the Election Commission. The independent and powerful federal institution, the Election Commission of India, has the responsibility

Table 3.15: Citizen Trust in Major Institutions in the World's Eleven Longstanding Federal Democracies: 'State Nations' versus 'Nation States'

Country and type	Mean rank among 11 countries	Mean trust score for six institutions
State Nations	4.8	46.8
India	3.0	49.3
Switzerland	3.7	48.5
Canada	4.0	52.5
Belgium	6.3	45.5
Spain	7.2	38.2
Nation States	7.0	38.2
Brazil	4.6	45.3
Austria	5.0	52.3
USA	5.9	40.2
Germany	7.6	35.9
Australia	8.0	37.0
Argentina	10.6	18.2

Note: See Table 3.12. For the two questions in which we do not have data for all eleven countries, we adjusted the rankings of the rest by multiplying the actual ranking by eleven, then dividing by the number of countries for which data exists.

Source: As in Table 3.14

for supervising the fairness and efficiency of the entire electoral process.[36] The fact that the Election Commission of India is a highly trusted institution helps give the democratic electoral process itself enhanced legitimacy. In comparative terms, even when we substitute the CSDS survey for the World Values sample, India's relatively high trust ranking holds up (see Table 3.16).

[36]   The 2002 riots in Gujarat, and the 2002 electoral outcome in Gujarat, raise many disturbing questions, which we discuss later. However, the central Election Commission emerged stronger in one respect. Against the ruling BJP's wish, the Election Commission managed to postpone the timing of the Gujarat elections. The Election Commission also gained prestige due to the positive role it played in conducting reasonably fair elections in Kashmir in 2002.

Table 3.16: Trust in Institutions in India, World Values Survey, and State of Democracy in South Asia Survey

	WVS 2001	SDSA 2005
Legal system	NA	59
Parliament	41	43
Political parties	28	36
Central government	49	62
Civil service	38	47
Police	34	42
Election Commission	NA	51
N	2002	5385

Note: Table entries except N are for the percentage, rounded off to the nearest integral of respondents who said 'great deal' or 'quite a lot' to a question about their trust in different institutions of India.

Source: *World Values Survey 2001, State of Democracy in South Asia Survey 2005.*

What does our survey data, linked to our knowledge of voting, and governing practices, indicate about India's overall political development in the last three decades? Contrary to observers who see growing signs of political disintegration in India, there are signs that in fact there is growing participation, growing sense of efficacy and, despite the proliferation of parties, especially state parties, growing commitment to Indian democracy as a way of managing diversity, among previously marginalized groups.

There is a general presumption, especially in American sociological literature, that the lower the education level and the income level, the lower the voting participation rates and the sense of personal political efficacy.[37] This is coupled with the belief that in the modern world, political trust in institutions has been declining for over three decades. Finally there is Samuel Huntington's famous axiom that if participation increases faster than institutionalization, there can be a crisis of governability. Most of these assumptions and or worries are true for the US, some are true for Western Europe, but none are true for India.

---

[37] See for example Sidney Verba and Norman H. Nie, *Participation in America: Political Democracy and Social Equality*, New York: Harper and Row, 1972. See especially p. 97.

Let us first examine the widely held hypothesis that the lower the socio-economic status, the lower is the voting turnout. In the US, this assertion holds true with brutal regularity. If we divide levels of income into five quintiles, for each quintile that income decreases in the United States, there is a monotonic decline in voter turnout, 77 per cent, 67 per cent, 59 per cent, 52 per cent, 43 per cent. The same holds true, even more sharply, for the six levels of education in the United States the percentage of post-graduate voters is 84, then for each descending level of education the percentages are 79, 66, 57, 43, and 38. Also, Blacks and Latinos vote less than Whites. In the non-presidential year of 1994, for example, 47 per cent of Whites voted, 37 per cent of Blacks voted, and 20 per cent of Latinos voted.

In sharp contrast to the US, in India, voting rates are not monotonic. Illiterates have a higher turnout than do post-graduates, who in fact have the lowest turnout rate. In terms of income, quintiles 3 and 4 vote at *higher* rates than do the two wealthiest quintiles, 1 and 2. In terms of ethnic/cultural community, in 1998 the Muslims, Sikhs, and SCs, *all* voted at higher rates than did upper caste Hindus. As Table 3.17 makes clear, the thesis linking lower socio-economic status with lower voting rate is confirmed for the US, but does not hold in India.[38] This has not happened in every election, as the Muslim turnout has dropped in the Lok Sabha elections held in 2004. But the basic pattern holds: those at the top of socio-economic hierarchy are not at the top of voting turnout tables.[39]

Another major thesis in US political sociology literature is that there is a general decline in voting rates in the democratic world and some believe that this decline is due to a decrease

[38] It should also be said that the reverse pattern in India is a longstanding one. See Samuel Eldersveld and Bashiruddin Ahmed, *Citizens and Politics: Mass Political Behavior in India*, University of Chicago Press, 1978, Table 14.5, p. 195.

[39] Yogendra Yadav, 'Understanding the Second Democratic Upsurge: Trends of Bahujan Participation in Electoral Politics in the 1990s', in Francine R. Frankel, Zoya Hasan, Rajeev Bhargava, and Balveer Arora, eds, *Transforming India: Social and Political Dynamics of Democracy*, New Delhi: Oxford University Press, 2000, Tables 14 and 15.

Table 3.17: Socio-Economic Status and Voting Turnout in USA and India

USA (1988)		India (1998)	
1998 Turnout 49% 1988 Turnout 60%		Turnout 62%	
(Turnout below expressed as percentage of voting age citizens)		(Turn out below expressed as percentage of electorate)	
Income:		*Income:*	
1) Lowest quintile	43%	1) Lowest quintile	57%
2)	52	2)	65
3)	59	3)	73
4)	67	4)	60
5) Highest quintile	77	5) Highest quintile	47
Education:		*Education:*	
No High School	38%	Illiterate	57%
Some High School	43	Up to Middle	83
High School graduate	57	College	57
Some College	66	Post-graduate	41
College Grad	79		
Post-graduate	84		

Community	1994 (Non-(Presidential Year)	% Voted 1996 (Presidential Year)	*Community:*	1971	1998
White	47%	56%	Hindu (Upper)	61%	60%
Black	37	50	Hindu (OBC)	45	58
Latino	20	27	SC	58	75
			ST	36	59
			Muslim	88	70
			Sikh	85	89

Sources: For India, Yogendra Yadav, 'Electoral Politics in Time of Change: India's Third Electoral System, 1989–99', *Economic and Political Weekly*, vol. XXXIV, August 21–8 1999, pp. 2393–9. For US, Jan E. Leighley and Jonathan Nagler, 'Socioeconomic Bias in Turnout 1964–1988: The Voters Remain the Same', *American Political Science Review*, vol. 86, September 1992, pp. 725–6.

in what is called a sense of 'efficacy' on the part of voters. In the US, the NES based at the University of Michigan has shown a general decline in the voters' sense of personal efficacy from the mid-1960s to the present. From 1952 to 1964, the average of four observations was 69.7 per cent. By contrast, the average of four observations between 1994 and 2000 was only 39.7 per cent.

The NES series in India uses the following question for measuring political efficacy: 'Do you think your vote has an effect on how things are run in this country or do you think your vote has no effect?' Unlike the data from the US, we do not have a large number of points to plot the time series for efficacy for India. But the Indian NES offers three observation points—1971, 1996, and 2004—that allow us to read a trend. The trend in India is quite the opposite of the US: 48 per cent of the respondents felt efficacious in India in 1971, 59 per cent felt efficacious in 1996, and 68 per cent felt efficacious in 2004. To be sure, efficacy is being measured here with reference to the worth of votes and the significant changes in this respect partly reflect the growing competitiveness in India's electoral politics in the last two decades. Yet, if significantly greater proportions of citizens feel that their vote makes a difference, this is undeniably positive for democracy and resonates well with the data on trust that we have examined.

Table 3.18 presents the data on changing levels of citizens' efficacy and legitimacy regarding the democratic system for some of the marginalized groups between 1971 and 2004. The most interesting thing about the Indian data is that if we select the groups that felt most marginal concerning their effective participation in 1971, virtually all of them express a growing belief that their 'vote has an effect on how things are run in this country', that is, in their efficacy as a voting citizen. Out of sixteen groups whose sense of efficacy was recorded in 1971, the seven groups which expressed the lowest efficacy, in ascending order from the bottom were, the STs, illiterates, women, the lowest economic quintile (the 'very poor'), the SCs, the second lowest economic quintile (the 'poor'), and the rural population. However, in 1996, *all* of these seven groups expressed significant increases in their sense of efficacy compared to 1971. Again in 2004, almost all of them expressed increased efficacy over 1996. This growing sense of efficacy could have expressed itself in a growing desire to be anti-system and since India is a longstanding democracy this might have meant an increasing dissatisfaction with democracy. In India however, what we see between 1971–2004 is a high correlation between the previously most marginal groups feeling more efficacious, and being more supportive of democracy (see Table 3.18).

Table 3.18: Growing Sense of Political Efficacy and Legitimacy of Democracy among Marginalized Groups in India: 1971–2004

	Political Efficacy			Support for Democracy		
Year	1971	1996	2004	1971	1996	2004
National Average	48	59	68	43	69	72
Group						
ST	31	48	59	41	66	68
SC	42	60	65	38	67	69
Illiterate	36	47	55	31	62	61
Women	36	51	61	32	64	67
Very poor	38	51	60	32	64	66
Poor	43	55	68	37	68	71
Muslims	50	60	66	40	72	73
Rural	44	57	66	39	69	70

Notes: All figures in row percentages rounded off to the nearest integral.

Source: India, National Election Study 1971, 1996, and 2004. The efficacy question was: 'Do you think your vote has an effect on how things are run in this country or do you think your vote makes no difference?'. The support for democracy question was: 'Do you think that the government in this country can be run better if there are no parties or assemblies or elections?

Thus we can conclude that there is growing participation, a growing sense of efficacy and, despite the proliferation of parties, especially state parties, a growing commitment to Indian democracy as a way of managing diversity, among previously marginalized groups.

Conclusion: India as a 'State Nation'; Past Accomplishments and Potential Threats

In our introduction to this chapter we argued that being a 'state nation' is an extremely important normative goal for culturally diverse, democratic federations, especially those with a multinational dimension to their diversity. We also argued that the relative presence or absence of a polity's state nation characteristics could be empirically observed by focusing on three of the most politically important attributes: (1), the degree of pride in citizen's *identification* with being members of the polity, (2) the degree of citizen's *trust* in the most important state institutions such as electoral procedures, the judiciary, and the civil service, and (3), the degree of citizens *support* for the democratic political system.

Notwithstanding the great linguistic, religious, ethnic, and caste differences within its diverse polity, India, as we have documented, is one of the world's democracies that scores most highly on these three state nation indicators of identification, trust, and support. We have seen that the evidence in this respect is quite strong. India also has extensive and rich patterns of *multiple and complementary* identities, which was our fourth indicator of a well-functioning democratic state nation. However, in a diverse polity, even if the average is fairly high, if within a major minority group, support for democracy is low, this can present a problem. Yet this is not the case in India concerning religious minorities because the major religious minority group, the Muslims, support democracy at a slightly higher level than the Hindus. Of the major longstanding democracies in the world, India has by far the lowest per capita income. If the poorest segment of the population had a very low support for democracy, in contrast to the rest of the population, this could also present a problem, but the very poor in India prefer democracy in about the same measure as anyone else. Finally, given India's caste system, it is important to note that even among the SCs (formerly called 'untouchables'), support for democracy is no different from other groups once we focus on valid responses. In comparative terms, therefore, the percentage of India's Muslims, of India's former 'untouchables', and of India's poorest strata, who answer that 'democracy is preferable to any other form of government', is about ten percentage points higher (for each of these potentially alienated anti-democratic groups) than the overall average of Latin America countries for 2001. More importantly, the proportion of those who may prefer authoritarianism, or are indifferent to the choice between democracy or non-democracy, is negligible in all the marginal social groups.

We would like to end this chapter however with a cautionary note. There is a significant element of 'social construction' in politics. What has been socially constructed can under some circumstances be socially destroyed. More than a quarter of a century ago Linz and Stepan edited a volume on the breakdown of democracy in twelve West European and Latin American countries. One of their major conclusions was that 'the independent contributions made to the breakdowns by political incumbents is a theme that emerges in almost all cases.'[40] Linz and Stepan also concluded that virtually none of the breakdowns was inevitable.

The authors of this essay have two major conclusions concerning India's political engagement with its socio-cultural diversity: (1) India is not a classic 'nation state'. (2) India has managed to create a functioning, democratic 'state nation'. In our judgment, the effort to attempt to forge a classic nineteenth-century French style 'nation state' in India would destroy the present functioning 'state nation', and not assure the creation of a democratic nation state. Worse, the attempt to forge a nation state in India would be extremely dangerous and ultimately unsuccessful; it would almost certainly produce at best, a lower quality democracy, an eroded state nation, and weaker attachments to the state. To the extent that the Indian state is not a classic nation state, and that India's federalism has historically recognized the diversity of people within the union, a nation-building campaign on the basis of a cultural, linguistic, or religious homogeneity, and the marginalization of those not sharing in this sought-after homogeneity, is a potential threat to the Indian state. Many loyal segments of the population in India, many groups, and many political administrative units, can be part of a state nation, but not part of a classical nation state.

However, some militant groups often referred to as 'Hindu fundamentalists' (such as the Rashtriya Swayamsevak Sangh [RSS], the Vishwa Hindu Parishad [VHP], and the Bajrang Dal), all of which are frequently—but not always—supported by the BJP often use a discourse, and carry out actions, whose socio-political consequences, if their project for India were ever implemented, would make India sharply less inclusive. In the Gujarat massacres of 2002, in which approximately 1,500 Muslims

---

[40]   See Juan J. Linz and Alfred Stepan, eds, *The Breakdown of Democratic Regimes*, Baltimore and London: Johns Hopkins University Press, 1978, p. ix.

were killed, many of the 'Hindu fundamentalist' groups supported, indeed helped coordinate, the anti-Muslim attacks, with the complicity of the BJP's state government of Gujarat. In the wake of the massacre, the BJP swept elections in Gujarat, and discussion of the 'Gujarat model' as the future electoral strategy of the BJP was frequently referred to in Indian political discussions. After the Gujarat elections, Ashutosh Varshney wrote the following, which we will quote at length to give an indication of the worries that some important observers had about the threats to pluralism and inclusiveness in India.

In effect, Gujarat's electorate has legitimized independent India's first unambiguous pogrom, a pogrom much more vicious than the killings of the Sikhs in Delhi in 1984, a pogrom that came closest to the classic, anti-Jewish pogroms of Russia and Europe in the late nineteenth and the first half of the twentieth century. The Congress Party, though deplorably involved in anti-Sikh violence in 1984, never had an anti-Sikh ideology. For purely electoral reasons, the Congress became contingently anti-Sikh for a while. In contrast, the VHP, the RSS and their stormtroopers, the Bajrang Dal, have an anti-Muslim ideological core.

Therefore, the victory of Rajiv Gandhi's Congress in 1985 was basically a strategic phenomenon, cynically parasitic as the Congress campaign was on Mrs Gandhi's assassination by her Sikh bodyguards. The BJP's victory in Gujarat, on the contrary, is ideological. It is about a larger vision of the polity, in which minorities, as the RSS put it earlier this year, must seek protection in the goodwill of the majority community, not in the laws of the land. The massive legitimization of an ideologically charged pogrom is a truly bruising embarrassment for all Indian liberals and a severe undermining of the pluralist national vision in Gujarat.'[41]

Clearly, if the Gujarat model ever became a dominant model in India this would bring about the socio-political destruction of India's state nation. We hope that this will not occur, and we do not believe it is inevitable that it will.[42] Much of what we have

---

[41]   Ashutosh Varshney, 'Will the Stallion Baulk in Mid-Gallop?', *The Hindu Magazine*, 30 December 2002.

[42]   Let us briefly mention some reasons that make us more confident than many others that the 'Gujarat model' is not bound to be successful in India's twenty-seven other states. Gujarat has many

discussed about India's institutions as well as the data we have presented here about the attitudes of citizens would support a more optimistic view.

_____

features that make it exceptional in India. (1) The Gujarat electoral model was aided by the fact that the BJP was ruling in Gujarat without the actual, or at least potential, constraint of coalitional partners. In all other major states where the BJP was then in power, it was in coalition with some other party or parties. (2) Ashutosh Varshney in his award winning book *Ethnic Conflict and Civic Life: Hindus and Muslims in India*, New Haven: Yale University Press, 2002, p. 97, presents data on deaths as a result of communal violence per 1,000,000 of urban populations in seventeen major states in India from 1950–95. Gujarat, by far, had the highest death rate. (3) Of the seventeen states for which we have survey data on support for democracy, the state that had the highest number of explicitly anti-democratic responses in 1998 was Gujarat. (4) Gujarat had emerged as the safest electoral bastion for the BJP, and had witnessed the most intense Hindu-fundamentalist mobilization of any state in the decade prior to the massacre. See Yogendra Yadav, 'The Patterns and Lessons [of Gujarat Election Verdict]', *Frontline*, 3 January 2003, 10–16. (5) The Godhra incident in which fifty-eight Hindus burned to death in a train returning from Ayodhya, one of the main symbols for Hindu fundamentalism, helped ignite the massacres. Without great complicity by incumbents, and unprecedented terrorism by civil society groups (whether Muslim or Hindu), a Godhra type incident will be an extremely rare occurrence. More generally, we can say that the leaders of the BJP as a political party (who were in a governing coalition with twenty-three partners) for reasons of parliamentary, coalitional, electoral, and even very important national and international investment imperatives, might well want to distance themselves from full association or complicity with, the projects of such groups as the RSS, VHP, and the Bajrang Dal. Finally, a non-BJP government at the centre, as presently exists, would probably not allow this not only out of a commitment to value India's tradition of inclusiveness but also for reasons of party competition. This would contribute to governability, a strong Indian state, and widespread support for a state nation. Such a government at the centre, in all likelihood, would not tolerate an individual state leader's incitement of a Gujarat type anti-inclusionary campaign and its attendant massacres. The BJP's defeat in the state assembly elections in

Himachal Pradesh in February 2003 rapidly demonstrated some limits to the Gujarat model. The BJP's defeat in the Lok Sabha elections held in 2004 was widely seen as an indicator of the failure of the Gujarat model. Many of the key allies of the BJP like the Janta Dal (United) and the Trinamool Congress lost Muslim votes and blamed the BJP's role in Gujarat for their electoral reverses.

4

Negotiating Linguistic Diversity
A Comparative Study of India and the United States

Neera Chandhoke

In these matters of language one has to be very careful. One has to be as liberal as possible and not try and suppress a language. We should not try to coerce anybody into using a language, as far as possible. Whenever an attempt has been made to suppress a popular language or coerce the people into using some other language, there has been trouble. Jawaharlal Nehru.[1]

INTRODUCTION

The aim of this chapter is to compare the way in which the US and India have addressed the issue of linguistic diversity, particularly since both states have been rocked on occasions by language movements which have pitted groups against each other and often against the state. Whereas the response of the state in India has been to pluralize languages, in the US twenty-three state governments have moved towards the imposition of what has come to be known as 'English Only' (EO) policies. This is

---

[1] Jawaharlal Nehru, *The Official Languages*: *Jawaharlal Nehru's Speeches 1949–1968*, Publications Division, Ministry of Information and Broadcasting, Government of India, 24 April 1963, vol. 3, pp. 16–32.

somewhat odd because from its inception the US as an immigrant society has been multilingual—Dutch, German, French, Spanish, and English were spoken and transmitted through complex systems of educational institutions, churches, associations, and clubs. The takeover of Louisiana, Mexico, and Puerto Rico by the American government, and the entry of successive waves of immigrants from different parts of the world, have increasingly expanded the range of languages spoken in the country. By the end of the twentieth century, the US has witnessed a dramatic transformation of its linguistic map. According to the 1990 census, 15 per cent of the American people over the age of five speak a language other than English at home. In California alone, one in every three persons is non-English speaking. However, whereas till about 1950 those who spoke German constituted a majority of non-English speakers, according to the 1990s census, speakers of Spanish constitute almost 50 per cent of non-English speakers. This percentage has increased since then, because according to the 2000 census the number of Hispanics in the country soared by 58 per cent in the 1990s. What is more significant is that most immigrant groups make the transition to English in a matter of two decades. Almost 94 per cent of Americans speak English. Yet the presence of a small minority of people who speak largely Spanish and Chinese, and who unlike earlier waves of immigrants refuse to transit to English, has propelled a somewhat disproportionate reaction in the form of 'Official English'(OE) policies by state governments, policies that have been often initiated by civil society groups.

On the other hand, India is historically constituted as a multi-lingual society. Indians speak languages or dialects that belong to five linguistic families: Indo-Aryan, Dravidian, Austro-Asiatic, Tibeto-Burman, and Andamanese. According to the 1991 census, 30.4 per cent of the people speak Hindi, 7.7 per cent speak Bengali, 7.6 per cent speak Marathi, 4.6 per cent of the population speaks Gujarati, 3.6 per cent speaks Oriya, 2.5 per cent of the population is Punjabi speaking, and 1.6 per cent of the population speaks Assamese. Among the Dravidian languages, 8.6 per cent of the population speaks Telugu, 7 per cent speak Tamil, 4 per cent speak Kannada, and 3.9 per cent speak Malayalam. The remaining 2.5 per cent of Indians speak English and 5.3 per cent speak Urdu.

The largest group in India thus speaks Hindi or related dialects, followed by Telugu, Marathi, and Bengali speakers.[2] These figures represent however a handful of languages spoken in India, which according to the 1961 census numbered above 1650.[3] The 1971 census records mother tongues that are not included within the Eighth Schedule of the Constitution—Bhili, Dogri, Gondi, Khandeshi, Oraon, Santali, and Tulu. What is more important is that percentages translate into very large figures; Robert King, for instance, points out Telugu is spoken by 68,000,000 people, which dwarfs the number of people who speak, say, Swedish and Hungarian and exceeds by almost 20 million the number of French speakers in France.[4] Given the plurality of the linguistic map in India, it is not surprising that attempts to legislate an official language catapulted into deep resistance, which often bordered on threats to secede from the Indian Union. Faced by unprecedented mobilization over language, the Government of India prudentially pluralized 'official' languages. This was accompanied by and often preceded by the formation of linguistic states as constituent units of the Indian Union.

This chapter maps out the politics of language in the US and in India. But before I proceed it may be worthwhile to register three issues that have some relevance to our understanding of political mobilization around language. (1) Language movements are essentially about the material opportunities that are available or not available to the speakers of a particular language. If one language is privileged as the language of material, social, cultural, and political transactions, it follows that the speakers of that language have an unfair advantage over others. Conversely, those who do not speak the language are disempowered; recollect for

[2] Robert L. Hardgrave Jr and Stanley Kochanek, *India: Government and Politics in a Developing Nation*, 5 ed., Forth Worth: Harcourt Brace College Publishers, 1993, p. 11.

[3] The 1961 census recorded 1,652 languages with 197 languages being dominant. The 1971 census spoke of 221 mother tongues being spoken in the country. This figure dropped to 106 in the 1981 census because the census commissioner from 1971 onwards omitted to list any languages that had less than 10,000 speakers.

[4] Robert D. King, *Nehru and the Language Politics of India*, Delhi: Oxford University Press, 1997, p. 3.

instance that the civil war in Sri Lanka initially broke out over the denial of the Tamil language. (2) Though the privileging of an official language opens the windows of opportunity for some and closes them for others, language has become a contentious political issue because it is the linchpin of identity. All human beings speak a language, but *all human beings do not speak the same language*. This is because language is connected to the shared understandings of a community, understandings that commonly go by the name of culture. Or, that language gives us an *identity* as members of a community, which is distinguished by certain shared understandings.[5] Therefore, if a state does not recognize or respect a language, the identity of the members of the linguistic community is devalued. This carries rather serious consequences for it leads to loss of belonging, alienation, discontent, and even revolt as in the case of Quebec and Sri Lanka. In sum, since language movements combine both identity and opportunity issues, they tend to prove explosive. (3) We must remember that language has formed the historical basis of nationhood as in the case of Italy and France in the nineteenth century. In the same vein, in the US and India the question of language has been wrapped up in another larger political issue, that of a homogenous, unitary, and strong nation versus fragmentation, disruptions, anomie, and even secession.[6]

[5]   Denise Reaume suggests that language can be valued intrinsically as a cultural inheritance and as a referral of identity simply because an individual member's use of language is at once participation in the accomplishment of a group as well as a marker of belonging. Denise G. Reaume, 'Official Language Rights: Intrinsic Value and the Protection of Difference', in Will Kymlicka and Wayne Norman, eds, *Citizenship in Diverse Societies*, Oxford: Oxford University Press, 2000, pp. 245–72, in p. 251.

[6]   Schmidt suggests that language policy conflicts are fuelled by a politics of identity in which competing rhetorical strategies are deployed on behalf of two competing public values: national unity on the one hand, and equality for all linguistic groups on the other. Conflicts over language policy thus emerge when a country is characterized by linguistic diversity, when ethnolinguistic groups compete over language, and where political actors motivated by concerns over group identity, national unity, and/or ethnolinguistic inequality push the state to do something about these facts. Ronald

It is true that most human beings tend to be bilingual because bilingualism is simply an intellectual, a cultural, and a material resource. In any case few people have the option of *not* being bilingual since multilingual societies are usually dominated by one language as the language of the media, of the state, of communication, of advertisements, of road signs, of billboards, and of commerce. Therefore, people who do not know the language come to speak it because it is there, around them like oxygen. Yet it is precisely bilingualism that takes a hard knock when one language officially becomes the medium of power. Language movements or decisions *not* to speak the dominant language are a response to this phenomenon. The question is: how do states and civil societies respond to language movements or to refusals to give up one's own language. This is the subject matter of this chapter.

THE CONSTITUENT MOMENT

The founding fathers of the American Constitution did not mandate an official or a national language. For, committed as they were to the twin ideals of freedom and the 'rights of man' the founders of the Constitution firmly believed that an official language policy was associated with authoritarianism, colonialism, and monarchy, all of which they were determined to break with.[7] It was generally felt that (1) it was not the business of a democracy to tell its people how to speak or what to speak and (2) though the choice of a national language defines and frames national identity, the act invariably excludes those who not speak the language. Therefore, it was not considered imperative to legislate an official tongue. There was some discussion about the need to distinguish American English from British English during the making of the Constitution. John Adams, for instance, believed that a language academy should be set up in order to establish official standards

---

Schmidt, Sr. *Language Policy and Identity Polity Politics in the United States,* Philadelphia: Temple University Press, 2000, pp. 68–9.

[7] S. B. Heath 'Why No Official Language?', in James Crawford, ed., *Language Loyalties*, Chicago: University of Chicago Press 1992, pp. 20–31.

for 'American' as distinguished from 'British' English. But this suggestion was rejected and the founding fathers made it quite explicit that they would rather rely on Noah Webster's attempts to codify a speller and dictionary of American English.[8]

In India matters were a little more complicated for the anti-colonial movement had thrown up a number of issues, all of which were to prove significant on the language front in the post-Independence era. For one, at the turn of the twentieth century, a movement for replacing English with Hindi as the national language made its appearance in north India. The leadership of the movement argued that Hindi should become the language of pan-Indian integration and the cornerstone of the national vision. One of the major proponents of Hindi as a national language was B.G. Tilak who at a meeting of the *Nagari Pracharini Sabha* at Benaras in December 1905 was to suggest: 'if you want to draw a nation together, there is no force more powerful than a common language for all.'[9] Tilak also pleaded for a common script for all Indian languages, that is, Devanagari. But the movement for Hindi

---

[8]   Webster felt that 'as an independent nation our honor requires us to have a system of our own, in language as well as in government.' A national language, he is reported to have said, is a band of national union. But then he set out to *compile* and not *found* a dictionary. Similarly John Jay in the Federalist Papers 1780 asked for the promotion of 'American' English. He was to coin the term 'Americanize' and his plea for a common language is often cited by the proponents of EO as reason for the politics of EO. There was also some talk of completing the revolution against England by opting for German, French, Greek, or Hebrew as the national tongue, but this was dismissed as idle talk, for it would require far too much investment in learning a new language. In 1923, in Washington, J. McCormick, a Montana Congressman, introduced a language proposal in the Congress to enshrine American as the national language instead of English in a bid to acquire 'mental emancipation'. 'Let our writers,' he stated, 'drop their top-coats, spats, and swagger-sticks, and assume occasionally their buckskin, moccasins, and tomahawks.' The proposal was not considered seriously, but in Chicago, American was mandated as the official language up to 1969 when English replaced it. Theodore Roosevelt felt the need to promote Americanized English in spelling, such a thru, altho, and tho, but this enterprise was confined to the office of the White House during his days as president.

[9]   Ram Gopal *Linguistic Affairs of India*, Bombay: Asia Publishing House, 1996, p. 175.

which was connected to the politics of emancipation from colonial rule and colonized mentalities also revealed a rankly communal face[10] for the movement was to position itself against Urdu.[11] Urdu, which derives from the Turkish word *Ortu* (a military camp) was developed during the closing years of Mughal rule in the cantonments and in the bazaars. A variety of people across religious and regional identities adopted the spoken language as a medium of communication. Urdu acquired a still more communicable *avatar* in the form of Hindustani, which could be written in both the Persian-Arabic as well as in the Devanagari script. In effect, Urdu/Hindustani became a link language in large parts of northern India.

However, even though Urdu evolved from *Khari Boli*, which is a branch of Hindi spoken in north India, and though the language is a *patois* since a Persian–Arabic vocabulary has been grafted onto to a *prakrit* syntax and grammar,[12] the movement for Hindi was to type it as associated with everything Islamic. It consequently sought to purify Hindi of all Urdu words, replacing in the process the spoken language with archaic vocabulary. In time, the idea of Hindi-Hindu-Hindustan posited not only a close link between language and nationhood but also between language and religion.

This development was contested by Gandhiji who initially had supported the move to make Hindi the national language. As early as 1909 he was to write in the *Hind Swaraj*: 'A universal language for India should be Hindi'. But by 1917 he was strongly arguing the case for adopting Hindustani as the national language, because Hindustani was neither Hindi nor Urdu, neither highly Sanskritized, nor highly Arabized. Anxious to pre-empt a communal divide on the issue, he stressed this point in speech after speech and editorial after editorial, dismissing in the meanwhile the problems that were likely to be encountered by non-Hindi speaking groups in the south and in Bengal. 'A spirit that is so exclusive

---

10   See Christopher King, *One Language, Two Scripts: The Hindi Movement in North India*, New Delhi: Oxford University Press, 1994.

11   Alok Rai has dealt with the complexities of the issue in his *Hindi Nationalism: Tracts for the Times*, New Delhi: Orient Longman, 2000.

12   See S. Maqbul Ahmad, 'The Politics of Urdu in India Today', in *Language and Society*, Shimla: Institute of Advanced Studies, 1969 pp. 147–51.

and narrow as to want every form of speech to be perpetuated and developed' he was to write, 'is anti-national and anti-universal. All underdeveloped and unwritten dialects should ... be sacrificed and merged in the great Hindustani stream. It would be a sacrifice ... not a suicide'.[13] Yet it was Hindi that became the official language of India.

The emergence of the Hindi movement was however not uncontested, it was paralleled by the eruption of regional language movements under the leadership of regional elites. Regional language movements challenged the claim that Hindi was the national language, on the ground that languages other than Hindi were also national. South Indian leaders in particular felt that the choice of Hindi as the national language privileged north Indians, that Hindi speakers would get an unfair advantage in jobs and in power, and that this would deny the status of 'national' to other languages. Even as the Congress repeatedly adopted resolutions suggesting that Hindi be the national language, opposition to the move mounted in non-Hindi speaking states. This was exacerbated in 1925, when under the insistence of Gandhiji, the Constitution of the Congress was amended to read that, '[t]he proceedings of the Congress shall be conducted as far as possible in Hindustani. The English language or any provincial language may be used if the speaker is unable to speak Hindustani.'

Simultaneously a sustained drive to introduce Hindustani in the south was initiated by Gandhiji and Rajagopalchari. This triggered off an expected backlash. As early as 1937, when the Congress-led provincial government mandated Hindi instruction in primary schools in the south, Tamil nationalists united under the Dravidian leadership to agitate against the move. During his visits to south India Gandhiji continued to insist that Tamils should study Hindustani, and the *Dakshin Bharat Hindi Prachar Sabha* was established for the purpose. Even Rajaji, who was an ardent Tamil nationalist, was to support Gandhiji in this endeavour. In time, the cleavage between the Congress leadership in Tamil Nadu, which supported the suggestion that Hindi was a symbol of national integration, and the resentment articulated by many Tamil nationalists that the imposition of Hindi led to the devaluation of the language and culture of the region, adopted formidable proportions.

[13] Cited in Robert King, *Nehru and the Language Politics of India,* p. 82.

The first anti-Hindi agitation by the Dravidian leadership which took the shape of a threat of secession and the formation of a Dravida Nadu occurred in the 1930s. In fact, the rise of the Dravidian leadership, the formation of the Dravida Munnetra Kazhagam (DMK) in 1949, and the decline of the Congress in Tamil Nadu was closely allied to the agitation against the imposition of Hindi on Tamil Nadu. For the Dravidian leadership saw this as an attempt to maintain Brahminical domination over the region.

Resultantly discussions on this issue in the Constituent Assembly were stormy: can Hindi or Hindustani be the official language? What would be the period of transition from English to the official language? What would be the status of other widely spoken languages? Ambedkar has confessed that at the time of the discussion of the draft constitution, there was no article that proved more controversial than the one that deals with the issue of Hindi as the national language. 'No article produced more opposition. No article, more heat. After a prolonged discussion, when the question was put, the vote was 78 against 78. The tie could not be resolved. After a long discussion when the question was put to the assembly once more the result was 77 against 78 for Hindi. Hindi won its place as national language by one vote.'[14]

But given the deep mobilization on the issue, the Constituent Assembly decided that the implementation of Hindi should be postponed till 1965, and that language commissions would be set up in 1955 and in 1960 to oversee the phasing out of English and supervise the progress of Hindi as the official language.[15] In the meanwhile English would continue as the official language of the Union, and states in the Union would use their regional languages. Regional languages were designated as 'official' languages by incorporation in the Eighth Schedule of the Constitution.

However, even as the time for the implementation of Hindi as the national language drew near, non-Hindi speaking groups

[14]   Cited in Selig S. Harrison, *India: The Most Dangerous Decades*, Princeton: University Press, 1960, p. 282.

[15]   These commissions would pay due regard to languages other than Hindi for purposes of examinations for the public services. In the schools, the three-language formula was institutionalized to further national integration. The formula failed for a variety of reasons. See Paul Brass, *Language, Religion and Politics in North India*, Cambridge: Cambridge University Press, 1974, pp. 213–15 on this issue.

readied for a massive confrontation in Tamil Nadu. Tamil leaders opposed the move as alien, detrimental to regional languages, and undemocratic. By 1963, the anti-Hindi agitation in Tamil Nadu assumed appalling proportions. The DMK, which in 1949 was founded on the twin planks of Tamil nationalism and anti-Brahminism/anti-Hindi, was to launch protest after protest from 1963 onwards. Those portions of the Constitution that dealt with the official language were burnt in the streets, and students, unions and political parties joined the massive protests against the decision to impose Hindi. The call of the DMK that was 26 January 1965—the date when the switch to Hindi was to be effected—should be marked by public mourning and the hoisting of black flags in many Tamil homes and public places.[16] Books written in Hindi were burnt, government offices and transport were attacked, and seven protestors committed suicide. The Congress government in the state responded with coercion, and sixty-six people were reportedly killed in police firing. By the middle of the 1960s, even as the central government prevaricated upon the continued use of English, even as agitation rocked the region, the DMK leadership lost control over the movement.[17]

The escalating protest over Hindi made it impossible to institute mono-lingualism in the country, and the central leadership compromised on the issue. The Official Languages Act in 1963 which represented this spirit of compromise, stated that whereas Hindi would become the official language of the country in 1965, English would continue as an 'associate additional official language'. A Parliamentary Review Committee would consider after ten years whether English should be retained if sufficient progress in extending the domain of Hindi as the official language had not been made. Prime Minister Nehru committed not to impose Hindi on non-Hindi speaking people in the country, but discontent did not abate because in 1963 the central government under Prime

[16] On this see Sumathi Ramaswamy, *Passions of the Tongue: Language Devotion in Tamil India 1891–1970*, Berkeley: University of California Press, 1997.

[17] For an excellent discussion of the link between the rise of the DMK and the language issue in Tamil Nadu see Narendra Subramanian *Ethnicity and Populist Mobilization*, New Delhi: Oxford University Press, 1999.

Minister Gulzarilal Nanda asked all ministries to report on the steps taken to make Hindi the official language in 1965.

When on 26 January 1965, Hindi became the official language, riots erupted in Tamil Nadu—sixty people were killed in police firing and two youths committed self-immolation. After a series of inter-party discussions, the central government assured the various states that Hindi would not be imposed upon them and that they could continue to use English for official purposes. This became the Official Languages Amendment Act of 1967, which provided for the following: (1) Hindi and English would be used in Parliament. (2) The central government would use Hindi in its communication with Hindi-speaking states and English for communicating with non-Hindi speaking states. (3) All policies relating to language were brought within the state list and under the power of the state government. (4) Articles 29 and 30 of the fundamental rights chapter of the Constitution protected minority languages.[18] The Commission for Linguistic Minorities was set up to act as a watchdog for protecting the languages of linguistic minorities within states. (5) The major languages of India are listed in the Eighth Schedule—the original Eighth Schedule contained fourteen languages; today it lists twenty-two languages.

The Eighth Schedule lays down that if any group sufficiently large in number moves the state to include its language for administrative and educational purposes; this can be done consequent upon a directive from the President of India. The Government of India retains the discretion of deciding whether

[18] The specific provisions for the protection of minority languages are the following: Firstly, any representation for the redress of any grievance to any officer or authority of the central or state government can be made in any of the languages used in the state or in the central government [Article 350]. Every state and local authority within the state is directed to provide adequate facilities for instruction in the mother tongue in the primary school level to children of minority communities. The President of India is authorized to issue whatever directions he considers necessary to secure such facilities [Article 350a]. A special officer for linguistic minorities is appointed to oversee the implementation of all safeguards for language minorities and to report to the president on the matter. The president can instruct that these reports be laid before each House of Parliament and also be sent to the government of the state in question [Article 350b].

the demand is legitimate, and whether sufficiently large numbers of people back the demand. This, not unexpectedly, has propelled moves for inclusion of languages in the Eighth Schedule. The problem is that no criterion has been specified for the inclusion of a language. It is *implied* that major languages which have literary scripts and traditions of their own, which are used in newspapers and radio broadcasts, and which are spoken by people in large contiguous areas, are candidates for inclusion. Secondly, classical languages of culture and heritage, and languages that are considered to be a resource or a root language for modern languages, such as Sanskrit, also find place in the Eighth Schedule. Thirdly, if a language is recognized as an official language in the states, such as Konkani in Goa, and Manipuri in Manipur, it is included in the Eighth Schedule.[19] And fourthly, if a sufficiently large movement backs the demand that a language be included in the schedule, the demand has been conceded as in the case of Sindhi and Nepali.

Conversely if a language is not backed by popular mobilization, if it is not the official language of a state, if it is not seen as a root language, or if does not have a literary tradition or script that is recognized by society, it does not find a place in the Eighth Schedule even though there may be very good reasons for granting it the status of an official language. The anomaly is that whereas Sanskrit with about 2,500 speakers finds place in the Eighth Schedule, several tribal languages with millions of speakers do not. Other valid questions can be raised. If languages with literary and cultural traditions find place in the Eighth Schedule, why are

[19]   Article 345 states that one or more languages in use in the state can be declared as the languages used for all or any of the official purposes of the state. Northeastern states and some union territories have declared English as their official language that is Tripura, Nagaland, Mizoram, Meghalaya, Arunachal Pradesh, Chandigarh, Andaman and Nicobar, Pondicherry, and Lakshadweep. Article 350 provides for every person to submit a representation for the redress of any grievance to any officer or authority of the Union or the state in any of the languages used in the Union or the state. Article 350a stipulates that every state and every local authority is directed to provide adequate facilities for instruction in the mother tongue in the primary stage of education to children belonging to linguistic minority groups and the president may issue such directions to any state as he considers necessary for the securing of such facilities.

Braj and Rajasthani not included? Braj, Rajasthani, and Awadhi, are the languages of a great tradition but they are subsumed under Hindi, whereas Konkani is regarded as distinct from Marathi.[20] Incidentally, whereas in the linguistic reorganization of states Punjab came to be known on the basis of Punjabi, and Tamil Nadu got its Tamil, Kashmiri, which is both a literary as well as a majority language did not go to Kashmir. Kashmir got Urdu, which logically should have gone to Uttar Pradesh.[21] Obviously, the inclusion of a language has to do with what kind of support it can garner.[22]

The other point is that whereas some languages are empowered by inclusion in the Eighth Schedule, others are dis-empowered simply because the former have immediate access to various privileges. Consider that whereas any Member of Parliament (MP) has the right to speak in Parliament in her or his mother tongue, the speech is translated simultaneously. If this language is included within the Eighth Schedule, Examinations to the central services are conducted in the twenty-two languages of the Eighth Schedule as well as in English. State and central governments fund the development of languages listed in the Schedule, and national radio and television networks encourage broadcasts in listed languages. Therefore, out of the 1,650 languages spoken in India, only a handful dominate the language scene because the Schedule empowers twenty-two languages in terms of access to recognition, prestige, education, judiciary, administration, trade, commerce, national communication networks, and access to funds for development.[23] Conversely, unless languages are granted recognition and given incentives to develop their script, grammar, and literary traditions, they can die out fairly rapidly, or relegated to the status of dialects or

[20]   R.S. Gupta and Anvita Abbi, 'The Eighth Schedule: A Critical Introduction', in R.S. Gupta, Anvita Abbi, and Kailash S. Aggarwal, eds, *Language and the State: Perspectives on the Eighth Schedule*, New Delhi: Creative Books, 1995, pp. 1–7.

[21]   Ibid.

[22]   Ibid.

[23]   Four chapters under part XVII of the Constitution, that is articles 343–51 spell out the language policy that is, the official language of the Union, the states, and the judiciary. This is the Eighth Schedule.

tribal languages such as Kharia, Ho, or Tangkhul Naga. But, on balance the constitutional recognition of twenty-two languages has managed to sort out what seemed at one point to be a rather intractable problem.

THE FORMATION OF LINGUISTIC STATES

By the turn of the twentieth century, regional language movements were contesting the claim of Hindi to be the national language. The agenda of these movements was however wider, for by the first decade of the twentieth century the movements began to demand linguistic states within the Indian Union in post-Independence India. This move was supported by the Congress leadership. For instance B.G. Tilak writing in 1891 in the *Kesari*, was to suggest that administrative units based on language would lead to homogeneity and aid development. The uproar in the aftermath of the partition of Bengal in 1905 was to prove decisive for this tension.[24] For the Congress began to conceptualize post-Independence India in terms of linguistically based administrative units. In 1908, a 'province' of Bihar was created in the organizational set up of the Congress and in 1917, Sindh and Andhra units were created as subdivisions of the Congress organization. The administrative implications of this arrangement were not slight, for Bihar was till then a part of the Bengal presidency, Sindh belonged to the Bombay presidency, and Andhra was part of the Madras presidency under the administrative framework of the colonial power. By 1920, Gandhiji was to declare his support for linguistic states though three years earlier he had dismissed the idea as not important for the Congress, faced as it was with more urgent issues. In 1920, however, the Telugu-speaking people of Andhra expressed their desire to be recognized as a separate state and very soon, Sindhi and Kannada speakers were to make the same demand. Therefore, whereas in a piece in *Young India* on 21 of January 1917 Gandhiji had argued that encouragement

[24]   The move to partition Bengal on the basis of religion was opposed on the ground that the Bengali language united all Bengali's irrespective of religious identities. This was to lead to the development of Bengali as a modern Indian language with the written word approximating the spoken word.

of regional languages would imperil the fate of Hindi as the national language, at the Nagpur session in 1920 he was to accept the idea of language as a basis for states within the Union in post-Independence India. Towards this end, the Congress was rearranged politically with the creation of twenty-one vernacular units in the form of Provincial Congress Committees.

In 1927, the Congress adopted a resolution suggesting that 'that the time had come for the redistribution of provinces on a linguistic basis' even as it accepted separate identities for Andhra, Utkal, Sind, and Karnataka. In 1928, the Nehru Constitutional Report reiterated that the principle of linguistic states was desirable: 'Language as a rule corresponds with a special variety of culture, of traditions and literature. In a linguistic area all these factors will help in the general progress of the province'. In 1930, the report of the Indian Statutory Commission. known better as the Simon Commission, opined that the arbitrary map lines drawn by the British administration needed to be rethought. The report recommended the creation of two provinces of Sindh and Orissa in response to demands of the Sindhi and the Oriya-speaking people. In 1936, these two provinces were created by the colonial power, though arguably in the case of Sindh the reasons had less to do with language than with the need to placate Muslim sentiment in the region. In 1937, the Congress reiterated the principle of linguistic reorganization of states, but now that Sindh and Orissa had been created as separate provinces, only Andhra and Karnataka remained on the agenda. Meanwhile the movement for linguistic states propelled its own trajectories for in 1938, Malayalam-speaking people demanded a separate linguistic province—the Congress accepted the demand in principle.

The demand for linguistic states was as a matter of course connected to other political demands. In Madras presidency, for instance, Telugu-speaking groups resented the fact that Tamil-speaking Brahmanical elites dominated jobs, education, and power. It is not surprising that the movement for Andhra was led by the very Telugu-speaking people belonging to the Kamma and the Reddy caste, who had been fairly marginal in the politics of Madras presidency. Similarly, the two powerful peasant proprietor castes speaking Kannada—the Lingayats and the Vokkaligas—were to demand a separate state, named Karnataka.

On the other hand, other groups resisted the making of linguistic provinces. For instance, Telugu-speaking groups in areas of the Madras presidency that were dominated by Tamil speakers, opposed the idea of a Telugu-speaking state, because they feared a backlash by the Tamil majority in their region. Conversely, both Tamil and Telugu-speaking Brahmins feared that the making of an Andhra dominated by the Kammas and the Reddys would put an end to their domination.[25] The so-called lower castes would have lost out in any case. 'Take Andhra' Ambedkar was to write, 'there are two major communities spread over the linguistic area. They are either the Reddis or the Kammas. They hold all the land, all the offices, all the business. The untouchables live in subordinate dependence on them.'[26]

To put it bluntly, the demand for linguistic states raised a host of other problems. For instance, groups that did not speak the dominant language within the projected state would lose out on both material opportunities as well as the chance to exercise power. Equally, linguistic states would provide new windows of opportunity for groups that did speak the language. 'Let us be frank,' wrote A.K. Mukherjee, 'and accept the Dal-Roti ... basis of this enthusiasm. It is the middle-class job hunter and place hunter and the mostly middle-class politicians who are benefited by the establishment of a linguistic state, which creates for them an exclusive preserve of jobs, offices, and places by shutting out in the name of the promotion of culture, all outside competitors.'[27]

Given all these complexities, it is not surprising that the leadership of the newly constituted Republic of India was to hesitate and prevaricate when the time came to realize its own commitment to linguistic states. States based on language may just have opened the proverbial Pandora box in a country that had been already divided in the name of religion, and further balkanized the country. The leadership feared that linguistic states would consolidate narrow, chauvinistic loyalties and thus endanger

[25]   J.E. Schwartzberg, 'Factors in the Linguistic Reorganization of Indian States', in P. Wallace ed., *Region and Nation in India*, New Delhi: American Institute of Indian Studies, 1985, p. 170.

[26]   B.R. Ambedkar, *Hindustan Times,* 3 September 1953.

[27]   K. Mukherji, *Reorganization of Indian States*, Bombay: Popular Book Depot, 1955, p. 31.

the unity and the integrity of the country. The leadership therefore went back on its commitment to linguistic states.[28] On 27 November 1947, Jawaharlal Nehru stated in the Constituent Assembly that though there were pressing issues facing the government, language was not one of them. Before the need for economic development and security, he was to say, the language issue paled into insignificance. In 1948, a committee consisting of Jawaharlal Nehru, Sardar Patel, and P. Sitaramayya was to conclude that the Congress had not examined the language issue in its full complexity during the freedom struggle, and that it should be rethought.

Nevertheless, the Constituent Assembly, under great pressure from various groups, appointed the Linguistic Provinces Commission, known as the Dar Commission—to look into the issue of the formation of Andhra, Karnataka, Kerala, and Maharashtra. The report of the Commission, which was submitted on 10 December 1948, strengthened the fears of the leadership. The report stated that in any linguistic province, only 70 to 80 per cent of people would speak the same language, leaving 20 per cent language speakers in the minority, and thus vulnerable. This would, it was apprehended, prove divisive. 'This is certainly not the time' reported the committee, 'for embarking upon the enterprise of redrawing the map of the whole of Southern India, including the Deccan, Bombay, and the Central Provinces.' The issue was, therefore, put aside for the moment.

In the meanwhile demands for linguistic states begun to mount. Sri Potti Sriramulu, a greatly respected leader of Andhra and a disciple of Gandhiji, went on a fast unto death for a separate Andhra state in 1952. Prime Minister Nehru was reluctant to concede to the demand since influential Tamil leaders particularly Rajagopalchari would have protested at the division of the state. But by 13 December of that year, discontent erupted in Andhra, even as the condition of Sri Sriramulu deteriorated. His death two days later prompted language riots in Telugu-speaking areas. On 16 December, Nehru announced that Andhra would be a separate state, and that it would be carved out of Madras state, excluding Madras city. Telengana was incorporated into the state.

---

[28] On Nehru's position on the language issue, see Robert King, *Nehru and the Language Politics of India,* chapter 4.

The formation of Andhra Pradesh propelled further moves for linguistic states and Pandit Nehru was forced into appointing a States Reorganization Commission on 22 December 1953. The Commission received and considered about 152,250 documents for or against linguistic states. The Report of the States Reorganization Commission, which ran into 267 pages and which consisted of four parts, was made public in October 1955. The report proposed the reorganization of states on a linguistic basis and in 1956, the Seventh Amendment to the Indian Constitution reordered the political map on the basis of linguistic considerations thus:

- Telugu-speaking Telengana area of Hyderabad became a part of Andhra to form the state of Andhra Pradesh.
- Mysore was enlarged by the absorption of Kannada-speaking areas of Hyderabad, Madras, and Bombay to constitute Karnataka.
- Bombay became a bilingual state by the addition of two Marathi-speaking areas: the Marathwada region of Hyderabad and the Berar region of the Central Provinces, as well as by the Gujarati-speaking areas of Kutch and Saurashtra, to the core region of the old presidency.
- Central Provinces, which was renamed Madhya Pradesh, lost Berar but gained by the merger of Madhya Bharat, Vindhya Pradesh, and Bhopal.
- Punjab was enlarged by merger with Patiala and East Punjab States Union (PEPSU) to form a second bilingual state in which the Hindi and Punjabi majority dominated in the north and in the south.
- Travancore-Cochin was enlarged by the absorption of a portion of the Malabar Coast of Madras to form the state of Kerala.

Other linguistic states that came into being without substantial reorganization of territory were the following: Uttar Pradesh, Rajasthan, Bihar, West Bengal, Assam, and Orissa. Other adjustments, which involved the transfer of entire districts, were made in order to ensure create linguistic homogeneity. Jammu and Kashmir, where Kashmiri and Punjabi are spoken, is one of India's bilingual states, but it was prudently left out of state formation for reasons that had to do with political stability.

The second round of linguistic state formation took place in 1956, when Bombay state was partitioned into Maharashtra and

Gujarat (the latter is incidentally one of India's most linguistically homogenous states). The States Reorganization Commission had earlier rejected the demand on the ground that Gujaratis were happy within Bombay, but the decision to maintain a bilingual state not only antagonized the Maharashtrians but also popular sentiment in Gujarat. In Gujarat, the Maha Gujarat Parishad began to gather strength by acquiring support from the vernacular press, from students, and from parties other than the Congress. Gujarati businessmen, who had a vested interest in an undivided Bombay, opposed separation, but in 1957 the Parishad took five parliamentary and twenty-nine assembly seats from the Congress. It is in this politically charged context that the decision was taken to divide Bombay.

Punjab remained bilingual till 1966, when again as a result of political mobilization on the issue of the Punjabi script, it was split into Punjab and Haryana. The latter consists of Hindi-speaking areas, except Hoshiarpur. The mountainous regions of the state, which are overwhelmingly Hindu and in which both Pahari and Hindi are spoken, were transferred to the new state of Himachal Pradesh, which was upgraded from a union territory. This was the last of linguistic states in India and subsequent state formation took place on other grounds. For instance, when the Naga Hills Tuensang area was formed in 1957, language was only one of the principles of state formation. In 1963, this area became Nagaland, where a number of languages are spoken.

Thus an issue, which had engaged political passions to a massive extent, was resolved by the leadership in India in the space of a decade with some success. Now even if they combine, linguistic minorities form not more than half, or in some cases one-sixth, of the population in these states. In Karnataka for instance, minority groups represent only one-third of the population. The districts in which the numerically predominant language differs from that of the state or union territory in which the district is located, account for only 9.6 per cent of the total areas of the Republic, and a mere 2.7 per cent of its population. Schwartzberg suggests that if we go by the 1981 census figures, the process of reshaping India's map to accord with the linguistic distribution of its inhabitants has run its course.[29]

[29]   Joseph E. Schwartzberg, 'Factors in the Linguistic Reorganization of Indian States', p. 155.

Paul Brass is of the opinion that most of the language conflicts in the Nehru period, some of which became at times bitter and violent, were ultimately resolved through pluralistic solutions. Moreover, the central government and the national leadership of the Congress have avoided direct confrontations with the language movements and have instead adopted the role of an arbitrator and mediator with strong leaders in the states playing the main role in such conflicts. At the same time, the Government of India has not tolerated any demand that is connected to religious divisions or that may lead to secession.[30]

To sum up the Indian experience with linguistic diversity at this stage: two historically constituted tensions have stalked the politics of language in India. The first component of this tension was to balance out the claims for either one or many official languages. The second component was the politicization of language groups in pursuit of forming their own state. The leadership in India has demurred on occasions, accepted the demands of civil society on most occasions, and compromised on many other occasions. The defining factor in every case has been the extent and the strength of political mobilization on the issue. And it is true that the Government of India have conceded precisely those demands which had been preceded by agitation, violence, political solidarity across party lines, and confrontation. For these reasons Arora and Mukherjee suggest that: 'The reluctant recognition of diversity resulted in the lack of a coherent policy frame for its integration ... policy shifts resulted from often violent pressures and protests from below, and political expediency frequently became the guiding principle. Asking ethnolinguistic groups to prove that they were important enough to be institutionally recognised was perhaps the most-counter productive method for promoting national unity ever devised'.[31]

This however may not necessarily be counterproductive for three reasons. (1) The central government has shown some discrimination in sorting out competing claims. (2) The leadership has shown some responsiveness to politicalmobilization on the language issue and has been willing to move to a more

[30] Ibid.

[31] Balveer Arora and Nirmal Mukherjee, 'Introduction', in *Federalism in India: Origins and Development,* ed., by ibid., Delhi: Vikas, 1992, p. 9.

accommodative attitude even as it has tried to evolve institutions that reflect the cultural diversity of the country. (3) As a result of the pluralization of languages, bilingualism has developed in India. The rate of national average of bilingualism in 1991 was as high as 19.44 per cent compared to earlier figures in the three censuses.[32] The national average for trilingualism in the 1991 census is 7.26 per cent. According to 1991 census figures, out of 838 million people in India (excluding Jammu and Kashmir where the census was not taken), 163 million are bilingual, and 61 million out of this figure are trilingual.

LANGUAGE POLITICS IN THE US

If linguistic politics in India has resulted in the pluralization of language policies, language politics have taken the US in another direction altogether—towards a narrowing of linguistic boundaries. Despite the fact that almost 94 per cent of the Americans speak English, in the 1980s the politics of 'EO' or 'OE' was to erupt on the scene of American politics. Language politics—clustered around debates on what it means to be American on the one hand, and around issues relating to affirmative action, citizenship, immigration, assimilation, and multiculturalism on the other— polarized civil society and brought it into confrontation with the state. The offshoot of these processes was the politics of EO, which many have interpreted as a conservative right-wing reaction to theories of multiculturalism and minority rights that dominated debates in the US from the 1960s. For instance, Gary Imhoff, a spokesman of 'United States English', an influential lobby devoted to making English the sole language of the public sphere, has launched a massive attack on multiculturalism. The post-civil rights period, he argues, has transferred the 'immigrant' paradigm into the 'minority' paradigm and attendant notions of minority rights.[33] Another defender of EO stated, after the 2000 figures became public, that 'the politically correct crowd won't

---

32   In 1961 the corresponding figure was 9.7 per cent, in 1971 it was 13.04 per cent, and in 1981 it was 13.34 per cent.

33   Cited in Susan J. Dicker, *Languages in America: A Pluralist View*, Clevedon: Multilingual Matters Ltd, 1996, p. 147.

be satisfied until the Washington Monument is replaced by the Tower of Babel.'[34]

The EO movement which gained tremendous mileage in the 1980s resulted in voters overruling their political representatives in at least four states in a bid to make English the official language. In California, Arizona, Colorado, and Florida, English language amendments to the state constitutions were placed on the agenda through the initiative process and adopted by popular vote. For instance, in November 1986, voters in California endorsed Proposition 63: an English Language Amendment (ELA) to the state Constitution. The popular initiative instructed the state legislature to enforce the status of English as the official language of California and make no law that 'diminishes or ignores' the role of English. Residents and people doing business in California now had legal standing to sue the state if the measure was not enforced.[35] Friction attended the adoption of the initiative, because all of the state's leading politicians, except for the Republican Senator Pete Wilson, opposed Proposition 63. Governor Deukmejian called it 'unnecessary' and warned that 'it would cause fear, confusion, and resentment among many minority Californians.' The Roman Catholic Bishops in the state urged the defeat of the motion on the grounds that it would enshrine prejudice in the law and jeopardize all forms of bilingual assistance. The state's attorney general called Proposition 63 an open invitation to hundreds of frivolous and hurtful law suits. The Los Angeles City Council termed it as contrary to the most basic principles of equality and opportunity, and stated that it would result in 'a sense of inferiority, debasement, and shame in one's own ethnic heritage'. The League of Women Voters, the

[34]   Joyce Howard Price, 'Spanish Language Joins US Culture', *Washington Post*, 20 May 2002.

[35]   Article III, section 6 of the Californian Constitution provides: (1) English is the common language of the people of the United States of America and the State of California. This section is intended to preserve and strengthen the English language, and not to supersede any of the rights guaranteed to the people by this Constitution. (2) English is the official language of the State of California. (3) The legislature was commanded to enforce the section by appropriate legislation, take all steps along with state officials to ensure that the role of English as the common language of the state is preserved and enhanced, and make no law that diminishes or ignores the role of English as the common language of the state.

local Chambers of Commerce, the state American Federation of Labour and Congress of Industrial Organizations (AFL-CIO), and the American Civil Liberties Union (ACLU) echoed precisely these sentiments and organizations of ethnic minorities repeated these charges, as did editorials in leading newspapers.

On voting day, however, 73 per cent of the electorate in the state, as well as a majority in every county of the state, opted for OE. Support for the move ranged across all distinctions of race, class, and education. An exit poll conducted by the Field Institute indicated widespread support for the amendment in almost every segment of Californian voters. More interestingly, the results of the poll showed that the vote was not dictated by economic competition over jobs and opportunities, since the measure garnered the backing of both the economically better as well as the worse off. Not surprisingly, Hispanics and Asians did not support the measure; but expectedly the Whites and the Afro-Americans supported it, as did the young and the educated. As expected, 84 per cent of Republicans favoured the amendment, but what was more surprising was the fact that 56 per cent of the Democrats also supported it. Two years later, the campaign for OE in Arizona, Colorado, and Florida closely followed the Californian initiative. Top elected officials of both the political parties, prominent leaders in education, religion, and the judicial system, important business and labour organizations, as well as the leadership of minority groups, and leading newspapers in the three states, saw the measure as unnecessary, divisive, racist, and destructive of bilingual services. But voters, in a rather spectacular display of popular power, adopted the amendment to the respective state constitutions. The Florida amendment not only received 84 per cent of the state-wise vote and not only did it carry the counties, but it also carried two-third of the vote in the heavily Hispanic Dade county. Colorado's version of OE passed by a three to two ratio of votes.

The amendment to the Constitution in California was more symbolic than substantive, for preserving, protecting, and strengthening the English language can be interpreted in a variety of ways, not all of which are destructive of bilingualism. In Arizona, however, a more restrictive version of OE was adopted in the form of an amendment to the state Constitution by a narrow margin of 51 to 49 per cent. The measure not only declared English to be the official language of the state—it also prohibited the use of other languages during performance of government business except for reasons of public health and safety. English was made the language of the ballot, of public schools, and of all government functions. The unstated presupposition of these moves is that (1) speaking English is a necessary prerequisite for full citizenship in the US, (2) non-English speakers should assimilate into the cultural and linguistic mainstream of American society, and (3) this should be the goal of official policy. 'Traditionally taken for granted,' writes Crawford, 'our national tongue emerged as a cause celebre, a civic passion touching nearly every state house, the United States Congress and numerous municipalities.' There is a rider attached to this formulation, for the fervour was not so much for English, believes Crawford, as against the growing prominence of other languages.[36]

Even as political passions have been yoked to these and related questions, the issue itself has taken on absurd proportions. For instance, complaining about signboards in languages other than English, one city council member in Monterey Park was to say: 'I've talked to a lot of people about this and they want to feel like it's their town too, not just a Chinese town. Why should Monterey Park be called the Chinese Beverly Hills? It's more than just EO; I want signs that look like we're in America.'[37] Concerned about the proliferation of signs in Asian languages that use Japanese and Korean characters, a number of local government officials proposed ordinances to limit or even ban the use of non-English signs in public places.[38] 'One community, in the visual enactment of formal equality, proposed that where non-English characters are used, equal square inches must be allotted to English characters.'[39]

The message is clear; the grant of citizenship rights depend upon assimilation into the national fold, which is strictly speaking

[36]   James Crawford, *Hold Your Tongue: Bilingualism and the Politics of 'English Only'*, Reading, Massachusetts: Addison Wesley, 1992, p. x.

[37]   Mari J. Matsuda, *Where Is Your Body? And Other Essays On Race, Gender, and the Law*, Boston: Beacon Press, 1996, p. 87– 88.

[38]   Ibid., p. 87.

[39]   Pomona City Ordinance section 3–7, no. 3467. Similar 'English Only' signs have been passed in states in the East Coast including New Jersey and Georgia. Matsuda, ibid., p. 87, and p. 100, note 15.

the fold of mainstream Anglo-centric, English-speaking America. Senator Huddleston who sponsored a proposed amendment to the federal Constitution in 1984 that would have made English the official language, stated as much when he said in the discussion on the bill: 'This amendment addresses something so fundamental to our sense of identity as Americans.' Senator Denton argued during discussion on the bill that OE laws will 'help to preserve the basic internal unity of our country.'

The second debate that clusters around the issue focuses on the liberal principles that serve as the foundations of the American political system. These are principles that privilege freedom over ghettoization, the subordination of the individual to the collective, and individual autonomy over exploitative ethnic leaderships. English, argue its defenders, belongs to an open and liberal worldview that happens to be the hallmark of the American character. Other languages are almost pre-modern, the languages of the barrio, of closed mindsets, and of allegiance to ascriptive norms. Entry into the modern democratic culture, it is further suggested, depends on the learning of English as the language of modern politics in the democratic mode.

The third debate has to do with the opposition between the contemporary waves of immigrants and earlier migrants who were ready to assimilate into the dominant American culture via the 'melting pot'. Today, unlike earlier years, runs the argument, immigrants increasingly from the south of the border as well as from East Asia refuse to learn the English language. They, in effect, show a determination to hold on to the languages of their national origin. This recalcitrance, reluctance, and determination to hold on to the culture of origin, challenges the very idea of a national culture and identity. It forces the realization that America's public sphere is divided on issues that are considered crucial to national unity and identity. This is the lament.

The catalyst for an outpouring of, sometimes openly, racist feelings was a movement that began from the political margins of American politics. Senator S.I Hayakawa of California, a Canadian immigrant of Japanese ancestry, felt that governmental concessions to bilingualism had gone too far. English, he believed, had been for long a unifying force of the American people but now bilingual education in public schools and multilingual ballots divided the people along linguistic lines.[40] On retiring from the Senate, in 1983, even as he warned that failure to maintain a common language in the US would produce the kind of unrest and polarization that had been experienced in Canada, Belgium, and other linguistically divided countries, Senator Hayakawa founded US English along with John Tanton, a Michigan ophthalmologist. Tanton was known for his opposition to immigration and had founded the Federation for American Immigration Reform in 1979 for this very purpose. The objective of the Washington-based lobby was to promote an ELA in the Congress and in the states, in order to ensure the preservation of English as the national language of the US by outlawing bilingual or multilingual ballots through a repeal of the 1975 amendments to the Voting Rights Act, to reform bilingual education, and to uphold language and civic requirements for naturalization.

In 1981, Hayakawa sought an amendment to the Constitution to make English the official language of the US and to give the Congress the power to enforce the official status of English. The ELA has been progressively reintroduced in different versions of the 'Language of Government' legislation. However, it was not until the Republicans had won a majority of seats in the 1994 mid-term elections, that the bill H.R. 123 dubbed 'The English Language Empowerment Bill', was voted upon and passed in the House of Representatives on 1 August 1996 by 259 to 169. The Bill aimed at repealing the federal requirement, which was stipulated in the Voting Rights Act (amended in 1975) that either bilingual or multilingual ballots be provided in jurisdictions with a significant number of non-English speakers. It also required the federal government to conduct all business in EO. Exceptions could be made in the case of teaching other languages, the conduct of international relations, in the interests of public health and safety, and in some judicial proceedings. The measure did not become law since the Senate failed to adopt it. But similar bills are introduced in every Congress and a total of twenty-three state governments have enacted and activated 'OE' laws. What is surprising is that the OE movement has won victories in regions

---

[40] A semanticist by profession, Hayakawa is known for his college text *Language in Thought and Action*, which explores a wide range of obstacles to effective communication.

where issues like immigrants and multiculturalism are remote. Of the states that have passed the official EO Acts, only four have a sizeable population of immigrants—California, Florida, Arizona, and Colorado. The rest like the western states of Montana, North and South Dakota, Wyoming, Indiana, and New Hampshire, and all the southern and border-states, except Louisiana and Florida, do not have substantial numbers of non-English speakers. The magnitude of support seems to increase even as the relevance of the issue diminishes. Witness, for instance, the 89 per cent majority that the measure won in Alabama where bilingualism is distant. This requires some explanation.

The main issue that has led to the EO movement is immigration. The repeal of the highly restrictive 1920s national origin quota legislation, which favoured Northwestern Europeans,[41] and the Immigration and Nationality Act Amendments of 1965, have promoted immigration from non-European countries. This has changed the racial and cultural balance of American society because by 1985, East Asia and South America were supplying more than 85 per cent of immigrants. These groups have brought with them their own ways of life, they are more unfamiliar to mainstream America, and their voices are more audible. Mainstream America worries that what Paul Kennedy has called the 'Hispanicization of the South-West' has resulted in the creation of communities, which find it unnecessary to either make the transition to English or assimilate linguistically or culturally. But more importantly mainstream Americans find that today's immigrants are doing what no previous immigrant group could ever have dreamt of carrying out—changing both the language and existing cultural, political, legal, commercial, and educational systems. 'What especially galls longtime Floridians' wrote one columnist, 'is not so much what they perceive as Hispanic Americans' slowness to learn English as the fact that native Americans are increasingly finding that they have to speak Spanish.'[42]

---

[41]   It took its first shape in the form of legislation to ban the Chinese through the 1882 Chinese Exclusion Act. This was extended to 1902, declared permanent thereafter and repealed only in 1943, when the Chinese were allowed naturalization.

[42]   Jeffrey Schmalz, 'Hispanic Influx Spurs 3 Ballots on Language', *New York Times,* 26 October 1998 in A1.

'EO' Bills were to legitimize precisely this resentment against non-English speakers. A natural offspring of this resentment is that American English has consistently lobbied for legislation to restrict immigration, which is perceived to reinforce the maintenance of certain languages, particularly Spanish. It is difficult to escape the conclusion that in the main, the movement has been fuelled by fear and prejudice directed against Hispanics.[43]

The proponents of EO, however, seem to exaggerate the enormity of the problem. For one, in terms of sheer numbers, the current wave of immigration is less than the wave in the early twentieth century. Dicker calculates that the total number of immigrants who arrived in the 1980s, both legal and illegal, was roughly 8 million, a figure not so different from that of 8.8 million who arrived between 1900 and 1910. Whereas in 1910, foreign-born residents made up 14.6 per cent of the population, in 1989 they made up only 7 per cent.[44] Secondly, the 1990 census figures that 1.9 million residents over 5 speak no English admittedly represent an increase of 41 per cent over the 1980s. But if we look at the issue historically we find that the figures are not stupendous—not if we compare them with the numbers in 1890, the year that was the peak of the 'great immigration' they are only a quarter higher than then. If we include among these figures those people who have limited English proficiency we reach only 6 million. This is not astonishing when we count the extent of recent immigration, and the difficulty that adults have in acquiring a new language, particularly when they work in menial jobs that do not require contact with English speakers. Thirdly, over 94 per cent—and possibly more—of the Americans speak English, which indicates a high level of linguistic homogeneity. There is no factual support that the learning of English is slowing down. In fact, when California passed the OE Act in 1986 it was estimated

---

[43] In a 1987 poll conducted by the *New York Times* and CBS, 71 per cent of Hispanics opposed a constitutional amendment because it types them as un-American and as inferior. In Texas, only 35 per cent Hispanics polled in 1986 favoured it, and only 23 per cent did so in 1988.

[44] Susan Dicker, *Languages in America,* pp. 148–9.

that 40,000 people were waiting for English classes in Los Angeles county alone.[45]

In fact, various surveys have shown that newer immigrants are learning English faster. The demographer Calvin Veltman has observed that now people learn English in two generations instead of three. The prototypical pattern is that of a three-generational shift to English with the first generation after settlement being predominantly monolingual, the second being bilingual, and the third being English monolingual.[46] The 1990 US census data shows that a high degree of speakers of non-English languages are proficient in the English language as well[47] in contrast to whites and Afro-Americans who tend to be monolingual. Other studies revealed that more than 90 per cent of first-generation Hispanics born in California have native fluency in English and that only 50 per cent of the second generation still speak Spanish. The Anglicization rate of the community seems to have been speeded up over the last century by 5 per cent per decade, involving in

---

[45]   C. Ingam, 'Proposition 63 Backers Aim at Bilingual Education', *The Los Angeles Times*, 24 November 1986.

[46]   Calvin Veltman, *Language Shift in the United States*, Berlin Mouton: Walter de Gruyter, 1983. Veltman points out that there are differences in the anglicization rates of the immigrants. Of those who arrived in the 1960s, by 1976 Chinese speakers were the least likely to have adopted English as their usual language (26.3 per cent), followed by Hispanics (29.1 per cent), Greeks (29.7 per cent), and Portuguese (29.9 per cent). Scandinavians, Germans, Japanese, Filipino's, Koreans, and Arabs came last.

[47]   Alejandro Portes and Richard Schauffler report that the most important finding in their ongoing study of language-use patterns among second-generation immigrant youths in south Florida, was the overwhelming dominance of English knowledge among children of immigrants. English learning has strong positive association with lengths of residence in the US, 'Language and the Second Generation: Bilingualism Yesterday and Today', *International Migration Review*, vol. 28 (4), Winter, pp. 640–61. Over 80 per cent of the respondents preferred to speak English over the language of their parents, and among Cuban American students attending private bilingual schools, over 93 per cent preferred to speak English to Spanish.

the process the rejection of the language and culture of one's parents. Further, few Hispanics reveal the kind of intense commitment to their mother tongue that earlier generations of Germans did. As seen in the general pattern of immigration, the loss of language begins to be felt keenly by the assimilated third and fourth-generation descendants of immigrants. But by then they have to struggle to gain even basic familiarity with the grammar of their own language.

More importantly, if we look at history, the allegation that immigrants today hold on to their native tongues, and earlier immigrants assimilated easily, just does not hold water. The same charge was made at the turn of the twentieth century when the US witnessed a series of backlashes against linguistic minorities, simply because they increasingly hailed from eastern and southern Europe rather than northwest Europe. It was felt that they resisted speaking English compared to earlier immigrants, for instance, Germans and Scandinavians, who reportedly assimilated easily. This again is not strictly true, for fewer people in the eighteenth century spoke English than today, and it was common to hear Dutch, French, and German being spoken by the settlers.

In fact, up to the nineteenth century, immigrants could hold on to their native language for several generations at no great cost, because they lived in isolated farming communities and had little contact with urban English speakers. Equally, it was easier for many groups not to learn English because they lived in one of the states that provided public schooling in their native tongues. Louisville Kentucky was one among several municipalities that translated city council minutes into German. Minnesota's 1857 state constitution appeared in five languages—English, German, Swedish, Norwegian, and French. Missouri published the governor's message in French and German, and Ohio and Pennsylvania did so in Welsh. Even Texas printed official messages in Spanish, German, and Czech. Earlier generations of 'nativists' were far too concerned about religion[48] or race to worry about language, therefore, immigrants could hold on to their own languages for generations with relative ease.[49]

[48]   Protestant leaders saw the influx of Roman Catholics, Greek Orthodox, and Jewish immigrants as a threat to law and social order.

[49]   For a detailed account see Heinz Kloss, *The American Bilingual Tradition*, Rowley Mass: Newbury House Publishers, 1977

In the light of all this, the EO movement appears an irresponsible and provocative move that represents nothing but anxiety over the changing linguistic landscape of the US as well as represents a determination to perpetuate the predominant culture, which is white and Anglo-American. Arguably, the movement is more of a response to other happenings in the US, such as the radicalization of racial issues in the 1960s, and what is called the 'revivalism of ethnicity'. The positive responses of the federal government in the form of affirmative action programmes and the introduction of bilingual education, ballots, and government services have arguably created great apprehension in the minds of the dominant sections of the population. Moreover, relatively new notions of multiculturalism that challenge older accepted and acceptable notions of the melting pot and the salad bowl, have created *frissons* of apprehension in mainstream America. This disquiet is aptly summed up in the work of Arthur Schlesinger Jr who laments the loss of the peculiar American genius for multi-ethnicity, which results in the creation of a brand new national identity and a new American culture. 'This vision of America,' he writes, 'prevailed through most of the two centuries of American history. But the twentieth century has brought forth a new and opposing vision, and a cult of ethnicity has arisen both among non-Anglo whites and non-white Americans to denounce the idea of the melting pot and to challenge the concept of one people. In the process, separate ethnic identities are being protected, promoted, and perpetuated.'[50]

The movement, therefore, has to be located in the politics of radicalized racial identities in the 1960s and its gains, such as affirmative action programmes. Writers such as Henry Giroux, who see the EO movement as a conservative cultural counter-revolution, argue that its 'more specific expressions have been made manifest on a number of cultural fronts including schools, the art world, and the more blatant attacks aimed at rolling back the benefits constructed of civil rights and social welfare reforms constructed over the last three decades. What is being valorized in the dominant language of the culture industry is an undemocratic approach to social authority and a politically regressive move to

---

[50]   Arthur M. Schlesinger Jr., *The Disuniting of America: Reflections on a Multicultural Society*, New York: W.W, Norton,1992, pp. 14–15.

reconstruct American life within the script of Eurocentrism, racism and patriarchy'.[51]

Above all, deep beliefs on what it means to be an American citizen originate from a highly Euro-centric culture and a singular notion of the nation, in American society. The beliefs go back to the inception of the US. Consider that in 1788, Alexander Hamilton, John Jay, and Madison in *The Federalist Papers* were to define the nation as 'one united people—a people descended from the same ancestors, speaking the same language, professing the same religion...very similar in their manners and customs.'[52] Since the basic values of the Constitution were derived from western European political traditions, it was the Europeans and particularly leaders of British origin who were to define the linguistic, cultural, and political profile of the young nation. This sentiment gained added salience from the revolt against the continued rule of Great Britan, a revolt which was constituted by European, but more importantly British values. Therefore, even though we find no mention of an official language in the Constitution, we do find that it is the deep beliefs of mainstream Euro-centric America that permeate the politics of language. Throughout history it is these very groups who have expressed unease at the fact that people speak a language other than English; this to them is simply non-American. As early as 1750, Benjamin Franklin had expressed displeasure at the refusal of the Germans in Pennsylvania to speak English. In the 1880s, there was a movement to ban German language schooling in the Midwest as, for example, in the efforts of the American Protective Association to legislate English as the medium of instruction. At the turn of the twentieth century, American society witnessed enormous attempts at Americanizing society. Laws regulating the speaking of English linked conformity to an Anglo-centric culture, to political allegiance, and the privileges of citizenship.

Even as laws at the turn of the twentieth century established a close connection between language and ideas of 'civicness', they undid the extensive bilingualism of the nineteenth century in civic and political domains. Theodore Roosevelt made this connection

---

[51]   Henry Giroux, *Border Crossings: Cultural Workers and the Politics of Education*, New York: Routledge, 1991, p. 15,

[52]   Ibid., pp. 89–90.

clear when he said: 'We must ... have but one language. This must be the language of the Declaration of Independence, of Washington's Farewell Address, of Lincoln's Gettysburg speech and second inaugural.' On another occasion he was to say:

For it is an outrage to discriminate against any such man because of creed or birthplace or origin. But this is predicated upon the man's becoming in very fact an American and nothing but an American. If he tries to keep segregated with men of his own origin and separated from the rest of America, then he isn't doing his part as an American ...We have no room for but one language here, and that is the English language, for we intend to see that the crucible turns our people out as Americans, of American nationality, and not as dwellers in a polyglot boarding house.[53]

The leadership of mainstream America, it is obvious, has historically been unable to accept linguistic diversity as part of a democratic vision of society. Therefore, a variety of mechanisms employed to melt people into the pot of American-ness were to progressively become harsher. For example, US immigration policies right up to the last decades of the nineteenth century did not use either the spoken or the written English language as a requirement for entry or for naturalization; the exception was the Chinese Exclusion Act of 1882. From the end of the nineteenth century onwards however, the idea of using a language requirement as a condition for immigration and naturalization began to be talked of. After 1890, matters were different simply because the origins of the new immigrants were different—Jews, Italians, Magyars, and Poles, who were now targeted because they were different from the predominantly English-dominated culture of the country.

Part of the resentment derived from the fact that it was generally believed that this stream of immigrants, unlike earlier ones, were rejects from their own societies and had come to the US for economic reasons and not for love of liberty. There seemed to be a general consensus that the new immigrants were insular, unlettered, and prone to nefarious and immoral behaviour. More importantly, immigrants from eastern and southern Europe such as Jews, Italians, Greeks, and Slavs, it was reported, resisted English

[53]   Cited in J. Crawford, *Hold Your Tongue*, p. 59.

acquisition compared to Germans and Scandinavians. Worried about the impact of what were considered the inferior races, the Immigration Restriction League founded by Senator Henry Cabot Lodge suggested that no one who could not pass the literacy test would be given citizenship. The test meant to prevent the entry of 'inferior' people into the country laid down that the candidate had to read forty words of any language in order to become an American citizen. In 1905, President Roosevelt, concerned about charges of bribery and fraud in naturalization procedures, commissioned a major study of naturalization procedures and requirements. The committee recommended an English literacy requirement for naturalization because the members believed that 'knowledge of English made fraud less likely and resulted in greater understanding and support of existing institutions'.

Two years later, a Federal Immigration Commission, the Dillingham Commission, reiterated the stereotypes about the new kind of immigrant to the US. The new wave of immigrants into the US stated the commission:

... as a class is far less intelligent than the old, approximately one third of all those over 14 years of age when admitted being illiterate. Racially, they are for the most part essentially unlike the British, German and other peoples who came during the period prior to 1880, and generally speaking they are actuated in coming by different ideals, for the old immigrants came to be part of the country, while the new, in large measure, comes with the intention of profiting, in a pecuniary way, by the superior advantages of the new world and then returning to the old country.

The commission, which produced a forty-two volume study over four years, recommended that a literacy test be taken in *any* language for immigration and not just English.

In 1913 and in 1915, in keeping with the recommendations of the Dillingham Commission, legislation that mandated literacy tests in any language as a prerequisite for immigration were adopted by the Congress. The legislation was however vetoed by Presidents Taft and Wilson, who saw the legislation as racially motivated. In 1917, a similar Bill passed by Congress over President Wilson's second veto *attached the condition that the candidate taking the test must know English*. The aim of the Bill was clear—to limit the number of immigrants, particularly from southeast Europe through literacy tests. In 1921, a quota system based on national origins was to limit immigration from eastern and southern Europe. In 1924, a decisive law on immigration intended to keep America in the hands of white Americans; conformity to Anglo-centric Americanism had been established as the acid test for naturalization. Naturally minority languages deteriorated, as did foreign language newspapers. Equally significant were the various state level statutes that laid down English language requirements for franchise.

It is difficult, therefore, to escape the conclusion that the EO movement is propelled by massive insecurity caused by large-scale demographic changes, greater mobility, the presence of immigrants who are visibly different, and the domination of public spaces in some areas by signboards in languages other than English. All this has disrupted Anglo-centric notions of the American nation. From being a nation that once prided itself on welcoming immigrants and on giving asylum to refugees from authoritarian regimes, mainstream America today is worried about the influx. *Arguably it is not the fact of immigration as the fact that immigrants are increasingly from what is seen as the third-world-boat people or people from south of the border that leads to anxiety.* They, it is said, stretch the resources of welfare schools, criminal justice systems, and health, but more importantly, they are seen as resisting any effort to Americanize them. The response has now taken the form of a renewed search for a unifying mechanism of nationhood in the shape of monolingualism.

The 'new nativism' indicates how far the American people have moved from political concepts such as the 'Jeffersonian Rights of Man' to emotional issues, such as language as a binding force. It almost seems to suggest that all that Americans need is access to resources that would allow them to talk to each other.

CONCLUSION

We can now proceed to draw the following insights from the comparative study of India and the US in this paper:

We have seen that civil societies in both countries have been wracked on momentous occasions by the politics of language. In India, if during the freedom struggle one set of movements were to present the one-language formula as essential for building a strong nation, another set of movements saw language as intrinsic to identity and opportunities. The tension between these two impulses led the central government towards the formation of linguistic states on the one hand, and pluralization of language on the other. This has meant that the role of Hindi as the unifier of the nation has been strongly diluted. India, in other words, has recognized the importance of language rights.

In the US, on the other hand, the deep belief that non-English-speaking groups will and should learn English as a matter of course, as an integral part of what it means to be an American citizen, has narrowed linguistic options. The US, in other words, seems to have no conception of language rights. The idea that many languages are a resource and an asset for any country, particularly one that seeks to lead the world in international relations, commerce, and media is obviously unknown to either the defenders of the movement or to policy-makers. It is true that the federal government in the US had in the 1960s, adopted a series of laws to institutionalize bilingualism in education, voters, ballots, and government services. This was in direct response to the wide-ranging agitation prompted by the civil rights movement in the US and the radicalization of ethnicity. But these measures were more a response to the recognition that non-English-speaking groups were also groups that were discriminated against on the basis of race, rather than on a recognition of language rights. It is the language of the first generation of rights, that is, civil and political rights, rather than the language of the third generation of rights, that is, cultural and language rights that has governed affirmative action policies in the US.

This is not to say that the federal government has not tried to protect the minorities. Congress, for instance, has not till now adopted English as the official language, and the Supreme Court has in important cases protected the rights of those complainants whose languages have been devalued through the adoption of OE legislation. But arguably, the concern of the Supreme Court has been prompted by the need to uphold crucial individual rights such as the right to freedom rather than the right to one's own language.

One last point may be in order here. Both the US and India are democracies, but understanding of democracy itself has undergone a shift. Given the massive mobilization over identities the world over, democrats have increasingly come to terms with categories that they had spurned as pre-modern, such as religion, culture, caste, gender, and language. Forced into realizing that it is not homogeneity but difference that rules a given society, they have had to accept that the public sphere should ideally reflect this diversity both in its symbolic as well as in its material practices. Democrats have had, in other words, to apprehend that democracy in complex societies is not about the *transcendence or bracketing* but of the *negotiation* of difference. The recognition of and respect for diversity, in other words, is an essential sine qua nom of genuine democracy. The price societies have had to pay for the imposition of homogeneity has proved far too costly, as the case of Sri Lanka, a pointer to this reality.

5

Minorities and India's Democracy

Nathan Glazer

WHO ARE THE INDIAN 'MINORITIES'?

A key test of a democracy in the twenty-first century is its treatment of minorities. How minorities fare economically, educationally, socially, politically, has become an international standard for the judgment and treatment of states: Note the universal condemnation of racism, and the role it played in the overthrow of the apartheid regime in South Africa. An increasingly effective world public opinion—exercised by international organizations, non-governmental organizations (NGOs), the academic world, the churches, the press, and other institutions— judges the competence and adequacy of a democracy by how its minorities fare. But beyond the influence of public opinion, and far more significant in placing the condition of minorities in a key position on national agendas, there is also the threatening reality that a deprived and discontented minority can produce disorder in a state, can threaten the state with physical disruption if the minority is concentrated enough territorially to demand autonomy or separation, or may undermine its national security through connection with its national enemies. These possibilities are no guarantee that even a democratic country will not discriminate against and oppress its minorities, but it is the norm that democracies do take the matter seriously, and if they do not they will be called to order by the community of democratic states. (Note the case of Turkey and its Kurdish minority: Europe requires better treatment of the Kurds as a condition of Turkey's entry into the European community.)

All these troublesome possibilities—and more—are present when we consider India's minorities in the perspective of an overall judgment of how India's democracy is faring. The groups that might be considered 'minority' in India differ greatly in the characteristics which define them as a minority, in their social and economic condition, in their place in India's politics and political structure. This diversity in kinds of groups that could be considered minorities makes it difficult to determine just which Indian minorities should principally concern us when we examine the effectiveness of India's democracy.[1]

The term 'minority' in general parlance refers to a part of the population of a state that is marked off by race, or language, or religion, or some other social characteristic defined by 'ascription' (that is, a trait one carries regardless of one's behaviour), which leads the people of the group to be looked on by the majority as somewhat different or 'other', and leads the minority to view the majority as both different and dominant. When applied to India, the term 'minority' encompasses groups of every possible type— racial, linguistic, religious, territorial—and in addition groups of a type unique to Indian society, minorities on the basis of inferior caste status.

In Indian official terminology, 'minority' has a more restrictive range, and refers only to the religious minorities. The official government Minorities Commission deals with the issues affecting the non-Hindu religious minorities—Muslims, Sikhs, Christians, Buddhists, and so on. A separate Commission for SCs and STs deals with the problems of groups of low social status, one which is reflected in their low economic and educational status. The 'SCs', in the term best known in the western world, are the 'untouchables'. Contact with the people of such a group will traditionally pollute upper castes, and in the traditional Hindu caste order contact with them is sharply limited and defined by various rules. How extensively these caste restrictions are

---

[1]   For an excellent and comprehensive accounting of Indian minorities, see Myron Weiner, 'India's Minorities; Who Are They? What do They Want', in Partha Chatterjee, ed., *State and Politics in India*, New Delhi: Oxford University Press, 1997, pp. 459–95.

practised today is not clear, but many of the old rules are apparently still observed in rural and village India, which is most of India. 'Untouchability', and discrimination on the basis of untouchability, is banned in India's Constitution. But there is no dispute that untouchables, or ex-untouchables, as Harold Isaacs dubbed them in an important study,[2] like blacks in the US, despite a substantial range of government programmes to improve their condition, which we will discuss below, bear the heritage of this past in terms of much poorer economic conditions, poorer education, poorer conditions of life generally, and a substantial degree of discrimination and abuse up to beatings, killings, and rapes, at the hands of upper—caste groups.

The brief of the National Commission for Scheduled Castes and Scheduled Tribes (NCSCST) also covers the range of groups that in India are called 'tribal'. Some tribal groups are parallel to American Indian tribes in the US, living on land and in areas reserved by law to them. They are seen as the indigenous inhabitants of the land, many of whom have been pushed into the mountains and forests by the expansion of traditional Indian agricultural society over the millennia. Others may be advanced in some respect (for example, educationally), and may be the dominant political group in some Indian states. This is true of the 'tribes' of the Northeast, Nagas, Mizos, and others. Increasing numbers of tribals are incorporated as unskilled agricultural workers into Indian rural society, or as unskilled workers in mines and factories, and have been exploited historically as severely as the untouchables. They are 'tribes' because they have a definition as separate groups with their own languages, have a form of self-government generally based on councils of elders and other adult males, are not a caste within Indian society, and are not divided within by caste. In various ways they are influenced by the varieties of Indian religion and the characteristics of Indian society, and in time the status of some groups becomes akin to that of a caste rather than a separate tribal people. But they do not form part of the traditional Hindu social ladder defined by caste. Tribal groups in India form about 7 per cent of the Indian population, and number some 70 million or so. (In contrast, American Indians are less than 1 per cent of the American population, about two million.)

---

[2] Harold Isaacs, *India's Ex-Untouchables*, New York: John Day, 1965.

'Minority' could be extended in the Indian context to refer to speakers of all the languages of India aside from Hindi, which, with English (though that in theory is to be phased out in time), is the official language of India. At times linguistic minorities have strongly protested what they see as discrimination, and this is still a contentious issue in India, though other kinds of contentions for the moment transcend it. Since Hindi may be spoken by only a minority of India's one billion people, and Hindi-speakers feel they face discrimination in achieving higher positions in government service, the private sector, the academic world, and elsewhere, even they may also on occasion and in some respects be considered a 'minority'. Speakers of the other major languages, which have official status in the states where their speakers dominate, have in their turn often protested what they see as the discriminatory results of the efforts to spread the use of Hindi; while speakers of minority languages within these states often face discrimination in public employment and elsewhere.[3]

It is thus not easy to properly bound an inquiry into the condition of minorities under India's democracy, and how well that democracy has dealt with minority problems. This chapter focuses on the two largest minority groups, which I find most comparable to the idea of 'minority' as it is understood in other countries: the SCs, and the largest minority religion, the Muslims. Other minorities are, by international standards, large enough to demand extended treatment: the STs, who include hundreds of groups and make up 70 million or more of India's population; the Christians, who number 19 million, and who have recently been reminded by some terrible atrocities, and by the rise of a party the BJP, emphasizing India's Hindu heritage and suspicious of all outside it, that they too are potentially a vulnerable minority in a majority Hindu society; the Sikhs, 16 million, closely related to Hinduism, of

---

[3]   See Myron Weiner and Mary Fainsod Katzenstein, *India's Preferential Policies: Migrants, the Middle Clases, and Ethnic Equality*, Chicago: University of Chicago Press, 1981. This book concentrates on preferences based on residence, designed to protect 'sons of the soil' (natives of a state) from competition for jobs or university entry by migrants, but in effect this becomes protection based on language and in complementary fashion discrimination based on language.

which they are an offshoot, but many of whom carried on for years a fierce and deadly insurgency demanding independence.

India's minorities are of enormous size—150,000,000 in the SCs, 120,000,000 Muslims—far transcending in absolute numbers any groups we might consider a minority in other countries. China also has minorities, but they are concentrated in China's border regions rather than spread, as India's major minorities are, throughout the country. And no minority group in China comes anywhere near the size of the SC population or the Muslim population. The third largest country in the world, the US, also has minorities, groups that have some kind of minority status in law or in official statistics or in popular understanding—Afro-Americans, Hispanic-origin Americans, Asians, and American Indians or Native Americans—who make up near 30 per cent of the American population, figures similar to the minorities of India—that is, SCs, STs, Muslims, and the smaller non-Hindu religions. But the largest minority, African-Americans, of some 35 million, about 12 per cent of the population, is much smaller in absolute numbers than the Muslims, the SCs, or the STs of India.

We need not linger long to consider why Muslims in India are properly to be considered a minority, with many of the problems minorities in other countries face, and with some special ones distinctive to the Indian scene. Some 12 per cent of the population, they are inevitably linked with the tragedy of partition and its heritage of deep hostility and division between India and Pakistan. Whatever their attitudes and the degree of their identification with and loyalty to India—and this identification and loyalty is extensive and pervasive, however threatened by a newly resurgent political emphasis on Hindu historic grievances against Islam—, Indian Muslims have to bear a burden, in terms of some identification with the national enemy, that even US blacks do not have to bear.

India's 'majority', in discussions of India's minorities, is taken to be the Hindus, given in the census as 82 per cent of the population. But that enormous percentage rarely makes itself evident in any great degree of common practice or action. The party that presents itself to the Indian electorate as distinctively Hindu in its orientation has never gotten more than a quarter of the vote, though in India's recent fractionated political situation this has been enough to enable this party, the BJP, to lead a coalition government. India's 'majority', the Hindus, refers to a complex mix of Indian religious practices and faiths that goes back a few thousand years, a mix which has always resisted formalization and standardization. 'The Hinduism of the "Hindu majority"', according to the authoritative scholars Lloyd I. Rudolph and Susanne Hoeber Rudolph, 'encompasses a diversity of gods, texts and social practices.... Without an organized church, it is innocent of orthodoxy, heterodoxy and heresy. Thus, until the transforming events and experiences that surfaced during the Janata government [the first non-Congress government of 1977–9 ... the "Hindu majority" remained an illusory support for a national confessional party....'[4]

That complexity still resists today the effort of ideological advocates of 'Hindutva'—'Hinduness'—to shape Hindus and Hinduism into something resembling the text-based and authoritatively structured religions stemming from the Middle East. Some Indian scholars, to emphasize how different Hinduism is from Christianity and Islam, refer to the latter as 'semitic' or 'semitist' religions, and emphasize their differences from diverse Hinduism. (While Judaism does not matter much in India—there are very few Jews in India—it is clearly the father of the 'semitist' religions. This is an odd twist in usage for the concept of the 'semitic', a term that has been adapted to many uses far from its origin as the simple description of a distinctive language group.)

THE SCHEDULED CASTES AND HINDUISM

The diversity of Hinduism has cast up what many would consider the most typical and distinctive minority in India, and the minority that will be at the centre of our discussion. In official terminology this is the 'SCs', in Western languages (and in Indian English, too) this is the 'untouchables', in Gandhi's now discarded term they are the 'Harijans'—this is now considered paternalistic—,and in the current most popular term among the militant defenders of the rights of this group, they are the 'Dalits'.

4   Lloyd I. Rudolph and Susanne Hoeber Rudolph, *In Pursuit of Lakshmi: The Political Economy of the Indian State*, Chicago, Illinois: University of Chicago Press, 1987, p. 37.

But what kind of minority are they? They encompass a great range of what in Western languages would be considered castes, in Indian terminology 'communities' or *jatis*, ranging from the most deprived to those scarcely different from castes formally above them. They are however listed in an official schedule, devised by the former British rulers, and not much revised since, they are counted separately in the census, they have a right to certain benefits, and in varying degrees are subject to various kinds of indignity, prejudice, discrimination, and abuse. Dalit leaders and organizations wanted to participate in the United Nations sponsored conference on racism in Durban a few years ago. They saw their fate as similar to and linked to that of other peoples in other countries, oppressed and disdained and discriminated against on account of race. The Indian government resisted the idea that the SCs or Dalits were a racial group and as such presented a question of *racial* discrimination. Whatever the case India could have made that it is trying to stamp out the status and accompanying disabilities of the SCs, it would not accept the idea that the Indian SCs could be equated with oppressed racial minorities: The SCs were unique to India. To the Indian government they were not a race different from other Indians (though our new sophisticated abilities to distinguish groups by genetic traces may well show a degree of separation that would qualify as racial).

There is a long history to the Indian nationalist and governmental resistance to separating the SCs from the Hindu majority, going back to the period when India was ruled by Great Britain, and the colonial rulers were introducing, to deal with the demands of the national movement, some degree of representative government. Muslims or Muslim leaders were already concerned with possible domination by what they saw as the Hindu majority in a free India. Muslims in undivided India made up a quarter of the population, and were the majority or near majority in some of the large states into which British India was divided. Possibly the divisions, social and political, among what appeared in the census as the Hindu majority, might have enabled Muslims to defend their rights through ordinary democratic politics. Nevertheless, Muslim leaders at the time demanded a separate electorate and guaranteed places in any legislative body in proportion to their numbers.

But what then of the untouchables or Harijans, as they were called at the time? Should they also have a separate electorate? The Christians, Sikhs, and Anglo-Indians also had rights to separate representation in the nascent representative institutions of British India. An epic struggle erupted between India's great national leader M.K.Gandhi, and B.R.Ambedkar, the leader of the untouchables. Gandhi insisted that the SCs were Hindus, that through his leadership and the leadership of the Indian National Congress their grievances would be met, and that separate electorates would introduce unacceptable divisions among Indians. Ambedkar insisted that separate electorates and representation were necessary to guarantee that untouchables could protect their interests and play a role in politics related to their numbers. In the end, the separate electorate was not created, but guaranteed seats for members of SCs in legislatures in proportion to their numbers in the population was accepted—and this still survives as a distinctive feature of the Indian political system.

The Indian census—that great achievement of India's colonial rulers—had already defined the untouchables through its elaborate listing of the population by caste, and the numbers were already available to fix the degree of their representation. The British colonial census officials may have been the first to worry over just who the untouchables were and how they should be classified. Were they within Hinduism, even though they are outside the four *varna*s described in classic texts, the Brahmins, Kshatriyas, Vaishyas, and Sudras, and thus below even the lowly Sudra? But they are a part—indeed an essential part—of Indian society in its classic form, for they enabled the higher twice-born castes to maintain their purity and caste status by doing the work that in Hindu perception was seen as polluting—disposing of dead animals, cleaning human waste, washing clothes, cutting hair, making pots.

'British census officials became obsessed with the question of whether untouchables were properly classifiable as Hindus, or whether they were a people *sui generis*. This may well have been the first time such a question was asked. Until Indian civilization was defined relative to the world outside, there was no need for a concept of 'Hindu' at all. That word and to some degree the very concept of the Hindu seems to have been supplied by Persians, Europeans, and Central Asians rather than Indians themselves. And while Brahminical ritual supremacy served to constitute untouchable castes as profoundly 'other', it did not constitute them as belonging to another non-Hindu religious community. Nor did the Muslim conquerors have much impact on the matter ... They displayed little interest in engineering relations among the non-Muslim population. It was the era of the British that sharpened all the deep ambiguities and tensions of Untouchable life in India.' [5]

The British census-takers worked hard at the task of defining the untouchables. British supervisors in the 1881, 1891, and 1901 census seem to have been exasperated by high-caste Hindu census enumerators who refused to record lower castes as Hindus at all, and simply listed their specific caste in the column for religion. But Indian national leaders were adamant that the untouchables were indeed Hindus: 'The spur to the change was the arithmetic of parliamentary representation that was begun under the Morely[sic]-Minto reforms of 1909–10: The Muslim League had sought to argue that the Hindu population was artificially inflated by inclusion of the Untouchables, and in response the Hindus now laid vehement claim to these people.' [6]

In 1911 the untouchables were called the 'Depressed Classes', in 1931 the 'Exterior Castes'. That was the last census in which caste was recorded generally for Hindus. But because of the 'reservations' for SCs, as they were later to be called, in political representation and in government jobs, which was maintained and expanded by independent India, the SCs (and STs) have continued to be counted and recorded in each census since independence.

The Indian census's silence on caste, aside from the SCs, reflects the commitment of the fathers of India's Constitution to the creation of a democratic society in which the hierarchy of caste was to be relegated to ancient history. When the 'backward (but not untouchable) castes' became assertive in demanding their share of government jobs and of entry places to universities, the only way to determine what their share might be was oddly enough to

---

[5]　Oliver Mendelsohn and Marika Vicziany, *The Untouchables: Subordination, Poverty and the State in Modern India*, New York: Cambridge University Press, 1998, p. 27 (henceforth, M and V).

[6]　Ibid., p. 28.

return to the base of caste figures given in the 1931 census, which is still done, by scholars as well as governmental agencies.[7]

SCHEDULED CASTES IN DEMOCRATIC INDIA

Even before India became independent in 1947, legislatures and governors' councils had been established in the states of British India, and in these legislatures and councils there was provision for the representation of minorities through the reservation of certain numbers of seats for them or through requirements to include members of these communities in councils. The minorities so protected not only included most prominently Muslims, but also Sikhs, Christians, and, a very small minority, Anglo-Indians (the descendants of British fathers and Indian mothers who had in effect evolved into a new 'community'). There were also reservations for untouchables, the 'SCs'. There was also another kind of 'reservation', of jobs in government, for persons from the lower castes. There were also some programmes to enable lower-caste persons to gain access to education.

These reservations were particularly prominent in the southern states, particularly in Madras Presidency (most of which is now Tamil Nadu) and in some important princely states. They reflected the social structure of the south, which is somewhat different from the north and east. In the south, the dominance of the Brahmins was particularly marked. They formed an upper class of landowners and administrators (though of course there were also Brahmin priests and Brahmin cooks and the Brahmin poor). Because of

---

[7]   The controversial Mandal Commission report, arguing for reservations for 'OBCs', referred back to the 1931 Census. Note that scholars of Indian politics in its relation to caste must also, seventy years after the fact, refer back to the 1931 census: See Dipankar Gupta, 'Caste and Politics: the Presumption of Numbers', in Veena Das *et al*, eds, *Tradition, Pluralism, and Identity*, New Delhi: Sage, 1999, p. 268 and elsewhere. See, too, on the issue of the Indian census and caste, Nandini Sundar, 'The Indian Census: Identity and Inequality', in Ramachandra Guha and Jonathan P. Parry, eds, *Institutions and Inequalities* New Delhi: Oxford University Press, 1999, pp. 100–27 and Laura Dudley-Jenkins, *Identity and Identification in India's Democracy: Defining the Disadvantaged*, London and New York: RoutledgeCurzon, 2003, Chapter 5.

their background they were particularly effective in gaining western education and in occupying places in administration and government under British rule. All other groups felt deprived because of this dominance, so the preferences called for in the south by the anti-Brahmin movements were primarily for non-Brahmins rather than for the most deprived, the untouchables. Anti-Brahmin movements swept through the south in the early part of the century, and one response of the government was to make arrangements for non-Brahmins to gain education and to find places in public employment.

But what was to be done with this complex mix of political, occupational, and educational reservations, varying from province to province, from state to state, in independent India? Marking the beginning of independent India was the shaping of a constitution, which was to become possibly the most effective and potent of the new post-war constitutions. Drawing from a variety of constitutions in the world—including that of the US, from which some key phrases were borrowed—accepting the basic forms of parliamentary government and of administration which had been introduced into India by its colonial British rulers, and dominated by the liberal democratic and egalitarian ideology that characterized the secular leaders of the Indian freedom movement, the Constituent Assembly which shaped the Constitution was drawn to the creation of a society in which all were equal and none bore the burdens—or privileges—of India's complex and differentiated social past. Ideally, all special reservations in political representation should have been swept aside, all preferences on the basis of caste or religion or language should have been eliminated. That was certainly what the liberal and democratic ideology of the time seemed to require.

India's Constitution did go far in this direction. All political reservations for religious minorities were swept aside. But reservations for the SCs were retained for ten years, presumably in the optimistic hope that by then the SCs would be so integrated into the nation that they would not need or want them.[8] As is typical of so many 'affirmative action' programmes intended to be in force for a number of years, this provision has since been

---

[8]   Granville Austin, *The Indian Constitution: Cornerstone of a Nation*, New York: Oxford University Press, 1972 [1966], pp. 149–51.

renewed regularly every ten years. (An odd special provision allowed the appointment of two representatives of the Anglo-Indian community to the lower house of the national legislature and state legislatures by the president and state governors.[9])

Despite these concessions to India's diversity, powerful bans on discrimination became a key part of the Constitution: 'The State shall not deny to any person equality before the law or the equal protection of the laws within the territory of India' (Article 14); 'The State shall not discriminate against any citizen on grounds only of religion, race, caste, sex, place of birth, or any of them' (Article 15); 'There shall be equality of opportunity for all citizens in matters relating to employment or appointment to any office under the State' (Article 16); 'No citizen shall be denied admission into any educational institution maintained by the State or receiving aid from the State on grounds only of religion, race, caste, language or any of them' (Article 29[2]).

But none of this meant that the various reservations and preferences in appointments and educational institutions for SCs and STs would disappear. These were already, primitive as they were in comparison to what was to follow, so fully institutionalized that such a radical change could not be envisaged. And the conditions of the untouchables so urgently called for redress in a liberal and democratic state that a place for substantial positive action had to be carved out. So another provision, which was indeed in some tension with the sweeping prohibitions of discrimination, asserted: 'The State shall promote with special care the educational and economic interests of the weaker sections of the people, and, in particular, SCs and STs, and shall protect them from social injustice and all forms of exploitation' (Article 46). And perhaps most crucially, as part of Article 16, requiring 'equality of opportunity for all citizens in matters relating to employment or appointment to any office under the state', a key exception was added on as part of the article: 'Nothing in this article shall prevent the state from making any provision for the reservation of appointments or posts in favour of any backward class of citizens which, in the opinion of the state, is not adequately represented in the services under the state' (Article 16[4]).

[9]   Ibid., p. 145, fn 1.

B. R. Ambedkar, the leader of the SCs, was given a key role in the shaping of the Constitution. An untouchable himself, he had won a law degree in England and two doctorates abroad— one at Columbia University in New York. His education and higher education came at a time when very few untouchables could receive any education at all owing to the fierce discrimination and prejudice to which they were subjected, and he achieved his position not only through his gifts and efforts but because of a kind of 'reservation', the patronage of the ruler of the princely state of Baroda. 'The special provision for backward communities, which is a distinguishing feature of the Indian Constitution, is clearly the handiwork of Ambedkar.'[10]

The tension between the expansive prohibitions of any discrimination by the state and the maintenance and expansion of the reservations for backward classes and castes meant that the Supreme Court of India would have a major role in shaping the regime of preferences. The Constitution had not been long in force when the Supreme Court had to deal with the contradiction: 'A pair of Supreme Court decisions in April 1951 shattered the legal foundations of the system of communal quotas which prevailed in South India. *State of Madras* v. *Champakam Dorairajan* struck down the Madras reservations in educational institutions.... *Venkataramana* v. *State of Madras* struck down the Madras quotas for all groups other than the Scheduled Castes and "Backward Hindus"....' (The reservations in Madras were basically anti-Brahmin and for all groups except Brahmins.)[11] Almost immediately, government responded to protect reservations, and the Parliament passed the first amendment to the Indian Constitution, Article 15 (4), allowing special provision for the advancement of any socially and educationally backward classes of citizens.[12]

---

[10]   Devanesan Nesiah, *Discrimination with Reason? The Policy of Reservations in the United States, India, and Malaysia*, New Delhi: Oxford University Press, 1999, p. 60.

[11]   Marc Galanter, *Competing Equalities*, Berkeley: University of California Press, 1984, pp. 164–5.

[12]   A very convenient and comprehensive edition of the Constitution is *The Constitution of India*, with selective comments by P.M. Bakshi, Delhi: Universal Law Publishing Company, 2002.

As one may see from the response to these cases, the principle of reservations for SCs and STs and for backward classes—not further defined—had strong political support and it has not really been challenged for fifty years. There are fringe issues that reach the courts on such questions as who can qualify for such benefits, whether reservations should apply to promotions, and other matters. The most seriously disputed question over the years has been how far up the caste ladder beyond the SCs and STs to include 'OBCs' should preferences reach. The Supreme Court has tried to limit beneficiaries to 50 per cent of the population, but in the southern states much higher percentages of the population qualify, including some castes that have achieved political power and who may only doubtfully be considered deprived.

Under this constitutional framework, a remarkable extension and institutionalization of reservations and special programmes for SCs and STs and, to some extent, OBCs, has taken place. The major conflict today around this regime of preference for the lower castes is over preferences for 'OBCs'. Are 'backward classes' to be defined as castes above the SCs in social status but still considered inferior, or by their economic status? 'Other backward castes' are not formally listed at the national level as are SCs and STs. What may be considered an OBC varies from state to state. The issue became particularly sensitive when in 1991 a liberal national government revived the recommendations of a national commission (the Mandal Commission) which had ten years earlier proposed national reservations for OBCs. (They already existed in southern states.) They have indeed been instituted. To determine to what extent these reservations are in force in government jobs, at the state and national level, and in educational institutions, both national and state-governed, is not easy. They are stronger at the state level, where castes above the SCs, and below the 'twice-born' upper three varnas, may achieve political power and in various ways can breach the Supreme Court limitation of 50 per cent on how many can receive preferences.[13]

---

[13]   For a full and comprehensive account of the complex political history of the efforts to extend quotas above the 50 per cent mark through the addition of castes above the SCs in Karnataka and Tamil Nadu see P. Radhakrishnan, 'Caste, Politics and the Reservation Issue', in Barbara Harriss-White and S. Subramanian,

Despite modifications, expansions, and political conflict, the regime of extensive preferences has remained in effect for over fifty years, and seems more solidly established than fifty years ago. This is in striking contrast to the fate of the somewhat parallel scheme of affirmative action in the US, where some of the programmes of affirmative action are under strong legal attack, and some indeed have been abandoned. In the US, in contrast to India, there is no clear basis in the Constitution and its amendments for affirmative action, the common name for what Indians call reservations. Affirmative action is based not on statutory law but on executive (Presidential) action, on regulations by government agencies, on the independent action of state and local governments, on voluntary action by institutions of higher education. It further differs from reservations in India in that the private employment sector is not exempt from affirmative action requirements, as it is in India. Further, there are no reservations formally in political representation (though action by the Department of Justice under its interpretation of the Voting Rights Act of 1965 has led to the carving out of constituencies that are expected to elect black or Hispanic representatives).

These key differences in the constitutional and statutory basis for reservations and affirmative action, and the reach of affirmative action in the US as compared with India (in particular, the extension to private sector employment in the US), reflect differences in the political, social, and economic structures of the two societies. In India, as I have indicated, preferences have moved upwards from the SCs and STs to cover a larger and larger part of the population, who are considered OBCs. In the US, there was a fear at the beginning that the preferences would be difficult to bound, and would be extended to others beyond the initial target groups. Affirmative action was instituted in the wake of and as a consequence of the civil rights' revolution, which was carried out by blacks and their liberal supporters to overcome their second class citizenship. But the Civil Rights Act (and the 14th Amendment to the Constitution, with its guarantee of 'equal protection of the laws') did not refer to any specific group that was to be the beneficiary of the ban on discrimination. Indeed, nothing in it

---

eds, *Illfare in India*, New Delhi: Sage, 1999, pp. 163–95 (in later references, *Illfare*).

had any suggestion of preference for any specific group on the basis of previous deprivation, and one provision banned quotas in employment based on proportions of each group in the population or the labour force. In contrast, quotas, for SCs, STs, and OBCs, are specifically mandated in laws pursuant to the Constitution in India. In the US, the listing of groups that were to be the beneficiary of affirmative action was an action of administrative agencies, and was never reflected in statutory law.

As against the upward expansion of benefited categories to include other possibly deprived ethnic and racial groups, as has occurred in India, in the US there has been a restriction of the scope of affirmative action. Asian-Americans, one of the four racial and ethnic groups originally considered by administrative agencies eligible for preference in employment or admission to colleges and universities, are no longer so considered, though statistics are still kept and reported on them. They are now, as a whole, overrepresented in elite occupations and in admissions to selective institutions of higher education. They still benefit from affirmative action in the granting of government contracts.

Affirmative action in the US is also undergoing restriction in its application to the initial and key target group, American blacks. Courts have abandoned mandatory programmes of school busing to equalize racial numbers in public schools. (While not usually regarded part of affirmative action, it is in essence a form a preference on the basis of race.) The Supreme Court has closely bounded affirmative action in the granting of government contracts, though this practice continues to some extent. Affirmative action in admissions to colleges and universities has been under the most severe legal and political assault. It has been banned by popular referendum in the states of California and Washington, by Federal Circuit Court ruling in Texas, and eliminated in Florida by action of the Governor and the legislature before a campaign for revocation by referendum could get under way. The assault on affirmative action in higher education—which was maintained by voluntary action of the institutions involved—reached the Supreme Court in 2003, and in a historic case it ruled narrowly that while quotas were impermissible, affirmative action could be maintained by colleges and universities. The ruling reflected the strong commitment of American elites, and in particular college and university administrators, to 'diversity', that is, the representation of previously deprived groups, and has helped maintain the numbers of black and Hispanic students who benefit from affirmative action in college and university admissions.

In the area of employment, the practices of affirmative action are so strongly institutionalized among large employers that they are hardly dependent any more on specific government action for affirmative action.

What explains why affirmative action in the US is under attack and being restricted, while in India it is solidly established for a large minority of the population and has been extended, through politically contested measures, it is true, to cover a range of groups that make up a majority of the population? The best explanation I think is that in the US the beneficiary groups—blacks, Hispanics, American-Indians, and Asians (they also include women, but women have not made common cause with deprived racial-ethnic groups in pressing for affirmative action)—formed a small minority at the time affirmative action was instituted. Nor could they expand their numbers: Those above them that might have redefined themselves as deprived and potentially eligible for affirmative action were already so well assimilated into the American population that they did not wish to claim victim status. In the areas where affirmative action is well established—among large private employers, and in admissions to colleges and universities—it is maintained not because of government and political pressure but because of judgments by those in a position to hire and admit that it is a good thing, and improves the business or college and university.[14] Undoubtedly the established two-party system of the US also plays a role in muting the reach of affirmative action. Both parties must try to appeal to a majority of the voters. While Democrats support it more than Republicans, Democratic political leaders must be careful to mute their support for fear of antagonizing large groups of voters hostile to affirmative action. The alliances that make possible extension

[14] On why the extension of affirmative action in the US was limited, see the interesting books by John Skrentny, *The Irony of Affirmative Action*, Chicago, Illinois: University of Chicago Press, 1996 and *The Minority Rights Revolution*, Cambridge, MA: Harvard University Press, 2002.

of reservations to larger proportions of the OBCs are not possible in the US.

Whatever the differences, it is striking that the two largest democracies in the world have also created the two largest programmes for raising of the condition of poor and deprived groups by means of positive action going beyond the simple ban on discrimination.

As a result, in both countries there has been impassioned controversy over the justice and legitimacy of programmes in which the individual's race or ethnicity or caste is a factor to determine whether that person will get a job or enter a university. The formal guarantee of the 'equal protection of the laws', present in both constitutions, is to the critic of reservations or affirmative action transgressed. Justice no longer wears a blindfold, as in its common representation. And in both countries, too, there is controversy over the pragmatic effects of these policies, whether and to what extent they have raised the condition of the target groups, and whether it would not have been better if their circumstances had been addressed by common policies for all the poor, or the illiterate, or the sick. Leading Indian intellectuals have been severe critics of the extension of reservations for employment and education upwards to include the 'OBCs', and the way this issue has become a political football. But the process, despite legal setbacks, is in India increasingly governed by crude efforts of the various parties to expand their appeal by extending reservations to caste groups whose position is well above that of SCs and STs.[15]

'Quotas' is not a dirty word in India, as it is in the US. Quotas for the SCs and STs are, despite widespread grumbling among the upper castes, solidly established and institutionalized and retain unchallengeable political support, which is far from the case in the US, where popular referenda in California and

---

[15]   See for example, André Béteille's essay, 'Equality as Right and as a Policy', in his *Society and Politics in India*, New Delhi: Oxford University Press, 1991, pp. 192–214; *The Backward Classes in Contemporary India*, Delhi: Oxford University Press, 1992, and some of his newspaper essays gathered in *Chronicles of Our Time*, New Delhi: Penguin Books, 2000, in particular pp. 201–41. Béteille has been the most consistent and effective critic of the extension of reservations beyond the SCs and STs, and the logic which attempts to justify it.

Washington have eliminated all preference by race and ethnic groups, though the implementation of that ban is limited by the fact that so many programmes are mandated by Federal courts or regulations.

In India, in contrast, the *principle* of reservations is scarcely challenged. As the distinguished Indian sociologist André Béteille notes:

> There is a great deal of disagreement in India, leading sometimes to violence, about how the policy should be made to work, and how far it should be extended, but the principle behind the policy is widely accepted as an important part of the commitment to equality. In the United States there appears to be far greater ambivalence about accepting the principle itself. This, no doubt, is partly because of the distinctively American conception of equality which, as Professor [Owen] Fiss has pointed out, is based on the 'anti-discrimination' rather than the 'group-disadvantaging' principle. In India, where collective identities are so much more marked, disparities between groups figure prominently where equality is a consideration.

> American courts, even while accepting affirmative action, have been hostile to racial and ethnic quotas. In India quotas or reservations are accepted by all branches of government as a necessary part of a policy of greater equality overall.[16]

The conflicts in India over reservations for OBCs have dealt with the size of the quotas or reservations, whether the most advanced communities dominate or monopolize the available jobs and university places, and have become in effect a 'creamy layer', and whether the quotas and reservations should be further compartmentalized so that the 'most backward classes' (MBCs) can get a larger share.[17] The uproar over the national extension

[16]   Béteille, *Society and Politics in India*, op.cit., p. 205.

[17]   See, for an example of current disputes, 'SC [Supreme Court] stays UP [Uttar Pradesh] order on jobs for MBCs', The *Hindu*, 22 January 2002, p. 1; and 'No jobs for backwards now, Supreme Court tells UP govt,' *Hindustan Times*, 22 January 2002, p. 1: Under a recent act, 'OBCs had been divided into three categories, backward, more backward, and most backward ... Senior Counsel Kapil Sibal said the government wanted to make 20,000 appointments under the new law before the elections and its motives were purely political.'

of reservations to the OBCs in the 1990s and the continuing opposition to its implementation does not affect the reservations for SCs and STs, to which we now turn.

WHAT RESERVATIONS HAVE ACCOMPLISHED

The regime of preferences and protections that has been created for SCs and STs consists of four major parts. (1) There is the reservation of seats for SCs and STs, in the national legislature, in the state legislatures, and in other elected bodies down to the lowest level. Nationally, these amount to about 15 per cent of the lower house of the national legislature, the Lok Sabha, for SCs, and 7.5 per cent for STs. The percentages of reservation for state legislature vary from state to state. (2) There are the reservations for posts and jobs with the national government, in a similar proportion, and for posts and jobs in state government, which vary with the numbers of SCs and STs in the state. (3) There is the reservation of places in institutions of higher education. (4) There are a host of special programmes, exemptions, provisions to help SCs and STs take advantage of reservations in government jobs and in institutions of education. These include special coaching or tutoring, loosening of age limitations for jobs, lowering of scores required in tests, special grants of assistance for books and the like, waiving of fees, publicly provided hostel (living) arrangements in colleges, scholarships at various levels, and indeed many others that would take pages to list.

Aside from the system of reservation and benefits is special legislation deigned to outlaw the practice of untouchability and to protect the ex-untouchables from the discrimination and abuse to which they are often subjected. Independent of all of these is a mass of legislation and schemes to assist the poor, among whom the SCs are disproportionately represented.

How has it worked? Our inquiry is grounded in the question—has democracy in India worked to raise the condition of and incorporate more effectively in Indian society its lowest strata, to make them equal in status and circumstances to other Indians? This inquiry must be set against the background of an Indian economic reality that must affect any judgement of how any group has progressed. India's prevailing poverty, and the relatively slow rate, until the last decade or so, at which its economy has grown, creates the limiting environment within which any group progresses, and sets limits to what government can do in any sphere, including lifting the lower strata. Further, the issue of untouchability is not only one of deep poverty and educational and economic disadvantage, severe as these are, but also one of lack of respect, of disdain, avoidance, refusal of social intercourse and contact, and in parts of the country, one of whether untouchables can assert their rights without risking physical attack and massacre. We have to consider what government has achieved in these respects.

The Constitution forbids untouchability, and Indian legislation forbids the practice of untouchability, and specifies a host of discriminatory acts that may not be practised, such as denying untouchables the right to enter temples, to use public wells and draw water, to use public roads or other public facilities, to use the customs and dress identified with upper castes, and many others. Such issues are far from the concerns of modern social policy with its pragmatic aims, but in India they are of the essence of the matter and deeply connected with the possibility of advancement in politics, in education, in the economic sphere.

These status issues were at the heart of the movements to raise the condition of untouchables in their origins. One's impression is that these status issues have in large measure been resolved, at least in the urban sector of Indian society, where people mix and do not necessarily know the caste backgrounds of those with whom they come in contact, and where indeed caste matters less. But we should recall that India is still two-thirds rural, that the great majority of Indians live in traditional villages, and the proportion of untouchables who live in such settings, generally in isolated parts of villages named for their community and where their status is marked and clear, is even greater. But untouchability in its classic forms does appear to be in decline.

Mendelsohn and Vicziany, in their excellent and comprehensive treatment of untouchability today, write that research in various locations shows that

Untouchables can now freely walk along virtually any public road, catch a bus or train, use the post office, eat in a cafe in a major city, and be admitted to a school which will not segregate them.... But ... in many regions discrimination persists at the water well, tea stall and temple, to name some prominent public sites. In the great cities of India, and in the special case of Bengal, there is now a civic culture that does not permit the open practice of ritual discrimination in public space.[18]

The issue of atrocities—attacks on and killings of SC villagers by upper-caste landowners and the thugs they hire, often occasioned by conflicts over land and labour—seems more important today than the classic issues of humiliation, which is not to say that the latter are not to be found. Much of the caste violence is occasioned by the refusal of untouchables to accept the treatment—such as molestation of untouchable women—that was once routine.

How to measure the improvement in the condition of untouchables in terms of social treatment and status is difficult. It is easier to describe the direct impact of the reservations, which have after all a quantitative goal or objective, and we can ask, have they been reached, and if they have, with what effect on the overall condition of the untouchables?

Concerning the reservations in political representation, we need no quantitative test of their success from the point of view of achieving PR of the SC population. The number of reserved seats is set to reflect the percentage of SC persons in the population, as determined by the census. There is no argument over how large the number should be, no great debate, as there is in the US, over determining the boundaries for electoral districts as to maximize (or minimize) the opportunity of a minority candidate to be elected. This process in India seems remarkably removed from direct partisan political considerations, when one compares it with the US. An independent commission sets boundary lines for electoral districts, and selects from among them the districts from which only a SC person may be elected. Proportional representation of this minority is thus guaranteed, and a host of conflicts with which we deal in the US are by the design of the scheme eliminated.

---

[18]   M and V, pp. 120–1. But there are less optimistic accounts on how things stand especially from Dalit sources. See, for example, G.S. Bhargava and R.M. Pal, eds, *Human Rights of Dalits: Societal Violation*, New Delhi: Gyan Publishing House, 1999, the proceedings of a conference held in Chennai and organized jointly by the Dalit Liberation Education Trust and the National Human Rights Commission, a central government agency.

To judge how much political reservations have done for the untouchables they are meant to represent is harder to determine. But when we recall that one measure of black progress in the US is how many blacks sit in Congress, in state legislatures, in city councils, and when we recall how far that number, despite enormous change, is from reflecting the proportion of blacks in the population, we may well consider that the mere fact that 15 per cent of the members of the Lok Sabha are from SCs is achievement enough. Political careers are thus opened up and made possible.

Has this arrangement advanced the condition of the SCs in general? That is harder to judge. Parliament in India has to begin with less power and resources than Congress in the US. For the first few decades after independence, SC voters formed a 'vote bank' for the Congress party, their legislators were almost uniformly of the Congress party, and this undoubtedly limited their effectiveness in promoting the interests of the group. In the last fifteen years, there has been a major change as the Congress party has declined, and new parties, including a specifically SC-led party, the Bahujan Samaj Party (BSP), have risen to some influence. The BSP has been able to form, in coalition with other parties, governments in India's largest state, Uttar Pradesh. Those governments were headed by an SC woman, which is some indication one would think of larger change. (As is the fact that the last president of India before the present one was an SC man; the current president is a Muslim.) SC voters now have the opportunity to vote for a party with SC leaders that appeals directly to them, and they do vote for it. Even if it gets only a small proportion of the vote, in the present climate where generally only coalitions can form governments, its influence increases. Further, we have seen some increase too in the number of SC candidates who are now elected from districts that are not reserved for them.[19]

[19]   'In the 11th Lok Sabha, there were 123 MPs belonging to SC/ST communities (as against 106 out of 545 seats reserved for members of SC/ST communities), which indicates that besides the reserved constituencies SC/ST candidates are elected against unreserved Lok Sabha seats also. It is a healthy sign of social transformation.' National Commission for SCs and STs, Fourth Report, 1996–97 and 1997–98, p. 30 (henceforth NCSCST).

Marc Galanter, in his monumental study of reservations, asserts that

The presence of reserved-seat legislators, if not in itself likely to raise the level of benefits [for SC/ST's], does seem to serve as a warrant of the continuation of these programs in their present levels. Furthermore, their presence in such numbers provides a quantitative basis for Scheduled Caste and Tribe participation in leadership at the cabinet level; it is unlikely that there would be many persons from these groups in cabinets were it not for the reserved seats. It appears that the initiation and expansion of programs for these groups is associated with the presence of group members in cabinet posts.[20]

This seems to me a balanced judgement. It was made almost twenty years ago. The effectiveness of SC voters and legislators one would think can only have increased in the new atmosphere of volatile voting and regime change.[21] But as we will see there are more pessimistic views on how much good electoral reservations have done the SCs.

Quotas in the sphere of legislative representation are so to speak self-enforcing: only an SC or ST may be elected from the designated constituencies and so the quota has been met. Meeting the quotas in government employment and in admission to educational institutions raises more difficult questions. In both areas, there is the problem of setting the boundary, of deciding who is legitimately SC and entitled to the benefit. Many Sikhs, Christians, and in particular Buddhists (Ambedkar led a movement for SCs to leave Hinduism and become Buddhists, and millions followed him) were SC before conversion, or their parents were before they converted, and their caste origin is still detectable through differential treatment by those within the new religious community or by others outside it. Do they qualify as SC? These cases can become wonderfully arcane—they are most fully treated in Galanter's *Competing Equalities*—but on the whole there seems to be no great problem in the identification or self-identification of the SC candidate for office, for jobs, for admission. Inevitably if there are benefits there will be some degree of fraud, but this

[20]   Marc Galanter. op. cit., p. 53.

[21]   See the excellent and more current treatment of the role of SC political actors in M and V, chapters 7 and 8.

does not seem to be a major issue, if one judges from public and scholarly discussion.[22]

But quotas in government employment and in admission to institutions of higher education are not self-enforcing, as are quotas in political representation: Someone must hire the candidate, or admit the applicant, and there has been much criticism of the administration of these benefits as being lax and inadequate. The figures are, however, actually quite impressive: The reservation targets for posts in government and places in institutions of higher education have on the whole been met. Thus, the most recent statistics I have seen for posts in the central government services, for 1998, show that 10.38 per cent of the Class A positions—the highest—are filled by SC persons, 11.73 per cent of Class B posts, 15.99 per cent of Class C, and 21.45 per cent of Class D.[23] Other figures are similar and have shown growth towards the quota goals, and even beyond them in the case of the less qualified positions, over the years. The pattern of fulfilment, with greater difficulty in filling the higher positions that require more education and more qualifications, is familiar and to be expected. It is not different from what we see in the patterns of black employment in the federal and other public services in the US.

One sees a similar pattern for public employment in some Indian states, though these matters are variable from state to state. In one recent and comprehensive study of Tamil Nadu, the employment figures are backed by figures for literacy and higher education, and the reasons for lesser representation in higher

[22]   See NCSCST, p. 26: 'False caste cases: ... Unscrupulous elements have made use of legal loopholes, prevalence of phonetically similar sounding caste names and lax administration to obtain false caste certificates thus cornering benefits and facilities meant for the poor SC/STs.... Commission has initiated enquiries into complaints of more that 1,000 false caste certificate cases received by it and has ensured dismissal from service and criminal action against more than 100 employees so far. Maximum cases are being reported from the states of Andhra Pradesh, Tamil Nadu, Karnataka, and Maharashtra.' And chapter VIII, 'False Community Certificates', goes into further detail on the issue.

[23]   National Commission to Review the Working of the Constitution, 'A Consultation Paper on Pace of Socio-Economic Change Under the Constitution', New Delhi, May 2001, p. p. 66 (henceforth NCRWC).

level posts becomes quite evident: Thus literacy among SC and other males is 58 and 78 per cent respectively; matriculation (entry into college) is 9 and 18 per cent; college graduation is 1.3 and 5 the percentage. The percentage of SC employees in Tamil Nadu in class A and B (the higher classes of employment) in 1999 was 13.4, the percentage in Classes C and D was 19.9. There is a rather understandable pattern of employment based on the deficiency in educational qualifications among the SCs. Large numbers of SCs, STs, and OBCs do gain government employment, and many at high levels. Upper caste domination in these positions has been radically reduced.[24] Mendelsohn and Vicziany write:

At the very apex of the public service, the fulfillment of quotas was ... relatively good. Thus by 1964 the quota of annual appointments to the Indian Administrative Service—an elite category within Class I—was reached, and this record has been maintained in the subsequent years. Recruitment in the other (slightly less elite) All India Services within Class I ... also reached their quotas from at least the early 1970s.

There are also quotas for employment in public sector undertakings, which in India include both the banks and large sectors of the industrial economy. Mendelsohn and Vicziany report: 'The record ... is worse in all areas of government employment other than the regular departments of state: ... the public banks, public sector undertakings, the armed forces, and the universities.' Reservations were introduced later for these areas than in the ordinary departments of government. There is no reservation in the armed forces, only 'advisory policy'. 'As late as 1973 only 29 out of 3,582 ... Class I officers of the Reserve Bank of India were from the Scheduled Castes.' With Indira Gandhi's nationalization of the banks in 1969 matters improved. 'By 1987 ... 7.29 percentage of officers, 13.77 percentage of clerical and 22.30 percentage of subordinate positions (exclusive of sweepers) in the banks were occupied by Scheduled Caste people.' The latest figures that Mendelsohn and Vicziany have for the armed forces are for 1981,

[24]   P.Radhakrishnan, 'Sensitizing Officials on Dalits and Reservations', *Economic and Political Weekly*, 16–22 February 2002, pp. 654–9. For other, earlier reports on the percentage of SCs and STs in government employmnt see Galanter, p. 89 (1953 and 1975); M and V, and p. 135 (1953, 1963, 1974, 1980, 1987); NCSCST, p. 177 (1995).

and only minuscule percentages (under 1 percentage) of officers were SC.

Mendelsohn and Vicziany conclude: 'Patterns of recruitment and promotion of Scheduled Caste persons now approximate to the designated quotas far more closely than they did in the immediate post-Independence years.' They assert improvement is not the result of 'increasing public and political acceptance of the reservation system: quite the reverse, resistance is growing in proportion to the uptake of benefits by the Untouchables. Presumably the improved performance derives from the cumulative pressure exerted by politicians, by bureaucratic oversight bodies, and most of all by the many Untouchable aspirants who are fully aware that a particular proportion of positions must in law go to them as a class.'[25]

Whatever the forces that make them effective, reservations in large areas of public employment have been effective. Every series of figures I have seen shows fairly steady progress towards ever higher proportions in government and in the public sector generally. Certain areas do lag far behind: faculty appointments in universities,[26] appointments as officers in the armed forces, the judiciary, and some other areas. But in view of the other failures of Indian government to which one can point, this strikes me as relative success. When contrasted with the steady resistance to affirmative action in the US, and its contraction at least in the area of admission to institutions of higher education, it is clear the reservations policy is in a much stronger position in India, and better buttressed by the Constitution, the laws, and political forces, than in the US.

[25] M and V, pp. 135–7.

[26] In particular, the national elite universities were for a long time exempted from the requirement to reserve faculty appointments for SCs. What happened in any institution depended on the vigour and commitment of the Vice-Chancellor. *The Chronicle of Higher Education* reported on 23 March 2000, that the 'University of Delhi had decided to set aside teaching positions for members of India's lower castes ... The powerful Delhi University Teachers' Union is fighting the ruling and said it would mean 1,400 jobs will have to go to lower castes'. Interviews with faculty members and administrators in January and February of 2002 seemed to indicate there were only about a dozen SC faculty members, but it was clear the policy was in place and being implemented.

We find a similar pattern of success in reaching quota targets in admission to colleges and universities. Here we also find a host of programmes to assist students in gaining higher education, scholarships, hostels, book-banks, coaching, and even overseas scholarships. Just what the figures are for SC enrolment in higher education is not clear from the report of the NCSCST: One table shows 1,058,514 out of a total enrolment of 7,955,514 in 'all courses of undergraduate, postgraduate and technical courses and professional courses' or 23.31 per cent, in 1995–6, far exceeding the 16.3 per cent of SC in the whole population in 1991, and a huge increase from 7 per cent in 1978–9. The running account on the next page, and another table, reports 496,872 out of 5,532,998, or about 9 per cent, in 'higher education', which I assume is a narrower category. But this is still respectable for a population that falls well below the average in literacy.[27]

One will find patterns similar to those in public service jobs. Those from the higher castes among the SCs and OBCs will do better than those from the lower groups in these categories (the problem of the 'creamy layer'). Dropouts of SC students will be higher. Those from educated parents will do better. Admissions to the elite national universities (the Indian Institutes of Technology, and others) lag behind, and admission to the more highly favoured and competitive professional and technical fields will also lag behind. Facility in English is a serious problem for SC and OBC students, who will more commonly have received their primary and secondary education in public institutions using Hindi or some other Indian language rather than in English-medium private schools or in elite public schools for high-level government officials and officers.[28] But in Tamil Nadu, even a few decades ago, the policies of preference for non-Brahmins was so effective that the letters to the newspapers were filled with mournful accounts of Brahmin students with very high marks who could not gain admission to the public universities in engineering and medicine and would have to go elsewhere for their education. Today in Tamil Nadu there is no problem reaching the quotas for SC and OBC students in engineering even as they go to 68 per cent.

---

[27]   NCSCST, pp. 60–1, 77.

[28]   See for a summary M and V, pp. 142–5.

Interviews suggest the language problem is particularly difficult for the SC and ST student, and here we see the conflict between two kinds of 'equality'. On the one hand, the educational system in each state—under state control—favours the use of the local language in the elementary and secondary schools, which raises the status of the local language and gives those who use it some advantage in education. But then university will be conducted in English, which creates difficulty for those who have been educated in another language, and gives an advantage to those who have attended private or the special national English-language schools, maintained for the children of upper civil servants and army officers and other elite groups.

To judge the success of reservations by considering the degree to which fulfilment of quota targets in public employment and colleges and universities are attained is to consider only one aspect of reservations policy. Whether this policy is wise or necessary or the best way of raising the condition of the SCs is another and larger matter. That some policy response to the very poor economic and educational and social position of the SCs was necessary, was originally universally accepted by the Indian political elite, and they had very good reason to make this a priority. In the late 1960s, a group of American and Indian social scientists tried to gauge the position of the SCs in India contrasted to that of Negroes in the US. This was done by national surveys in both countries. It seemed clear that the SCs were farther behind compared to other Indians than blacks were in the United States compared to whites. Thus, for example, '81 per cent of Harijans [the term used in this study] were in the two lowest [of seven] income levels, ... only 53 per cent of blacks.' Almost no Harijans were in the three highest income levels, against 13 per cent of caste Hindus, while in the US, 15 per cent of blacks were in the three highest income levels, against 39 per cent of whites. The authors concluded: 'The absolute difference ... is quite striking between the two deprived groups. Harijans are absolutely much worse off than blacks ... They are more concentrated in the lowest categories of the [educational and economic] hierarchies.'[29]

[29]   Sidney Verba, Bashiruddin Ahmad, and Anil Bhatt, *Caste, Race, and Politics: A Comparative Study of India and the United States*, Beverly Hills: Sage Publications, 1971, pp. 90, 95.

Was the concentration on appointments to government jobs and admissions to universities the right response? Why was the private sector not also targeted for jobs? And why was not more done to prepare students through primary and secondary education for either higher education or the chance for better jobs for the great majority who would never enter university? Recently the extension of reservations to the private sector has been proposed, by among others the President of India, in his Republic Day address in 2002. He pointed to the US as a model, where a large part of the private sector, all those who are government contractors, are subject to affirmative action requirements. The Congress-led government that leads India at the time I am writing seems sympathetic to such an extension, but no specific policy proposal has emerged.[30] In view of the widespread feeling—difficult to demonstrate—that the efficiency of the public services has declined because of reservations, and the understandable scepticism about government's ability to implement and monitor such a scheme, it is sure to be strongly resisted by the private sector.

It should be noted however, on this issue of whether the private sector should be covered, that in India public employment, if we include the great range of public sector undertakings, covers a much larger share of the labour force in the 'organized sector' of the economy than in the US and other advanced industrial societies. The 'organized sector', in Indian statistics, refers to the jobs outside the agricultural and family-enterprise sectors, that is, jobs in formal bureaucratic organizations and in large manufacturing and service enterprises, with regular salaries and wages and benefits. Only 10 per cent of workers in India have this kind of job. The rest are farmers or farm workers, or artisan and service workers in family enterprises. Of the jobs in this 'organized sector', two-thirds are in government or public sector undertakings: If these are targeted for reservations, one has covered most of the economy that can be subjected to this kind of requirement or regulation.[31] However the expansion of the non-

---

[30] For some discussion of the issue, see the articles in *Seminar*, May 2005, by André Béteille, Gopal Guru, Sukhadeo Thurat, and D.L. Sheth.

[31] See Rudolph and Rudolph, op. cit., p. 22–3, and in particular the enlightening footnote 6, on p. 412 on the organized sector and its meaning.

governmental sector in the last decade and the possibility of the privatization of some public enterprises will add urgency to the demand to expand reservations to the private sector.

One can see the effect of the movement of substantial numbers of SC workers into government and the public sector in ethnographic accounts of change in SC communities: An entire community can be raised thereby, not only economically, because of the stability of government jobs, but also socially and politically, as these serve as bases for social advancement and political action. There are a number of accounts of such transformations of SC communities that are quite impressive.[32]

Perhaps the most potent criticism of reservations as the key policy means of raising the position of the SCs is that the emphasis on government jobs and jobs in large organizations and admissions to universities does not touch the great bulk of the SC population, in the villages and in the agricultural sector. In 1991, 49 per cent of SC workers were agricultural labourers, 25 per cent cultivators, working their own land or others' lands as sharecroppers, 10 per cent in the manufacturing sector, and 13 per cent in trade, commerce, and transport. Only 19 per cent of the SC population lived in urban areas in 1991.[33] With access to schools and good schools very difficult for the great majority of this population living in villages, with their scanty level of services for health and sanitation leading to debilitating illness, and with their generally very low level of nutrition, what chances did these SC people have to advance to jobs that demand literacy and more than literacy?

[32]   See, for example, Jonathan P. Parry 'Two Cheers for Reservation: The Satnamis and the Steel Plant', pp. 128–69 in Ramchandra Gupta and Jonathan P. Parry, *Institutions and Inequalities: Essays in Honour of André Béteille*, New Delhi: Oxford University Press, 1999, on the striking change in the Satnami community as a result of reserved jobs in the huge Bhilai Steel plant; and M and V, pp. 169–75, on the rise of a number of SC communities in Behror in Haryana. Only part of this rise is owing to jobs in government and the public sector, but it has played a role.

[33]   Pravin Visaria and Leela Visaria, 'India's Population: Its Growth and Key Characteristics', Delhi: Institute of Economic Growth, Occasional Papers in Sociology, No. 3, November 2000, p. 24; M and V, p. 31.

There are, it is true, many public programmes designed to overcome poverty among this great mass of the SC population—and not only the SC population, since poverty is the condition of a very large part of the Indian population—but no one has given them very good marks in effectiveness. Thus there are major programmes to distribute land to the landless,[34] to provide some modest capital in the way of a cow or buffalo or a sewing machine to enable the poor to rise out of poverty, and there have been programmes to distribute development funds so as to favour SC groups. Their effectiveness seems to be limited, as one reads the literature, by the general weaknesses in Indian administration, and by the power of the local elites to engross most public funds for their own benefit. Thus of one such programme, the 'Special Component Plan', designed to direct development funds, such as, for example, road construction, so as to aid SCs and STs, Mendelsohn and Vicziany write:

The planning and implementation mechanisms for such a policy are simply not in place ... Implementation was left largely to regular District administrative machinery....This was another way of condemning the initiative to death. The District administration is overburdened, often grossly inefficient, and always subject to the intense pressure of local notables who tend to oppose the transfer of benefits to Untouchables. In short, it is highly doubtful that any significant flow of funds occurred through the operation of the Special Component Plan.[35]

The rise of the SCs—and there has indeed been improvement, whether one looks at census and other national figures, or ethnographic accounts—has been substantial, but from a base so low it will not appear impressive to any observer acquainted with the much more rapid rise of the poor populations of some other countries.[36] One could argue that it would have been better if Indian governments had adopted policies effective in increasing the rate of economic growth generally, in providing a sound universal

---

[34] See, for example, Sanjeeb K. Behera, ed., *Dalits and Land Reforms in India*, New Delhi: Indian Social Institute, 1999.

[35] M and V, pp. 165–6. One can find many similar reports in evaluations of anti-poverty measures by independent scholars.

[36] Thus, literacy of SCs has risen from 10 per cent in 1961 to 37 per cent in 1991, while literacy generally has risen from 24 to 52 per cent

elementary schooling and universal literacy, in providing safe
drinking water and other basic services to the great mass of the
Indian population in the villages. Such policies could well have
done more for the SCs than the prevailing policies of political
and educational reservations that have played so large a role in
Indian politics. But India's democracy and the way it has evolved
has meant other emphases. Thus, despite the hopes and expectations
of India's founding fathers that caste considerations would fade
away, we have seen in politics, and particularly in state politics,
an increasing emphasis on caste.[37]

---

the same period (M and V, p. 141). But this is not very impressive
when other countries as poor have achieved close to universal
literacy. As is often noted. there are great differences from state to
state, with near universal literacy in Kerala, and a much poorer
record in north India. As in so many other cases where one depends
on official and census figures, just what the numbers mean is
doubtful, despite the propensity to report them to two decimal places.
Thus, Robert Cassen notes: 'While official figures for gross enrollment
in primary education are well over 90 per cent for boys and over 80
per cent for girls, the census tells us that little over 50 per cent of
the age group are actually in school. And the quality of much of the
education is fairly dire ... In 1991, according to government figures,
just over two-thirds of males and one-third of females aged 6 and
over were literate. This is hard to reconcile with other evidence for
1981, when it was found that the mean educational attainment for
the labour force was 1.9 years, only 7 per cent had completed primary
education and only 15 per cent had ever attended schools.' Robert
Cassen, 'Population and Development Revisited', p. 56, in *Illfare*.
Even more devastating are Myron Weiner's contrasts of official
reports of near universal enrolment in schools with how few are
actually present or complete elementary education, *The Child and the
State in India*, Princeton University Press, 1991, pp. 65, 68, 71, 72, 74.
All this does give one pause in depending too heavily on official
figures. Yet accounts from observation generally do show
improvement. And if Indian education were as disastrous as the more
critical view of literacy statistics suggest, it would be hard to explain
how India manages to fill its enormous higher education system and
turn out hundreds of thousands of engineers and doctors who seem at
least minimally competent.

[37]   Thus, considerations of caste, operating in the selection of
candidates to run, seemed to dominate the upcoming election in
Uttar Pradesh, India's largest state, in January and February 2002.

Caste has declined as a social or religious concern affecting people's behaviour, but has strengthened as a political resource, creating the 'vote banks' that Indian politicians try to manipulate and Indian political analysts study. Elections at the state level become competitions in attracting votes by caste-based parties and even parties with a broader base select their candidates on the basis of which caste or religious group they need to appeal to in order to put together a governing majority. Is this the best way to advance the interests of the group? Probably not, but it is the way that is favoured in a democracy of political competition for the spoils of government. And it is the spoils of government—office, jobs, bribes, and the like—rather than the larger policies that would advance the fortunes of the poorest that seem to have become, certainly in many states and for many participants, the chief object of politics.

In the last piece he wrote before his premature death, the distinguished student of Indian politics, Myron Weiner, was particularly discouraged by what Indian democracy had managed to achieve for the poorest and weakest:

The incorporation into the political system of backward caste elites and members of the scheduled castes has apparently done little to reduce the enormous social and economic disparities that persist in India's hierarchical and inegalitarian social order. That raises the fundamental question: If there are now so many OBC and scheduled caste bureaucrats and politicians, why is this not reflected in state policies to promote the well being of their communities? Why have state governments given so little attention to the expansion and improvement of primary education...? Why has so little attention been given to the plight of low-caste child laborers and why are child labor laws not enforced? Why has public investment in public health, sanitation, and the provision of safe drinking water remained so

---

For example: 'BJP ticket for MBC's ... ', *Hindu*, 18 January 2002; 'With a view to expanding its voter support base, [the BJP] has given a large number of seats to the 'most backward castes' and the 'most oppressed' among the dalits'. Or: 'Cong. [Congress] accommodates caste groups'. *Hindu*, 20 January 2002. 'The party appears to have made an earnest attempt to give adequate representation to all the major caste and social groups in Uttar Pradesh'.

inadequate? Why has the increase in political power for the lower castes done so little to raise these communities?[38]

Ironically, these despairing questions appear in a book titled *The Success of India's Democracy*. Many political scientists have laboured at understanding why the formal success of India's democracy—its regular dependence on elections, the maintenance on the whole of civil rights and civil liberties—has not been accompanied by a larger concentration on what the critics of India's democracy see as a more effective course towards economic success and the raising of the condition of the poor. Weiner goes on to write:

A central theme of this paper is that India's democratic system has proven resilient in its capacity to incorporate hitherto excluded elements, and that the lower castes have indeed moved into positions of power in the administrative services, in parliament, and in executive positions. But ... the material benefits to the lower castes have largely gone to their more advanced members.... Those who wield political power among the lower castes have tended to use their positions for self-benefit and to provide symbolic benefits to those who have been left behind.[39]

This is a harsh judgement, but not very different from that which could be made in some other democracies when members of deprived groups begin to achieve power.

ATROCITIES

The SCs, the Dalits, now have a much louder voice in Indian politics, through parties they dominate, parties which appeal to them, through their own movements and organizations, than they had when India gained its independence, or twenty years ago. Much of this voice is now expended in decrying and denouncing a rising and steady tide of 'atrocities', as they are regularly termed, deadly attacks by higher castes, not necessarily much higher, against Dalits. These attacks are quite different from the more

[38]   Myron Weiner, 'The Struggle for Equality: Caste in Indian Politics', in Atul Kohli, ed., *The Success of India's Democracy*, Cambridge and New York: Cambridge University Press, 2001, pp. 211–12.

[39]   Ibid., p. 223.

traditional abuse of untouchables, though there are elements in common. The traditional attacks on untouchables were instigated when they attempted to escape the degraded sphere to which they had been confined by upper castes, such as coming too close to or entering a temple, drawing water from a well, using a dress to which they were by the traditional order not entitled, adopting a marriage custom (the bridegroom riding a horse) which was banned to them, and the like. This kind of thing continues, though there is less of it than there was. But it is not this kind of attack in defence of the ritual caste order that people have in mind when they refer to Harijan atrocities, nor what is targeted by the 'Prevention of Atrocities Act' of 1989. The atrocities to which this act was addressed arose less out of the old effort to keep untouchables down than as a response to the new fact that untouchables no longer accepted their condition and were trying to rise up.

Many of these atrocities are initiated as a result of conflict over land. The untouchable agricultural worker generally works the land of others, since he has none or too little of his own to work. With more effective land reform, many have gained access to some land, taken (with compensation) from those who had land exceeding the land ceilings set in the legislation of the state (the states are responsible for land reform), or owned by the state, or belonging to a religious institution. This land was distributed to the landless, a disproportionate number of whom were SCs, though many of course were not. The superior castes fought to prevent the poor agricultural worker from becoming independent by gaining land that he could work on his own and for his own benefit. They operated through local political influence, on administrators, magistrates, and police; they used force and threats of force; they might accuse those gaining access to the new land of being in league with revolutionary Naxalites. They organized private armies to attack poor agricultural workers, and if these were SC workers, upper-caste disdain of untouchables and outrage at their attempt to move above their ordained lower status gave additional force to their enmity.

Direct conflicts over who had rights to the land, who might farm it, was supplemented by additional conflicts as SC workers withdrew their labour in order to work their own land or demanded higher wages for their labour. The outcome of such conflicts was often an attack on the SC hamlet, leading in the more extreme cases to the massacre of its inhabitants, men, women, and children, accompanied by the burning of their houses, rape of their women, and other atrocities. The police or constabulary, if it was evident at all, come too late, or stood aside, or sided with the attackers.

In large measure, this is a new phenomenon of the last twenty-five years or so. Mendelsohn and Vicziany write:

Immediately after the cessation of Indira Gandhi's Emergency in 1977, [Harijan violence] became the stuff of front-page news. A series of particularly gruesome 'Harijan atrocities' genuinely shocked national opinion makers.... We need to ask whether these incidents, and the routinely high level of violence apparently suffered by Untouchables, is the summation of age-old subordination, or whether it arises from a new consciousness and resistance on their part.[40]

Mendelsohn and Vicziany clearly take the latter interpretation, and connect it to the more effective pace of land redistribution during the emergency, and under the governments that followed it. These atrocities result in the deaths of hundreds of SCs each year, the maiming of thousands, the destruction of property. Cases registered with the police from 1995 through 1997 showed 1,617 cases of murder, 12,591 of hurt, 2,824 of rape, 3,102 of arson, over this period of three years. The number of cases does not vary much from year to year. Bihar is particularly notorious as a centre of outrages against untouchables, though these crimes are widespread.[41]

This atmosphere of violence and assault prevents the poor and the SCs from taking advantage of the benefits that government at the higher levels is making available to them. One report tells us: 'In 1996 a nongovernmental organization undertook a door-to-door survey of 250 villages in the state of Gujarat and found that, in almost all villages, those who had title to land had no possession, and those who had possession had not had their land measured or faced illegal encroachment from upper castes. Many had no record of their holdings at all. Even those who had been offered land under agrarian reform legislation refused to accept it for fear of an upper-caste backlash.' This account is

[40]   M and V, p. 44.
[41]   NCSCST, p. 240, and ch. X generally.

followed by one from Tamil Nadu, where, in the Madurai district, Dalits were able to acquire at auction land belonging to a Hindu religious endowment: One month later, and in broad daylight, one hundred members of the Kallar community, an upper-caste group, invaded and destroyed nine acres of paddy (rice) fields belonging to the Dalits. In subsequent attacks, the Kallars murdered two Dalit men and assaulted three Dalit women ... [42]

There are scores of accounts of such and worse outrages, by upper-caste militias, by upper-caste landowners, by the police, and of the impunity with which these outrages are committed, and covered up by bribes, lying, and intimidation. Very few of the perpetrators ever come to justice. Energetic NGOs document and report these atrocities, the papers report on them, the national authorities decry them. But any effective response seems to be beyond the grasp of Indian democracy. It is one thing to fail at raising the social, economic, and educational level of a depressed group. Social uplift is always a difficult and chancy project. But one would think personal safety from assault and bold-faced robbery and murder and rape should be within the reach of government, and indeed should be its first duty, whether it is democratic or otherwise. For SC people in the villages, this does not seem to be the case, though of course India is large and even the documentation of hundreds of cases means that in thousands of other villages these outrages do not occur, or occur rarely.

Nor are these outrages limited to rural India, though they are predominantly to be found there. The police in the cities are not much more respectful of the rights of the poor and untouchables.[43] There are investigations and reports and recommendations. One does not see a downward trend. Perhaps one can take some satisfaction in the fact that many atrocities are occasioned by more aggressive action by Dalits, new demands, organization, self-assertion, protest. In many places Dalits can appeal to a politician of their own group or sympathetic to it for relief. (That is clearly one reason caste-based politics is so effective: one can vote for someone who one may appeal to for help against the

---

[42]   *Broken People: Caste Violence Against India's 'Untouchables'*, New York: Human Rights Watch, 1999, pp. 28–9.

[43]   Ibid., ch. VI.

police, or other authorities.) But the overall picture is one of a state that cannot yet effectively protect a large part of its citizens.

THE MUSLIM MINORITY

Ashutosh Varshney, in his important study of Hindu–Muslim conflict in India, describes the typical governmental response, a worthy one as far as it goes, to the recurrent Hindu–Muslim riots that have convulsed India again and again since partition, and that are perhaps unique phenomena among democratic polities:

[T]he inquiry commissions and research reports typically present the following conclusions...: state governments should not undermine or interfere with local law enforcement; speedy and firm action to control rioters should be taken at the first sign of trouble; prosecutions of offenders should be taken at the first sign of trouble; prosecution of offenders should not be withdrawn by the state for political reasons; communal political parties should be banned or regulated by the state; civil and police officers should not be transferred for reasons other than the requirements of service; the police force should be made professional so that its communal biases are eliminated; the press should be stopped by the state from making false and deliberately inflammatory statements; and the state should cleanse school textbooks of communal interpretations of history.[44]

All very good, as far as it goes. And yet when disorder breaks out, it rapidly reaches a phase in which, typically, however started, there are mass assaults on Muslim homes, businesses, and families, of terrible and uncontrollable cruelty, in which neighbourhoods are destroyed, businesses are looted and left in ruins, and hundreds of people may be killed in the most abominable ways. After each such outburst, one hopes it may be the last. But on 27 February 2002, one of the worst broke out in Gujarat. Its immediate initiating cause was horrifying enough: a train with Hindu enthusiasts from the disputed site of the destroyed Babri Mosque in Ayodhya was set on fire at a stop in Gujarat, and fifty-seven women and children and men were burned to death. The retaliation on Muslim communities began shortly thereafter and

---

[44]   Ashutosh Varshney, *Ethnic Conflict and Civic Life*, New Haven: Yale University Press, 2002, p. 287.

spread to Gujarat's largest city, Ahmedabad, and beyond. Large Muslim areas were destroyed, more than 700 people were killed, and more than 100,000 people, the great majority Muslim, were left homeless and in refugee camps. (These were from early reports; the number killed seems much larger from later reports.) Again, as is typical, there were charges that the retaliation was organized by Hindu nationalist groups, that the police stood by, suspicions that higher levels of government encouraged the attacks—Gujarat had a BJP government—and the result was the fixing among the minority population of a fearful conviction that Muslim lives were endangered in democratic India.

The most serious minority problem in India is that of the Muslims, and their most serious problem is the occasional explosion of hatred against Muslims which leads to riot, arson, and death for large numbers. As in the case of the SCs, government has not been able to devise means to prevent or stem these outbreaks, though there are large periods of peace, and some parts of the country—in particular, the south—are less afflicted by Hindu–Muslim conflict than the north.[45]

Muslims form the same percentage of India's population as do the blacks in the US—12 per cent—but in India that amounts to an enormous population of 120,000,000 or so. They are a diverse group and consist of Bengali-speaking Muslims in West Bengal, a large number of Urdu-speaking Muslims (Urdu is a distinctively Muslim variant of Hindustani) in the populous Ganges valley, and in the former princely state of the Nizam in central India, Malayalam-speaking Muslims and Tamil-speaking Muslims in Kerala and Tamil Nadu. They are most concentrated in the north and northeast (Assam, West Bengal, Bihar, and Uttar Pradesh) and in the southeast (Kerala) but are found everywhere in India.[46]

Muslims have a distinctive background for a minority. Muslims ruled most of India for 250 years. They came from Afghanistan

[45]   For a comprehensive collection of material on Hindu–Muslim riots, including selections from official inquiries, see Iqbal A. Ansari, ed., *Communal Riots: The State and the Law in India*, New Delhi: Institute of Objective Studies, 1997.

[46]   Myron Wiener, 'India's Minorities ... ' (op.cit., pp. 467–71); N. A. Siddiqui, 'Spatial Pattern of Minorities in India', pp. 1–8 and Lubna Siddiqui, 'Distributional Pattern of Muslim Population of India', pp. 27–46, in M. Hashim Qureshi, *Muslims in India Since Independence*, New Delhi: Institute of Objective Studies, 1998.

and Persia and Turkestan and further afield, first as raiders then as conquerors and rulers. Some came peacefully as traders. Great numbers of the local population were converted to Islam, which led to an oddly bifurcated Muslim population, with rulers, administrators, and landowners at the top, and a large mass of lower-caste background—the typical source for converts from Hinduism to any religion—at the bottom, with very little of a middle class in between (though some Muslim communities, as in Surat in Gujarat, were oriented towards trade). A degree of political cooperation between Hindus and Muslims during the nationalist movement broke down and British India was divided as the British gave up rule, a division accompanied by huge population movements, as Muslims fled to the new Pakistan, and Hindus and Sikhs to the newly independent India. This move amounted to flight for most to escape murder, as the partition was accompanied by terrible killings that took the lives of hundreds of thousands.

Refugees, from India to Pakistan, from Pakistan to India, play a major role in the politics of both countries. Many—more in India than in Pakistan—have been able to move up and rebuild their lives. Hindu refugees still come, in particular from Bangladesh, the former East Pakistan. There are very few Hindus left in the former West Pakistan, which now bears alone the name of Pakistan. Many thousands born in what was once a common India and what is now to them a foreign country form part of the elites today in India and Pakistan.

One major princely state remained in contention between India and Pakistan at the time of the partition, Kashmir, which has been divided between India and Pakistan since the partition. It is the source of continual enmity and conflict between India and Pakistan, and was the the cause of a number of wars.

The Muslims of India are thus a unique minority, unique in their size, unique in their relation to a foreign nation which is seen as the permanent and unchanging enemy of India, unique in their history as a once dominant group that is now reduced to one that has lost power, property, and dominance. This is a difficult background for a minority. Muslims lag behind the majority in income, in education, in participation in the major institutions of the country—public and private. Is this lag the result of Muslim educational backwardness, of lack of Muslim energy in taking advantage of whatever opportunities India affords, of discrimination by the dominant Hindu minority? How is one to sort out the effects of these and other factors that make Muslims, despite the existence of a well-educated and cosmopolitan elite, on the whole poorer and more backward than other Indians, and one that is permanently uneasy about its status as Indians?

There are no reservations for Muslims, either in politics or in public employment or in admission to universities, though that, in the wake of Congress victories nationally and in some states in 2004, is beginning to change.[47] It seems likely there will be some reservations in public employment and university admissions at least in some states. There are no special public programmes for Muslim welfare (though one notes surprisingly that the government provides assistance to Muslims who wish to make the pilgrimage to Mecca). Insofar as they are poor, they should benefit from programmes targeted to the poor. An analysis of the relative shares of Muslims in public employment shows that they have considerably fewer of the posts in government and

[47]   Muslims call for them, and, surprisingly, A.B. Vajpayee, Prime Minister of India, said in February 2002 that 'the government was actively considering bringing an amendment to give the scheduled caste status to the most backward among Muslims'. *Hindu*, 4 February 2002, p. 1, 'We will never compromise on Loc, says Vajpayee.' After the installation of a Congress-led coalition national government and new state governments following the elections of 2004, Muslims were incorporated into the list of backward classes or castes in Kerala, Tamil Nadu, and Andhra Pradesh, and limited reservations of some kind were instituted for them; see Zoya Hasan, 'Reservations for Muslims', in *Seminar*, May 2005. The Andhra Pradesh Congress-led government introduced a 5 per cent quota for Muslims, but it was held up by action by the High Court: 'Quota Muddle', in daily *Hitavada* (Nagpur), 5 February 2006. In February 2006 a committee set up by the national government to investigate minority welfare asked the armed forces to provide information on how many Muslims served in them, at various levels, which aroused a wave of discussion: The armed forces had always been exempt from reservations. See Shishir Gupta, Sunday *Express*, 12 February 2006, 'How Many Muslims do you have, Govt asks armed forces'; Shekhar Gupta, 'Kitne Musulman Hain?', *Indian Express*, 18 February 2006; Sundeep Dikshit, 'Muslims and the Indian Army', *Hindu*, 20 February 2006. See the discussion of Muslim demands for reservations in Dudley-Jenkins, op.cit.

public sector undertakings than their share of the population. For example, they have only 13 per cent of the Class I posts in Central Government they might expect on the basis of population share, rising to 43 per cent of Class IV. They are somewhat behind in literacy, though not as far behind as SCs. Their enrolment in elementary schools is lower, and even lower in secondary schools—35 per cent of what would be a share equal to their percentage of the population. They do better in enrolment in universities—83 per cent of expected share. But they lag behind in the preferred business courses and engineering courses. Similarly with representation in administration and faculties. The numbers of company directors is minuscule.[48] Muslims do sit on major judicial benches, hold posts as ministers in central and state government, have served as president (a Muslim is President today), are leading journalists and academics, but there is no question their presence in India's elites is much less than might be expected on the basis of their numbers.

Muslims, like other groups, form a 'vote bank' and have political influence. They are appealed to by various parties, who put up Muslim candidates to demonstrate their goodwill and to attract Muslim voters. While the Congress party was dominant, Muslim voters saw that as their best bet for their security. With the collapse of Congress dominance, Muslims make other kinds of alliances, but on the whole their representation in the Lok Sabha, the representative lower house of India's Parliament, has shrunk.[49] And they look fearfully at the rise of the BJP, which has twice led national coalition governments, and which is a party which has achieved dominance in part by appealing to anti-Muslim sentiment with its campaign, since the 1980s, to build a Hindu temple on the site of a Muslim mosque in Ayodhya.

It is not easy to explain or plumb the character of Hindu resentment and hostility to Islam and Muslims. (Of course, not all

---

[48]   All these figures are taken from C.A. Abdussalam, 'Muslim Backwardness: A Quantitative Analysis', in Iqbal A. Ansari, ed., *The Muslim Situation in India*, New Delhi: Institute of Objective Studies, 1989, pp. 80–8.

[49]   Muslims in the Lok Sabha rose from a low of 4.4 per cent in 1952 to a high of 9.2 per cent in 1980, and have since shrunk to a low of 5.6 in 1999. Iqbal A. Ansari, 'Minority Representation,' in *Seminar #* 506, October 2001, pp. 37–41.

Hindus share it—the leading figures in the fight against the rise of 'communalism' and its appeal to anti-Muslim sentiment are themselves Hindu. We are trying to explain an occasional and a minority sentiment, but one strong enough to help make a specifically Hindu party one of the largest national parties in India.) Clearly history plays a role: Muslims were the conquerors, who in the style of the day destroyed temples and built mosques from their ruins, looted temple sanctuaries, forced conversion. They exhibited a range of attitudes towards Hinduism, from fierce intolerance to enlightened acceptance.

But it is not history 'as it truly was', in all its complexity, that determines dominant Hindu attitudes, but history as interpreted, rewritten, popularized. There is a perpetual war over India's ancient (and more recent) history being waged in India, which expresses itself in conflicts over school and university curricula and textbooks. When the Hindu right is in power, as it was in the late 1990s and up through 2002, the war was particularly intense. In addition to history, as interpreted and reinterpreted and rewritten, one must add the permanent tension with Pakistan, and the fear that the large minority Muslim population is at heart on the side of the enemy.

Why should India's 800 million Hindus (I am taking the most expansive measure, that used in the census) fear its 120 million Muslims? But then there is Pakistan, and Bangladesh, and the Muslim world beyond, and many Hindus see India as an island surrounded by a hostile Islam. In view of its size, it might better be described as a continent. Each census since independence has shown an increase—a very modest increase—in the proportion of the population that is Muslim, from 9.92 per cent in 1951 to 12.12 per cent in 1991, and a complementary shrinkage in the Hindu percentage, from 84.96 to 82.01.[50] Each such modest advance in the Muslim percentage leads to a good deal of discussion and some alarm. (Possibly the increase in the Muslim percentage could be accounted for by the Muslim concentration in the high fertility regions of India, and other demographic

[50]   Siddiqui, op.cit., p. 30. The author points out that in 1941 the percentage of Muslims in the area that became India after partition was 13.34, higher than it is today—the shrinkage was owing to the migration to Pakistan p. 31.

adjustments, but it is the gross change that seizes the public imagination.)

There is also resentment at what is considered the 'pampering' of Muslims. This idea of pampering was particularly encouraged by the Shah Bano case, dealing with the conflict between Muslim religious law, which gives minimal assistance to a divorced wife, and India's Supreme Court, which ruled that a divorced wife should get greater assistance. The decision of the Supreme Court angered the more traditional Muslims, and Rajiv Gandhi, Prime Minister at the time, arranged for a law to restore the Muslim religious law in this case, which then angered many Hindus.[51] It was clearly a political action, but along with the case of the Babri Mosque it seems to stoke a great deal of anger among Hindus.

At any rate, there is a well of hostility and ill-feeling that can be tapped. Some Hindu–Muslim riots are sparked by insignificant causes, some by only rumours of disrespect to sadhus, or temples, or cows, or alternatively disrespect to mosques or Muslim holy sites. Their escalation into a deadly riot may be spontaneous but increasingly, it is charged by the defenders of secular India and it is believed by Muslims, the rioters are inflamed by extremists and in particular by people connected with the group of militant Hindu organizations whose political expression is the BJP. It is clear the rise of the BJP to national power was spurred by its campaign to replace the Babri mosque with a Hindu temple. When indeed the mosque was finally destroyed by a mob, riots broke out in which hundreds of Muslims were killed. Overall, matters have gotten worse, not better, since independence. Ashutosh Varshney writes, reviewing the pattern of these riots since 1950: 'The statistics ... show no trend at all between the early 1950s and the mid 1970s... After the mid-to-late 1970s, ... we do see an unambiguous and rising curve of violence peaking in 1992, when the mosque in Ayodhya was destroyed.' He does report a very low level in 1994 and 1995, 'but in order for that decline to be called a trend, good data on several more years will have to be

---

[51]   For one account of the case, see Robert D. Baird, 'Gender Implications for a Uniform Civil Code', in Gerald James Larson, ed., *Religion and Personal Law in Secular India*, Bloomington: Indiana University Press, 2001, pp. 185–8.

recorded. It is a judgment to be made in the future.'[52] That judgment alas was made in February 2002, when perhaps the worst anti-Muslim riots since partition were launched, hardly restrained by the police, and leading to perhaps 2,000 deaths, the destruction of great quantities of property, the driving of 150,000 or more Muslims into refugee camps.

In contrast to Dalit atrocities, which are largely rural affairs, Hindu–Muslim riots are concentrated in the cities. But both reflect a weakness in Indian democracy of a very grave character. The Indian state or states are not very effective at controlling public violence against minorities. The police are not effective and the minorities fear they are in league with those who would do them harm. They are either not present when they should be, or take no forceful action, or in the worst cases may participate in the violence. The army is often needed to bring matters under control. Fortunately the army is not considered to be 'communal', that is, in favour of Hindu rioters, even though the Muslim percentage of officers and men is minuscule.[53]

We should remind ourselves that India is large, that Hindu–Muslim violence is mostly concentrated in a belt of northern states, but it is not easy to minimize the scale or seriousness of this problem. Matters were worsened by the election in Gujarat in December 2002, in the aftermath to the Gujarat riots, in which the BJP state government unapologetically defended its abysmal performance, appealed to Hindu enmity against Muslims, and won a great victory. This reinforced a pervasive sense of insecurity in the Muslim population. But in the subsequent national election of 2004 the BJP-led coalition government was turned out of power to be replaced by a Congress-led coalition. In the national campaign, the BJP eschewed the tactics that had led to victory in Gujarat, and in general it has moderated its anti-Muslim stance in its search for allies with whom it can form governments in the Indian states. The BJP national government was restrained by its coalition partners, and the logic of democracy may continue to impose this restraint upon it. It is not clear how far the BJP is committed

[52] Varshney, op.cit., p. 95.

[53] See Omar Khalidi, 'Ethnic Group Recruitment in the Indian Army: The Contrasting Cases of Sikhs, Muslims, Gurkhas and Others', *Pacific Affairs,* vol. 74, Winter 2001–2, p. 547.

to a course that must increase hostility and conflict between Hindus and Muslims. The imperatives of democratic competition and democratic rule may well in time correct the matter, and we may see Indian leaders hastening to reassure Muslims, as American leaders did after 11 September 2001, that they have nothing to fear and are fully accepted by their country. Some Indian leaders can be depended upon to act in such a manner, and we may in time see BJP leaders playing this role.

Conclusion

How does one draw up the balance sheet on Indian democracy and minorities? In certain respects, it is a good record. The Indian Constitution balances well the commitment of a democratic and liberal state to equal status for all, and the need to take account of weaker and more backward groups. A strong judicial system has played an important role in setting the rules for how to reconcile the commitment to equality with policies designed to assist specific backward groups. The Indian political system supports the compromise between these two objectives, though elements in it push towards one side or another. At the formal level of Constitution and legislation, India has done well—and no one should depreciate the role of the formal arrangements, even if they are not fully implemented, and often transgressed on the ground. From an American point of view, the steady expansion of reservations and quotas, from SCs and STs to OBCs, and perhaps now Muslims, all fed by political competition, is regrettable, but this is the way Indian democracy has evolved and works. 'The worst system,' as Churchill said, 'except for all the others....'

But our review of the circumstances facing two minorities does bring us up against two major failings of Indian democracy in its first half-century. It has not done as well as it could have in establishing a basic minimum of decent living standards for all. In a poor country, this minimum we know must be low. But when reviewing what other poor countries have done, one could have expected and should have expected a better record on literacy, more and better elementary schools spread throughout the country, a more successful effort to provide some minimum in health standards, in drinking water, in access to electricity. This has hurt all poor Indians. It has hurt the poorest strata, the SCs, the most. And when one sees how some countries as poor as India at the time of its independence have fared since, it is clear that India need not have remained as poor a country as it is for so long. Clearly some wrong policies were set, and adhered to too long, and Indian democracy was not able to change the course in good time.

And second, there is still much work to be done in establishing, on a sound and universal basis, the first condition of a good society, security of persons and property ensured by a professional and disinterested police force, by public security officials, and courts. At the highest levels in all these areas India does well. But the principles and procedures so well set forth in state documents and expressed by high officials does not filter down to set the conditions under which the great mass of the population must deal with the state. In their intercourse with police and government officials and the courts, this great mass—and not only the poor, but these are hurt most because they have the fewest alternatives—strongly doubt they can receive disinterested and impartial treatment.

Critics, analysts, economists, social scientists, high government officials have studied both these matters and improvement is undoubtedly possible. This is not the place to make proposals, and in any case, this writer is not qualified to make them. But certainly, for the sake not only of India's minorities but also the country at large, a better record on both these matters is required.

6

Democracy within Parties and the Accommodation of Diversity
Comparing India and the United States

E. Sridharan

India since 1989, and especially since 1996, has had a party system that is more competitive than most other established democracies, with more parties represented in parliament, and still more represented in state assemblies, and still again more contesting elections at national and state levels. It has also had the largest coalition governments in the world since 1996, when the coalition of governing and supporting parties has ranged from thirteen to twenty-four parties. This poses obvious problems of governmental stability and policy coherence. India has had six general elections between 1989 and 2004 in what would normally have been three parliamentary terms. There is vigorous political competition between a large number of parties, especially between the historically dominant Congress party and the BJP, which leads the National Democratic Alliance (NDA) coalition. Yet no party today can hope to dominate the scene or be sure of its prospects. Nor is there any real democracy within political parties—they function in a top–down style with the key decisions about political strategy, election nominations, and the raising and distribution of money excessively controlled by the party leadership.

This is in contrast to most parties in Western democracies, where the trend over the past four decades has been towards decentralization and greater internal democracy. The two American parties have been the polar opposite to those in India in terms of decentralization and internal democracy, particularly with respect to nominations and finance, to the point where the American parties as coherent organizations are threatened, and increasingly tend to become collections of candidate-centric structures. In the Indian case, the lack of internal democracy has been accompanied since the late 1960s at least, by repeated splits in major parties or their state units, the emergence of new and minor parties, and the frequent merger of small and new parties with other parties. This has continued to happen despite the anti-defection law (the 52nd Constitutional amendment) of 1985. It is tempting to conclude that the absence of internal democracy has caused many of these splits.

The issue of internal democracy in parties is vital for India for several reasons. Are party splits, endemic in Indian parties, due to the Hirschmanian logic of exit, voice, and loyalty?[1] That is, do factions, leaders, and voters exit a party after a period of declining loyalty when they find that they lack a voice within the party? Or do they exit because of the lack of democracy within parties and the instability of coalitions? Is there a link between the lack of democracy within parties and the capacity of governments to take a long-term view on policy issues, particularly policies which may be unpopular in the short run but may yield dividends only in the long run? And, central for this chapter (but related to all of the above), is the accommodation of cultural, religious, and ethnic diversity. Can political accommodation of diversity take place by the formation of a multitude of small parties, each based principally on particular social groups and forming coalition governments, despite the lack of internal democracy within parties? And/or can single state-based parties merge across state boundaries to form federal parties[2] to achieve the same political accommodation unless there is greater democracy within the

---

[1]   Albert O. Hirschman, *Exit, Voice and Loyalty*, Princeton, NJ: Princeton University Press, 1970.

[2]   Douglas V. Verney, 'How has the Proliferation of Parties Affected the Indian Federation: A Comparative Approach', in Zoya Hasan, E. Sridharan and R. Sudarshan, eds, *India's Living Constitution: Ideas, Practices, Controversies*, New Delhi: Permanent Black, 2002.

existing parties? The evolution of the party system to two or three broad-based federal parties would appear to require intraparty democracy. This is important in the context of the almost universally accepted opinion that there is no possibility of a single-party majority government in the foreseeable future.

Given the polar contrast between the functioning of the two major American parties along the dimension of internal decentralization and democracy, and their absence in Indian parties, this chapter seeks to explore the reasons why this is so. Also explored is the link between intraparty democracy and the capacity to accommodate religious, racial, ethnic, caste, linguistic, and regional diversity. Is it the weight of history? Political culture? Particular institutional arrangements? Or is it a combination of these factors? Is it in a particular historical sequence? The chapter also brings in comparisons from trends in intraparty democracy in European parties, mostly intermediate on the spectrum between top–down and polyarchal/decentralized/democratic styles of functioning.

In the following sections, we outline: (1) A typology of parties and party evolution from the point of view of party democracy. (2) The main features of the evolution of the two major American parties, including the question of whether/how the internal processes of the parties conduces to intraparty democracy and the accommodation of diversity, and why newly-mobilized interests have not opted for or successfully formed third parties. (3) The evolution of the Indian party system and the major Indian political parties since Independence, focusing on their internal democratic processes. We attempt to link this to whether there is accommodation of social diversity, repeated splits in parties, and the rise of new parties. Lastly, we draw some tentative conclusions for Indian parties, reflecting on the experience of American and European parties.

A TYPOLOGY OF PARTIES AND THE EVOLUTION OF THEIR INTERNAL FUNCTIONING

Parties historically emerged as an organizational form most suited for the performance of certain functions. The key functions performed by parties are candidate nomination, electoral mobilization, both constituting elite recruitment, and other related functions like issue structuration, societal representation, interest aggregation, forming and sustaining governments, and societal integration.[3] There are a vast variety of party typologies but a state-of-the-art, rich but parsimonious typology would be the following, based on Diamond and Gunther.[4] Their typology and the sequence of party evolution outlined further below does not necessarily fit every country but is the best for our purpose. They divide political parties into fifteen types or species clustered into five broader genuses— elite, mass-based, ethnicity-based, electoralist, and movement parties.

The first genus of (traditional) elite parties consists of either parties of local notables or clientelistic parties based on local notables. These are weakly organized, mobilizing support through the personal resources of notables or vertical patron–client networks, and making election nominations based on loyalty. Typically, they exist in premodern or early modernizing rural polities.

The second genus of mass-based parties, or the mass party[5] is a party created outside the legislature, typically an industrial working-class party but could also be a peasant or religious or nationalist party in some circumstances, well-organized, and with a mass membership. There are six species here—three pairs of socialist ideological parties, nationalist ideological parties, and religious ideological parties. Each of these pairs has an organizationally thin, pluralist type and an organizationally thick, proto-hegemonic type. Thus there are 'class-mass' socialist, social-democratic, and labour parties, and there are Leninist revolutionary communist parties, both mass parties of the working class. There are broad-based nationalist mass parties, and ultranationalist or fascist parties, Christian Democrat-type religious mass parties, and religious fundamentalist parties. This genus of party is controlled by its professional bureaucracy, has a variety of mass organizations, which it uses for mobilization, and its nominations for elections are controlled by the top of the party bureaucracy.

---

[3]   Larry Diamond and Richard Gunther, eds, *Political Parties and Democracy*, Baltimore: Johns Hopkins University Press, 2001, pp. 7–9.

[4]   Ibid., pp. 3–39.

[5]   Maurice Duverger, *Political Parties: Their Organisation and Activity in the Modern State*, New York: Wiley, 1963.

The third genus of ethnicity-based parties can be either mono-ethnic parties that follow an ethnically exclusivist or even polarizing strategy, or broad, multi-ethnic coalitional or congress parties. The first type may be well or weakly organized but they are typically not internally democratic. They tend to be controlled either by organized religious hierarchies or charismatic leaders, and nominations for elections are made by the top. Examples of the second type are the Indian National Congress up to the mid-1960s, the Malaysian Barisan National, and the Tanzania African National Union, all of which are multi-ethnic parties characterized by national integration ideologies combined with particularistic benefits. Nominations tend to be decentralized and part of a pattern of power-sharing in multi-ethnic societies.

The fourth genus are the electoralist parties. These may be personalistic, programmatic, or catch-all parties. Personalistic parties are merely vehicles for the ambitions of leaders and are purely election-oriented, for example, Silvio Berslusconi's Forza Italia or Benazir Bhutto's Pakistan People's Party. Programmatic parties are also election-oriented and thinly organized but are more ideologically or programmatically coherent, for example, Thatcher's Conservative party or the post-1980 Republican party. The catch-all party[6] is not a class party but essentially a machine oriented to winning elections. It tends to cut across class and other cleavages and make direct appeals to voters through the mass media.

Lastly, the fifth genus of the movement party consists of parties that have evolved from contemporary social movements such as the Green Party in Germany or the various anti-immigrant extreme-right parties in Europe such as the Austrian Freedom Movement, which straddle parties and movements. They tend to be catch-all in character but with a distinct, often single-issue, programme.

Katz and Mair[7] using many of the above party types, argue for an evolutionary sequence of party types, based on their relationship to civil societies and states in different stages of development in

[6] Otto Kirchheimer, 'The Transformation of the Western European Party Systems', in Joseph La Palombara and Myron Weiner, eds, *Political Parties and Political Development*, Princeton: Princeton University Press, 1996, pp. 177–200.

[7] Richard S. Katz and Peter Mair, 'Changing Models of Party Organization and Party Democracy', *Party Politics*, 1995, vol. 1, no. 1, pp. 5–28.

the context of European history, but their typology and staging can have useful insights for developing-world democracies too. They argue that the mass party,[8] which is often taken as the benchmark, is a product of industrial working-class societies and is only a stage in the continuing process of political evolution. The mass party, typically working-class based, led to the development of Kirchheimer's catch-all party[9] in what was essentially a reaction of older, less organized, conservative or liberal parties, or even clientelistic parties of notables, focusing on broad appeals cutting across class barriers to counter traditional class-based mass parties. The catch-all party, as a type, made its appearance and grew in the post-war boom era with the growth of the middle class and the relative decline of the old, industrial working class. The catch-all party or the electoral-professional party[10] tended to pitch its appeal wide, concentrating on electoral mobilization through the media rather than by grassroots' organizations in an era of the spread of television and the rise of a professional political class. In the electoral-professional party,[11] the party in government has also tended to become stronger than the extra-parliamentary organization, unlike in the older mass party.

Katz and Mair[12] posit the rise of cartel parties in the post-1970s period when established parties, both of the moderate left and the right, which are closely integrated with the bureaucracies of a managerial state deeply involved in the economy, collude to limit competition. Some cartel parties, in their view, are part of the adaptation of the old mass parties to the rise of catch-all parties.

There has been a general trend over 1960–90 towards greater decentralization and transparency within parties.[13] In several

8   Duverger, *Political Parties*.

9   Kirchheimer, 'The Transformation of the Western European Party Systems'.

10   Angelo Panebianco, *Political Parties: Organization and Power*, Cambridge, UK: Cambridge University Press, 1988.

11   Ibid.

12   Katz, 'Changing Models . . . '. Also, Richard S. Katz, 'The Problem of Candidate Selection and Models of Party Democracy', *Party Politics*, 2001, vol. 7, no. 3, pp. 277–96.

13   Lars Bille, 'Democratizing a Democratic Procedure: Myth or Reality?', *Party Politics*, 2001, vol. 7, no. 3, pp. 363–80; Lawrence LeDuc,

major parties in the democratic world, including both major British parties, particularly Labour, in the Spanish Socialist Party, and the Progressive Conservative Party in Canada, there have been movements by local and middle-level party activists and by the rank-and-file to reduce the power of entrenched party elites, whether legislative or party-bureaucratic. There have been strong movements within parties to democratize nomination and leadership selection processes and make them open to broader and more inclusive selectorates.

Four caveats about the importance of intraparty democracy need to be recorded here. (1) There may be a danger of overemphasizing the importance of intraparty democracy for accommodativeness and representation. It may well be possible for accommodation and representation of all group interests to take place under an oligarchical leadership that is so inclined, while on the other hand, an emphasis on intraparty democracy— in a context of majoritarianism in both the rules of intraparty democracy and the prevailing social ideology—may marginalize minority interests in intraparty dynamics. This can result in internal democracy without the accommodation of social diversity. (2) Intraparty democracy may not be entirely benign. It may help better representation but under certain circumstances, particularly in ideologically extreme parties, it may help extremists control parties since these will be the most active in getting themselves and their followers voted to party office and can up the ideological ante in intraparty debate. (3) In any comparison of India and the US, it needs to be taken into account that in a parliamentary system, the major function of parties is to provide government, unlike in the US presidential system. Parties would need a degree of coherence. Therefore, in the US, a highly decentralized candidate-centred party may not matter as much to governance as it would in a parliamentary system. Thus, intraparty democracy may pose the problem of responsiveness

---

'Democratizing Party Leadership Selection', *Party Politics*, 2001, vol. 7, no. 3, pp. 323–41; Jonathan Hopkin, 'Bringing the Members Back In? Democratising Candidate Selection in Britain and Spain', *Party Politics*, 2001, vol. 7, no. 3, pp. 343–61; Gideon Rahat and Reuven Y. Hazan, 'Candidate Selection Methods: An Analytical Framework', *Party Politics*, 2001, vol. 7, no. 3, pp. 297–322.

versus responsibility. (4) The argument can be made[14] that in a very heterogeneous society and federal state, a multiparty system would quite likely evolve anyway despite Duverger's law and even if there was intraparty democracy in the major parties.

THE AMERICAN PARTIES

In this section, we view the American parties in the light of this background. The two major American parties, the Republican party and the Democratic party, are the world's most decentralized, and least top–down in their internal functioning. This is so even in comparison to European political parties at the beginning of the twenty-first century, despite their recent democratizing reforms— and certainly in comparison to all Indian political parties. How did they become so? And is this characteristic at the expense of party coherence? Are the decentralized structure and functioning of the American parties due to a particular sequence of historical accidents? Or is it due to political culture, the relationship of parties with civil society, institutional features such as federalism, the system of primaries, or state regulation of party processes?

My understanding is that the decentralized and internally democratic nature of the two major American parties is due to a combination of the above features in a particular historical sequence, that is, a path-dependent evolution resulting in the outcome described. This internally democratic character, in turn, facilitates the accommodation of newly mobilized social, including racial, ethnic, and cultural, constituencies. Also, the structure of the parties and the party system as well as the single-member district, simple-plurality electoral system in combination with the presidential system, inhibits the formation and electoral success of third parties, thereby encouraging newly mobilized groups to try to carve out space within the existing parties.

[14]   Rein Taagepera and Matthew Soberg Shugart, *Seats and Votes: The Effects and Determinants of Electoral Systems*, New Haven: Yale University Press, 1989.

Verney, Douglas V., 'How has the Proliferation of Parties Affected the Indian Federation: A Comparative Approach', in Zoya Hasan, E. Sridharan, and R. Sudarshan, eds, *India's Living Constitution: Ideas, Practices, Controversies*, New Delhi: Permanent Black, 2002.

The historical origins of the party system in the 1790–1800 period are crucial. Parties emerged, like in England, from legislative factions. They were loose, factional coalitions of legislative notables without elaborate organization, ideology, or discipline. In fact, the elites were highly pluralized. They functioned in a political regime of generally accepted norms about political freedom, and the state was a federal state with separation of legislative, executive, and judicial powers and a system of checks and balances. The political culture that evolved was one that tolerated party factionalism and dissent, and both the more elitist Federalists and more grassroots Anti-Federalists were ideologically flexible and encompassed a breadth of societal interests.

The period from 1824 to 1860, when the suffrage was expanded and mass participation grew, was also one in which embryonic party structures were established. The power to control and direct the party organization was increasingly transferred to state and local party leaders upon whom national leaders depended for electoral mobilization, with the powers over the party organization increasingly transferred from parties' legislative leaders to state and local leaders who were not members of Congress or the state legislatures.

This was also the period when the earliest versions of the now well-established party structures, beginning with the Democratic party, emerged. The first national convention, based on delegates from state units, appeared in 1831–2 to coordinate party activities and the first national committee (of the Democrats) appeared in 1844. These structures transferred power from Congressional and state legislative party caucuses to non-legislative national, and crucially, state and local party leaders. Thus, decentralized state-level party structures, which were embryonic in the 1800–24 period, evolved and took root alongside the massification of parties during the period of 1824 to 1854, beginning with the Democratic party due to the efforts of Andrew Jackson and Martin Van Buren.[15] The Democratic party became the first national mass party in history. By 1840, the US had two national mass parties in place, the Democrats and the Whigs, with a turnout of 78 per

[15] John W. Aldrich, *Why Parties? The Origin and Transformation of Political Parties in America*, Chicago: University of Chicago Press, 1995.

cent of the eligible electorate.[16] The development of national party organizations was substantially due to the imperatives of competing for the presidency. As Epstein[17] puts it, '... the very office meant to be nonpartisan is primarily responsible for the existence of national parties as well as for their special nature.' This is in addition to Duverger's law.

The post-Civil War period up to 1896 saw a consolidation of the Republican–Democrat two-party system (the Republicans emerging as a contender for the presidency in 1852 and rapidly replacing the Whigs). The significant developments were the development of urban political machines in the big cities, the adoption of legislation to protect the integrity of elections and, with that, the regulation of party organizations.

The next major period 1896–1932, saw the emergence of primaries, which ultimately took the leadership-nomination function out of the hands of the party organizational leaders and put it in the hands of registered party voters. However, formal nomination for presidential elections remained in the hands of the national convention, though increasingly influenced by primaries. The first state direct primary was held in 1903—by 1912 a majority of states had adopted mandatory primary laws and by 1917 all but four states had direct primary laws for at least some state offices.[18] By 1955 all states had such primaries, though they were far from homogenous, being characterized by a bewildering variety of rules and practices from state to state. The first presidential primary was held in Florida in 1904 and today the great majority of states have presidential primaries. The 1896–1932 period also saw a movement towards non-partisan elections for municipal offices and moves to regulate campaign finance activities.

To elaborate on the growth of primaries and their effects on the nomination function in political parties—if we consider the whole period of 1832–1968, the era of presidential nomination by the party national convention—it is useful to distinguish two periods, one until 1912 and the other from 1912 to 1968. In the first period virtually all convention delegates were chosen within each

16   Ibid.
17   Leon D. Epstein, *Political Parties in the American Mold*, Madison: University of Wisconsin Press, 1986, p. 83.
18   Ibid.

state by party caucus, district convention, state convention, executive committee, or some combination of party organs. From 1912 to 1968, the system can be called mixed, following the spread of presidential primaries. However, from 1912 to 1968, in twenty-one seriously contested Republican and Democratic nominating contests (when incumbent presidents were not automatically renominated) on twelve occasions the winners of the largest number of primaries failed to secure the nomination. After 1968, the primaries determined the results.

The important point, in comparative perspective, is that primaries in the US are subject to state law and operated by state and local officials and financed by public funds, in contrast to party primaries in the 1980s and 1990s in Europe, which were regulated by party rules and operated by party officials and funds.

The period 1936 to the present, began with the New Deal coalition effecting a basic party realignment (though some scholars argue that a new party system came into effect from 1968). The major characteristics of this period are the much-debated 'decline' of parties, affecting both major parties, or in other words, the decline of traditional mass parties. This has been constituted by, and complexly caused by, a range of inter-related developments, among which we can list the following: the decline of urban political machines, the increase in the proportion of convention delegates selected by direct primary elections from one-third to four-fifths over 1968–98—along with the spread of presidential primaries—the increase in ticket-splitting by voters, growing non-partisan voting in Congress up to 1980 at least (see Rohde,[19] for the re-emergence of partisanship in the 1980s), the growing dependence on television, the greater regulation of campaign finance, and the rise of candidate-centred elections.[20]

To sum up, the principal factors, in our understanding, that have created and sustained highly decentralized and (by the standards of most other countries, certainly India) internally democratic parties, to the point of a decline of party coherence, are: first, the creation of pluralistic parties in a federal state with

[19]   David W. Rohde, *Parties and Leaders in the Postreform House*, Chicago: University of Chicago Press, 1991.

[20]   Martin P. Wattenberg, *The Decline of American Political Parties, 1952–1996*, Cambridge: Harvard University Press, 1998.

separation of powers from the outset, even before the growth of mass parties and the evolution of the two-party system consisting of the Republican and Democratic parties after the 1860s; second, the institution and spread of direct primaries and presidential primaries through the twentieth century; third, the decentralized wealth of a wealthy country; fourth, the spread of new media-dependent campaigning since the 1950s.

How have the two parties responded to and accommodated social diversity, especially race, the most significant ascriptive socio-political cleavage, particularly since the Civil Rights Movement? The Voting Rights Act of 1965 began a new era of substantial empowerment for African-Americans. The ending of formal constraints on political participation resulted in large increases in voter registration and voting in the states of the deep south. It also brought about large proportionate increases in the number of black elected officials, particularly to state and local political office such as state legislators and mayors.[21] It also led to the inclusion of black political agendas in national, state, and local politics.

However, all this took place within the existing political parties, principally the Democratic party, in the same two-party system, indicating successful accommodation *by the parties* of a hitherto excluded group. A similar pattern characterizes the increasing political participation of Hispanic groups from the 1980s onwards. So much so that some scholars have pointed to the rise of 'deracialization' or a dropping or toning down of black political agendas as a political phenomenon associated with the campaigns of many successful black politicians, the best recent example being L. Douglas Wilder, the first black governor of any state (Virginia).[22] Why have politically emergent and assertive social groups either not opted to form third parties or been unsuccessful in doing so? And why has there been no phenomenon like the BJP in India, that is, a calculated attempt to create a majority–minority polarization over race as the BJP has attempted over religion and culture?

21   Robert B. Albritton, George Amedee, Keenan Grenell, and Don-Terry, Veal, 'Deracialization and the New Black Politics', in Huey L. Perry, ed., *Race, Politics and Governance in the United States*, Gainesville: University of Florida Press, 1996, ch. 11, pp. 179–206.

22   Huey L. Perry, ed., ibid.

To elaborate on the parties and race since the Civil Rights movement, it is not that race has disappeared as a determinant of party strategies. Indeed, since 1968 there has been a steady shift of white voters throughout the eleven southern states from the Democrats towards the Republicans as lower middle-class and working-class whites threatened by desegregation and affirmative action, particularly in the issue areas of jobs, housing, crime, and schooling, have gravitated towards the Republican party.[23] The Republicans have been largely successful in effecting a shift of white votes in the south to themselves, reducing the Democrats to the votes of blacks plus liberal whites, who are not a majority in most of the south. However, the Republicans did not raise these issues in terms of race but in terms of opposition, on liberal-individualist and free-market grounds, to quotas, busing, and law and order, maintaining that they were actually talking about these issues when they raise them and not about race[24] although the coded message was about race. In the southern states in 2002, electoral calculations of candidates of both parties were crucially about percentages of the white and black vote needed to win or deny victory.[25] However, in the US, both parties are basically catch-all parties that do not seek to *polarize* even when they may be indifferent or lukewarm to the empowerment aspirations of the principal racial minority. There have been episodic exceptions, but even here such polarization is attempted only in coded language as in the Bush campaign's use of the Willie Horton case in 1988.[26]

---

[23]   E.J. Dionne, *Why Americans Hate Politics*, New York: Simon and Schuster, 1991; Alan I. Abramowitz and Kyle L. Saunders, 'Party Polarization and Ideological Realignment in the US Electorate, 1976–1994', in L. Sandy Maisel, ed., *The Parties Respond: Changes in American Parties and Campaigns*, 3rd edn., Boulder, CO: Westview Press, 1998.

[24]   See Dionne, ibid.

[25]   David Broder, '50–50 America: The Southern Battleground', *Washington Post*, 13 October 2002.

[26]   See Dionne, *Why Americans Hate Politics*; Mark Clapson, 'Suburbia and Party Politics', *History Today*, September 2000.

Diamond, Larry, and Richard Gunther, eds, *Political Parties and Democracy*, Baltimore: Johns Hopkins University Press, 2001.

The striking fact remains that despite the presence of both ethnic diversity and federalism, third parties have been resoundingly unsuccessful in the US. This is so even at state level (unlike in Canada and India) and even in district-level minority pockets. In fact, third parties have disappeared even more noticeably in state and congressional elections than in presidential elections.[27] The reason for this is probably that,

For state as for national third-party leaders, the direct primary no doubt made it easier to reenter Republican or Democratic ranks than would an older organizational control of nominations. Thus early abandonment of evidently failing third parties may be encouraged by the same intraparty electoral opportunity that appears to make third parties less useful in the first place'.[28]

In presidential elections, the twenty-six presidential elections in the hundred years from 1864 to 1964, saw only four minor party candidates (and no independents) win over 5 per cent of the vote. But in the ten presidential elections from 1968 and 2004, the 5 per cent margin was exceeded four times (Wallace in 1968; Anderson in 1980; Perot in 1992 and 1996). However, third parties can arise in circumstances in which the electoral relevance of major parties declines. This can happen when they do not address issues perceived to be salient[29] or if there is strong dissatisfaction with major party candidates, both of which appear to be the case in 1968 due to deep divisions in the Democratic party as a result of the Civil Rights movement and the Vietnam war.

However, blacks and other minorities are distributed as minorities in all states (except Asians in Hawaii), are not united, and are mostly in a minority even at the level of congressional districts. Therefore, third parties with a strong minority agenda would tend to lose, and there would be a strong incentive to work within major parties. The latter too would have incentives to accommodate minorities since there are no formal barriers to voting although blacks vote overwhelmingly for the Democrats. However, this outcome

[27]   Epstein, *Political Parties*, pp. 124–5.

[28]   Ibid., p. 132.

[29]   James L. Sundquist, *Dynamics of the Party System: Alignment and Realignment of Political Parties in the United States*, 2nd edn, Washington DC: Brookings Institution, 1983.

is a combination of class, race, and geographical effects—not race alone. Even at levels below the presidency, or perhaps particularly at these levels, serious candidates for Congress and state legislatures might prefer to attract resources from the major parties, rather than trying to build support without those valuable resources. The power of Congress and state legislatures leads to a built-in preference for working with established parties. Critics, however, have pointed out that a major reason behind these outcomes is that since the late nineteenth century both major parties have acted in concert to tighten ballot access rules and voter registration rules in most states, making the system, in effect, anti-working class and anti-poor, indirectly anti-immigrant and anti-minority.[30]

Lastly, it can be argued that the remarkable stability of the Republican–Democrat duopoly since the Civil War, masks diversity expressed in the intense electoral competition within parties as well as shifting alignments and realignments within and between parties over the course of nearly a century and a half. What it also reflects is the absence in American society of social blocs irreconcilably attached to particular ideologies and the prevalence of more pragmatic interest group politics.

THE EVOLUTION OF THE INDIAN PARTY SYSTEM AND INTRA-PARTY DEMOCRACY IN THE MAJOR PARTIES

The Indian electoral system follows the Anglo-American pattern of single-member districts and a simple-plurality system. There are 543 constituencies that send a single member each to the Lok Sabha (two members are nominated). This FPTP system, in common parlance, was adopted shortly after Independence, following debates in the Constituent Assembly (1946–9) and parliament (1950–1) just before the adoption of the Representation of the People Act, 1950 and 1951, and the first general elections of 1952. Two- and three-member constituencies which accounted in aggregate for a third of the seats in 1952 and 1957, were abolished in 1961.[31]

---

[30]   Micah L. Sifry, *Spoiling for a Fight: Third-Party Politics in America*, New York: Routledge, 2002, pp. 9, 14, 52, 227–8.

[31]   E. Sridharan, 'The Fragmentation of the Indian Party System, 1952–1999: Seven Competing Explanations', in Zoya Hasan, ed., *Parties and Party Politics in India*, New Delhi: Oxford University Press, 2002.

This electoral system produced a party system, in the elections from 1952 to 1984, in which the single largest party won a majority of the seats, and formed a single-party majority government, despite only a plurality of votes. In all elections from 1952 to 1984, the single largest party (which formed a majority government) was the Congress party, except for 1977 when it was the Janata Party— formed by uniting almost the entire non-Communist opposition. No Indian party has ever won a simple majority of votes, the maximum percentage of votes received being 48 per cent by the Congress in 1984. However, it always got a majority of seats, several times a two-thirds and (in 1984) even a four-fifths majority.

Since 1989, the party system has changed. The past six general elections in India—1989, 1991, 1996, 1998, 1999, and 2004—have resulted in hung parliaments and, as a consequence, minority and/or coalition governments. Even the Congress government of 1991–6 was a minority government for the first two-and-a-half years of its term.

In the rest of this section, we outline the trajectory of intra-party democracy in the major Indian parties, focusing on the Congress party. Is the reconstruction of an umbrella party like the Congress party was in its heyday, with coalition politics being played out within the party, and electoral politics not being played out along lines of social cleavage, possible at all? And can the present national party system evolve towards the development of what Verney[32] has called federal parties, that is, parties formed by the merger of single-state parties so as to form, first, a cross-state spatial coalition, followed eventually by unification into a federal party. For either of these developments to happen, a minimum condition would be that parties must be internally democratic and run their affairs according to transparent, rule-based democratic procedures so that there are incentives to work within the party and for newly-mobilized interests to seek to work within existing parties rather than float new parties.

The Congress Party[33]

The Indian National Congress, or Congress party, was founded in 1885 by a group of English-educated Indian lawyers, journalists,

---

[32]   Verney, 'How has the Proliferation of Parties . . .', p. 147

[33]   The account of the Congress in this section draws on Sridharan (Note 31); E. Sridharan and Ashutosh Varshney, 'Toward Moderate

businessmen, and other members of the emerging intelligentsia. It gradually grew from a collection of urban-based notables pressing for an improvement of the position of Indians under the colonial regime into both an umbrella party and a mass movement for independence. It also sought to include all religious communities, castes, linguistic and regional groups, and classes, as well as a variety of ideological strands.

The Congress was a broad, multi-ethnic coalitional or congress party, in our typology, with an elaborate organizational machinery at the provincial, district, and lower levels. The organization went all the way down to the village in large parts of the country. It faced parties with a much narrower social and geographical base and hence unable to compete with it electorally. These parties at best offered localized challenges.

Internally, the Congress was a grand coalition of the major political and social forces. What held it together was a set of significant factors: its image of being the party which won India its independence; the name recognition and genuine popularity of its leaders, especially Gandhi and Nehru; a host of competent provincial stalwarts, who had participated in the national movement and managed the party organization at the state level; intraparty democracy which, however imperfect, allowed all significant voices to be heard, facilitated internal bargaining and conflict resolution, and accommodated demands of various groups. Ideologically, the party was centrist, committed to democracy, secularism, federalism, and a mixed economy. The Congress as an internal grand coalition faced by a motley

---

Pluralism: Political Parties in India', in Larry Diamond and Richard Gunther, eds, *Political Parties and Democracy*, Baltimore: Johns Hopkins University Press, 2001; Atul Kohli, *Democracy and Discontent: India's Growing Crisis of Governability*, New York: Cambridge University Press 1991; Richard Sisson and Ramashray Roy, eds, *Diversity and Dominance in Indian Politics: Changing Bases of Congress Support*, vol. 1, New Delhi: Sage, 1990; James Manor, 'Parties and the Party System', in Atul Kohli, ed., *India's Democracy*, Princeton: Princeton University Press, 1988; Rajni Kothari, *Politics in India*, New Delhi: Orient Longman, 1970; Stanley Kochanek, *The Congress Party of India*, Princeton, NJ: Princeton University Press, 1968; and Myron Weiner, *Party Building in a New Nation*, Chicago: University of Chicago Press, 1967.

collection of smaller, narrower-based parties, was described in its ideal-typical phase—roughly the first two decades after Independence—by Kothari,[34] as a 'party of consensus' surrounded by 'parties of pressure'.[35]

At the grassroots, membership was open to all who paid nominal dues and were not members of any other political party. This rule, therefore, opened the party to the masses as primary and active members. The latter category referred to those primary members who qualified by certain criteria of party activism. Above them was a hierarchy of local (sub-district, that is, panchayat or block), district, state, and all-India Congress committees. The last three were called the District Congress Committees (DCCs), Pradesh Congress Committees (PCCs), and the All India Congress Committee (AICC). At the annual Congress session, held in a different parts, of the country every year, the delegates were the members of the PCCs. They elected one-eighth of their members to the AICC for a two-year term and the AICC delegates elected the president of the party and a certain number of their members to the Congress Working Committee (CWC).

Thus, at the apex were the party president and the CWC, collectively described as the 'high command', which ran the party at the national level on a day-to-day basis. The structures described above and the periodic internal elections at all levels facilitated a two-way communication between the leadership and the grassroots, and resolution of the factional conflict on personality, caste, regional, ideological, and other lines of cleavage.

The organization gradually disintegrated during the 1960s over the issue of bogus memberships, as party leaders at all levels, especially the local, District Congress Committee (DCC), and PCC levels, recruited large numbers of unverifiable members to swell their 'vote banks' for party elections. This was entirely possible in a poor, illiterate population, without registration of births and deaths in the villages, and without reliable forms of identification. These bogus members' votes would swell the vote of local bosses in intraparty factional competition. In 1969, there was a major split in the Congress party—between the faction led by the then prime minister Indira Gandhi, and the leaders in control

---

[34] See Kothari, *Politics in India*.

[35] Ibid., p. 179.

of the party organization. It led to an organizational crippling of the Congress, from which it has still not recovered. Indira Gandhi used her personal popularity to win national elections, and defeat the organizational wing of the party. By the early 1970s, the organizational Congress was decimated in electoral politics, and Indira Gandhi's party gradually became recognized as the real Congress.

Confident of her charismatic ability to keep winning elections, Mrs Gandhi decided to suspend the decades-old organizational principles of the Congress party, especially the norm of intra-organizational elections. Between 1972 until 1992, the Congress party was progressively turned into what Diamond and Gunther,[36] basing themselves on Kirchheimer,[37] call a catch-all party. This was election-oriented rather than oriented to social integration and transformation. Office-bearers at all crucial levels were no longer elected but appointed by the prime minister and Congress president, both the same person. Party nominations for elections, and increasingly even for state assembly elections, had to be approved, if not decided, by the party high command, especially Mrs Gandhi (until her assassination in 1984). The criterion increasingly became one of personal loyalty to the leader over all other considerations. Earlier, party nominations for elections were decided by the state party leadership with the CWC sending observers to act as arbitrators between major state-level faction leaders in the event of factional clashes. These centralizing tendencies weakened the party's leadership at the state and local levels.

In 1992, after a gap of twenty years, attempts were made to repair the organization and intra-party organizational elections were finally held. In 1997, they were repeated again, but after that the CWC has been nominated by the party president. The latest development in the Congress party is the rise of Sonia Gandhi, Rajiv Gandhi's Italian-born widow, now a naturalized Indian. In the 1998 campaign, she sidelined the formally elected party president, who simply could not lead the party organization and had to give in to her rising popularity. In retrospect, it is clear that Sonia Gandhi's

---

[36] Diamond and Gunther, *Political Parties and Democracy*, pp. xv and 25.

[37] Kirchheimer, 'The Transformation of the Western European Party Systems'.

election campaign energized the party organization and prevented a further drift of Congress voters to other parties. After the elections, she was installed by the CWC as both party president and leader of the Congress parliamentary party, leading to the ouster of the existing party president. In November 1998, her stature rose even further, as the Congress under her leadership and campaign did extremely well, defeating the incumbent BJP state government in two states and winning the election for the incumbent Congress government in a third state. However, in 1999, despite a rise in its vote share to 28.3 per cent from an all-time low of 25.8 per cent in 1998, it fell to an all-time low of 114 seats, recovering to 26.2 per cent and 145 seats in 2004.

Sonia Gandhi's role in Congress politics is paradoxical. She became party president and leader of the Congress parliamentary party in 1998, despite never having won an election as a MP—this was in line with the long-term de-institutionalization of the party. However, her declared goal and her first acts as party president were to rebuild the party organization, state by state, and increasingly at the district levels. At this she has been only partly successful but, the reversion to nomination of the CWC indicates that the attempt to restore intraparty democracy is over for the time being, as of 2006.

The long-term trend towards organizational decay has been accompanied by a change in party finance and election campaigning styles.[38] Private donations by companies and wealthy supporters were the mainstay of party finances since party dues by individual members were never an adequate source of funds in a poor country. Indian laws after 1969 banned company donations to political parties and since then, there has been an increasing resort to illegal means of raising election funds. In the absence of state funding, the ban on company donations, mandated by Indira Gandhi, left no legal source of large-scale finance for elections. With the increasing cost of elections, this has led to an increasing reliance on kickbacks on licences and state contracts in a highly regulated economy. The increasingly

---

[38] Based on extensive interviews conducted by the author. For details, see E. Sridharan, 'Toward State Funding of Elections in India: A Comparative Perspective on Policy Options', *Journal of Policy Reform*, 1999, vol. 3, issue 3.

regulatory policy regime of the 1970s strengthened the political leadership's hands vis-a-vis the private sector. Indira Gandhi's plebiscitary style of campaigning increased the need for money, devaluing the tradition of door-to-door campaigning. It also led to centralization of party finance, party office appointments and election nominations.[39] The increasing 'Americanization' of campaigning, beginning under Rajiv Gandhi in 1989, that is, reliance on television and radio, advertising, and criss-crossing of the country by national leaders by air to address mass rallies, accentuated the neglect of the party organization and its year-round grassroots political activity by a multitude of party workers.

The re-legalization of company donations in 1985 made no difference to these trends because the system had by then become too deeply entrenched. Election finance remains essentially unreformed, despite a reduction in the campaign period to fourteen days since the 1996 elections, an increase in the expenditure ceiling for candidates, and the availability of some free television and radio time in the 1998, 1999, and 2004 campaigns. The existing system strengthens the hands of the national party leadership, and reinforces the centralization of nominations.

The lack of internal democracy in both factions of the Congress since the split of 1969 and the suspension of organizational elections for two decades from 1972 was a major contributory factor to a series of splits in the party. Earlier, there were minor state-level splits. The first major Congress split was that of 1969 which took place at the national level in what was essentially an intra-leadership struggle, which was cast in ideological and policy colours, as well as in parliamentary versus organizational wing colours. The victorious Indira Gandhi-led Congress (I) that emerged as the main faction took most of the Congress vote with it to emerge with a two-thirds majority in the 1971 elections (43.7 per cent and 352 seats versus 10.4 per cent and 16 seats for the losing Congress organization). On the eve of the post-Emergency 1977 elections, the Congress split again, with veteran SC leader Jagjivan Ram leading a faction called Congress for

---

[39] Further, the amendment of the law governing election expenditure limits in 1975, effectively making party and supporter expenditure on behalf of a candidate not count towards the candidate's election spending ceiling, removed all effective checks on election expenditure.

Democracy into a merger with the newly-formed Janata party. The next major split took place in February 1978 when the Congress was in the opposition with only 154 MPs after its defeat in 1977; the Congress (I) that emerged had only 78 MPs. The breakaway faction led by K. Brahmananda Reddi and Karnataka chief minister Devaraj Urs called itself the Congress (U), split again to merge with the Congress, leaving a rump that became the Congress (Socialist) in 1981, confined to a pocket in Kerala.

The next significant splits in the Congress took place during the Narasimha Rao government as the 1996 elections neared. Former UP chief minister Narain Dutt Tiwari left the Congress to float a party called the All India Indira Congress (Tiwari) which cut into the Congress vote in a small way (3–4 per cent) in Madhya Pradesh, Uttar Pradesh, Assam, and Rajasthan, winning four seats in 1996 and one in Rajasthan in 1998. Former cabinet minister Madhavrao Scindia floated a faction called the Madhya Pradesh Vikas Congress which won one seat in MP in 1996. However, these factions soon rejoined the Congress, on the latter's terms. In Haryana, former Congress leader Bansi Lal broke away before the 1996 elections to form the Haryana Vikas Party (HVP), but returned to the Congress in 2005.

However, the most significant and damaging split was in the Tamil Nadu unit of the Congress just before the 1996 elections, in revolt against the decision to ally with the All India Anna Dravida Munnetra Kazhagam (AIADMK). The major faction that emerged from this split formed a new party, the Tamil Maanila Congress (TMC). This split cost the Congress dearly, as the TMC won 27 per cent votes (against the official Congress' 18.3 per cent) and twenty seats in alliance with the DMK (25.6 per cent and seventeen seats) while the official Congress' AIADMK ally got none and 7.8 per cent votes. With the TMC's twenty seats, and those of the Tiwari Congress (four) and the Madhya Pradesh Vikas Congress (one), the Congress could have emerged as the single largest party in 1996, ahead of the BJP. Splits were now a serious concern for the Congress.

Another important state-level split took place in the UP unit of the Congress when nineteen out of thirty-seven MLAs broke away to form the Loktantrik Congress Party (LCP) in October 1997 and allied with the BJP to form a coalition government. Two other significant splits took place just before the 1998 elections as the

Congress appeared to be disintegrating under the presidency of Sitaram Kesri between the fall of the United Front (Gujral) government in November 1997 and the February 1998 elections. The major one was the breakaway in West Bengal of the faction led by Mamata Banerjee to form the Trinamul Congress, which then proceeded to ally itself with the BJP in the state and won seven seats and 24.4 per cent votes in 1998 while the official Congress won only one and 15.2 per cent votes. Clearly, the bulk of the state Congress went over to the Trinamul Congress. The provocation for the split was an intense conflict in the state unit of the Congress in which the central leadership of the Congress backed the less popular formal leadership of the state unit against Mamata Banerjee. This could never have happened if the party practised the basic internal democracy that would leave such decisions on state leadership to democratic processes within the state unit. In Arunachal Pradesh, again just prior to the 1998 elections, the chief minister Gegong Apang broke away to form a new party, the Arunachal Congress, which won both seats in the state and 52.5 per cent votes against 23.9 per cent for the Congress. The Arunachal Congress split again in 1999, the bulk of it merging with the Congress again.

The most damaging recent split in Congress was the May 1999 split led by the Maharashtra political heavyweight Sharad Pawar, former Lok Sabha Speaker, P. A. Sangma, and Bihar leader, Tariq Anwar. Ostensibly against Sonia Gandhi's fitness to be projected as the Congress prime minister in the event of victory in the 1999 elections on account of her foreign birth, the trio called for a constitutional amendment to bar foreign-born citizens from high political office. The move was triggered off by Congress president Sonia Gandhi's implied claim to prime ministership in the event of the Congress forming a government in the aftermath of the BJP-led government's resignation in April 1999, without due consultations within the CWC. The trio were expelled and went on to form the Nationalist Congress Party (NCP).

These splits are not only about personality clashes or power struggles at the top but also, crucially, about defection of erstwhile segments of the party's social base to other or new parties, and the inducements offered for such defection by new parties formed by newly mobilized and assertive groups. The decline of the Congress has also been due to social reasons. Key segments of the traditional Congress voter base have been moving to other parties in the 1990s.[40] The first major social constituency to go over to the non-Congress opposition was the emerging rich-farmer constituency, largely belonging to 'lower castes', or the so-called 'middle castes', in the Green Revolution belt of northwestern India. The rising 'lower' or 'middle' caste peasantry resented the domination of the Congress organization by the 'upper' castes, principally Brahmins and Rajputs, especially in the very large state of UP.[41]

The second major challenge to Congress dominance came from the regional parties, beginning with the victory of the DMK in the state of Tamil Nadu in 1967. Regional parties have focused on regional or linguistic identity and on demands for greater state autonomy in India's federal system. As the Congress party centralized decision-making under Mrs Gandhi, regional parties gained strength.

The SCs (ex-untouchables), constituting 16.5 per cent of India's population, are the third major constituency to move away from the Congress in several parts of India, particularly in the crucial states of UP and Bihar, and to a lesser extent Punjab, Haryana, and Madhya Pradesh. Their growing assertiveness and organized political activity in north India is identified with a new party, the BSP.[42]

Finally, the Muslims, comprising over 13 per cent of the total population, are the fourth major social constituency to part ways

[40]   Subrata Mitra and V. B. Singh, *Democracy and Social Change in India*, New Delhi: Sage, 1999; Oliver Heath, 'Anatomy of BJP's Rise to Power: Social, Regional and Political Expansion in 1990s', *Economic and Political Weekly*, 21–8 August 1999; Anthony Heath and Yogendra Yadav, 'The United Colours of Congress: Social Profile of Congress Voters, 1996 and 1998', *Economic and Political Weekly*, 21–8 August 1999.

[41]   Paul Brass, 'The Politicisation of the Peasantry in a North Indian State', in Sudipta Kaviraj, ed., *Politics in India*, New Delhi: Oxford University Press, 1997.

[42]   Kanchan Chandra, 'Mobilising the Excluded', *Seminar*, 480, August, 1999; Kanchan Chandra, 'The Transformation of Ethnic Politics in India: The Decline of Congress and the Rise of the Bahujan Samaj Party in Hoshiarpur', *Journal of Asian Studies*, 59:1, February 2000, pp. 26–61.

with the Congress in several states, crucially in the two largest states of UP and Bihar. The alienation of the Muslims began in the late 1980s, when the Congress did not resolutely challenge the rising Hindu nationalist movement, culminating when the Congress government failed to prevent the demolition of the Babri Mosque in 1992 by the Hindu nationalists. The Muslim vote has gravitated to viable anti-BJP parties where they exist, like the Samajwadi Party and BSP in UP, or the Rashtriya Janata Dal in Bihar, but has tended to remain with the Congress in states where it is the only viable anti-BJP formation.

In addition to this, the post-1990, post-Mandal (reservation) policy led to a partial consolidation of the new, policy-created OBCs (in effect, 'backward' castes, below the traditional upper castes but above the SCs in the traditional caste hierarchy, comprising small farmers and artisans) around parties other than the Congress, which had for them the unattractive track record of ignoring their aspirations.

The gradual erosion of the party's base due to the desertion by erstwhile support groups, the failure to incorporate newly mobilized groups, and the substantially related phenomenon of repeated splits in the party or its state units, due to factional fights in the absence of clear rules, pose the central question of whether democracy within the party could have produced compromises that may have averted such developments.

The Bharatiya Janata Party[43]

The BJP overtook the Congress to become the largest party in the lower house of parliament in the 1996, 1998, and 1999 elections. It came to power in March 1998, leading a large coalition of pre- and post-election allies, and yet again in October 1999, leading much the same coalition in an early election, and governed until May 2004. The BJP began as the Bharatiya Jana Sangh (BJS), founded in 1951 as the political arm of the RSS, a tightly centralized secretive organization formed in 1925 dedicated to the creation of a Hindu nation. It conceived of India as a Hindu nation in which Muslim and Christian minorities were essentially aliens and towards whom it was explicitly hostile,

---

[43] For this and the next two sections I draw heavily on Sridharan and Varshney, 'Toward Moderate Pluralism . . .'.

particularly to the former, regarding Muslims as descendants of invaders and Christians as converts, whose holy places lay outside India in distant Arabia and Palestine. The RSS did not take part in the independence movement, choosing to target the Muslim community rather than resist British rule. It also took no part in electoral politics until 1951 when the BJS was formed. The BJP is the new name adopted by the party in 1980 after its demerger from the Janata Party into which the BJS had merged in 1977. The BJP is the political party of the family (*parivar*) of civil society organizations spawned by the RSS (called the Sangh Parivar). It can be described as a Hindu nationalist party, its ideology of *Hindutva* or Hinduness being close to both classical fascism in many respects, minus the leader cult, and to the ethnic party type with ethnicity being defined by Hindu religious and cultural markers in this case. It mobilizes people and conducts propaganda against Muslims and Christians, ranging from criticism to hatred and even periodic violence, and characteristically employs Hindu–Muslim, and less frequently Hindu–Christian polarizing electoral strategies.

The BJP organization has a layered, multi-level organizational structure from the village and district levels to the state and national levels. The core urban unit is the *mandal* or ward. Intraparty elections take place regularly, though these are rarely contested and leadership succession is usually settled by consensus at all levels. The party has remained one of the most cohesive of Indian parties.[44] Intraparty conflicts lay dormant for decades until recent years when the party enjoyed power for six years and has since been out of power for two years at the time of writing. This is quite in contrast to the Congress as well as the Janata parties.

With its growth as a mass party in the 1990s, internal factionalism has increasingly come out into the open. The first major split was that of its Gujarat unit in 1995 in which a major state-level leader and former chief minister, Shankarsinh Vaghela split the party, taking a large chunk of it with him, and eventually joined the Congress. Differences have been both over ideology between extremists and moderates and over the fruits of office, especially in its stronghold states in northern, central, and western

[44]   Walter Andersen and Shridhar D. Damle, *The Brotherhood in Saffron*, New Delhi: Sage Vistaar, 1987; Thomas Blom Hansen, *The Saffron Wave*, New Delhi: Oxford University Press, 1999.

India. During the years in power, the BJP, as the party in power, gained ascendancy over the RSS and the rest of the Sangh Parivar, a trend that was resented by the latter as signifying among other things, ideological dilution in the interest of managing a diverse coalition and staying in power. This is not surprising and parallels the gap between the governmental and organizational wings of the party and its front organizations that has been seen in a variety of mass parties in democracies.

The Janata Family of Parties[45]

The Janata family of parties can be traced back to the Congress Socialist Party of the 1930s, a faction within the larger Congress-led national movement. It was pro-land reform, rural-based, and wanted to steer the centrist Congress party towards its own more pro-poor peasant, socialist-ideological ends. After 1947, some of the socialists left the Congress to form socialist parties, which became the single largest group of non-Congress parties by vote share during in the 1950s. They disliked the landlord- and upper-caste dominated organizational machinery of the Congress party at the district and state levels, as well as its promotion of big industry instead of agriculture. Ram Manohar Lohia, a socialist MP advocated the coming together of all non-Congress parties in a broad-front anti-Congress alliance to avoid splitting the non-Congress majority vote which repeatedly converted the plurality vote of the Congress into a seat majority. These developments led to the formation of non-Congress coalition governments in several major Indian states in the period 1967–71, when the Congress lost eight major states to such alliances in the state assembly elections. In the general elections held after the lifting of the Emergency

[45] This account of the Janata family of parties draws heavily on E. Sridharan and Ashutosh Varshney, 'Toward Moderate Pluralism: Political Parties in India', in Larry Diamond and Richard Gunther, eds, *Political Parties and Democracy*, Baltimore and London: Johns Hopkins University Press, 2001, and on state-wise accounts of Congress dominance and decline in Richard Sisson and Ramashray Roy, eds, *Diversity and Dominance in Indian Politics*, vols I and II, New Delhi: Sage, 1990; Francine R. Frankel, 'Middle Castes and Classes', in Atul Kohli, ed., *India's Democracy*, Princeton: Princeton University Press, 1988; Francine R. Frankel and M. S. A. Rao, eds, *Dominance and State Power in Modern India*, vols I and II, New Delhi: Oxford University Press, 1989.

(1975–7), in which democratic freedoms and civil liberties were suspended, four non-Congress parties came together to form the Janata party, also a broad, multi-ethnic coalitional or Congress party, and won a thumping victory.

The Janata party of 1977–9 has by now split into so many parties that it is best to describe the entire set as the Janata family, although its offshoots are in different coalitions and they do not constitute a political cluster or front with a common programme. In terms of vote share for the period 1977–89, the Janata family of parties was collectively the next largest to the Congress, losing that position to the BJP from 1991. All the various splinter groups are essentially based on particular state-specific caste blocs, mobilized through primordial ties and the promise of a share in power, and are somewhere between multi-ethnic coalitional parties and ethnic parties.

However, the original Janata Party was a fractious party composed of incompatible elements ranging from the Hindu nationalist right to the socialist left. It failed to develop an organization, let alone conduct party elections, and in July 1979 it split into two factions. In the 1980 elections, the two factions of the Janata party won 19.0 per cent votes (thirty-one seats) and 9.4 per cent votes (forty-one seats) respectively, as against the Congress' 42.7 per cent and 353 seats. After this defeat, the Janata party disintegrated. In 1989, after a gap of eight years, the party was reborn as Janata Dal, led by V.P. Singh, former finance minister (and prime minister later in 1989–90), and was given a lower-caste-based, peasant orientation once again with the August 1990 decision to reserve 27 per cent of government jobs for OBCs based on caste criteria, in addition to reservation for the SCs and STs. In the 1989 elections the Janata Dal had won 17.7 per cent of the vote and 142 out of a total of 543 seats.

However, personality clashes between ambitious leaders tore the party apart. In 1991, reduced by a split, the rump of the party that retained the name Janata Dal received 11.8 per cent of the vote and fifty-nine seats. In the 1996 elections, after another split, the rump that again retained the name Janata Dal got 8.1 per cent of the vote and forty-six seats. Before the 1998 elections, it underwent two splits, and was more or less was decimated. The rump that yet again retained the name Janata Dal won only six seats and 3.25 per cent of the vote. In the 1998 and 1999 elections, an apparent disintegration of the Janata family of parties took place, with the virtual collapse of the United Front. Several Janata family splinters, less ideological and more power-oriented, aligned with the BJP-led coalition of parties. A year after the BJP's exit from power, the various offshoots of the Janata family of parties remain in different coalitions led by the BJP and the Congress with some major offshoots like the Samajwadi Party in the key northern state of UP remaining independent.

The support base of the Janata family of parties has consisted of small peasant proprietors of the lower castes, whose interests were not adequately represented in the caste coalitions that underpinned the Congress, and whose special demands for social justice, subsequently, were not recognized by Hindu nationalists. This peasant proprietor base went in different directions in different states during the successive splits suffered by the party— to the Samajwadi Party in UP, to the Rashtriya Janata Dal and Samata Party in Bihar, and to the splinter Biju Janata Dal in Orissa, as the BJP successfully attempted to co-opt intermediate caste peasant proprietors, playing on their fears of job quotas for some castes and the mobililization of SC landless labour.

However, the main weakness of the Janata family of parties is and has always been organizational. They have been the most weakly organized of the major political parties in India, and have never had credible organizational elections. Why has the Janata family of parties not been able to put together a cohesive front? Their potential unity has problems of both a vertical and a horizontal nature and the lower castes have their own internal hierarchy, varying state by state, for they include the OBCs as well as the SCs. As a result, an internal differentiation within the presumed 'lower caste' unity has emerged. In some states like UP, the SCs have openly rebelled against the lower castes, calling them the new oppressors.

There are also problems of horizontal aggregation across states since the 'lower castes' in one state may have little to do with the 'lower castes' elsewhere because the specifics of the caste hierarchy as well as particular castes themselves are unique to particular states, as are their 'oppressor' castes. And as part of being less institutionalized, the Janata family parties are even less allied to formal civil society organizations.

The Left Parties, Regional Parties, and the Bahujan Samaj Party

As far as organization, nomination of candidates, fund-raising and distribution, and other key political decisions, the Left parties, the various regional parties, and the SC-based BSP, one of the fastest rising parties in India in terms of votes, are as top–down in their functioning as the major parties described. This does not mean that they are as weakly organized as the Janata family parties. Some of them, such as the Left parties, the DMK in Tamil Nadu, the fascistic Shiv Sena in Maharashtra, and some others may be relatively tightly organized, but they remain essentially top–down, not decentralized or internally democratic. Key decisions like nominations, finance, and electoral strategies are decided by party leaders or oligarchies. All of these parties, beginning with the CPI in 1964, have undergone at least minor splits, most them quite a few times, and in many major cases over clashes between rival leaders.

CONCLUSION: DEMOCRACY, THE ACCOMMODATION OF DIVERSITY IN INDIAN PARTIES AND THE AMERICAN AND OTHER INTERNATIONAL EXPERIENCE

In this section we try to put forward some tentative conclusions from the American and European experience for the prospects of democracy within the major Indian parties, principally for the Congress party and other middle-of-the-road national parties and its implications for the political management of diversity. As far as the BJP is concerned, it is essentially controlled by an extra-parliamentary, secretively-run, highly ideological and hierarchical organization, the RSS,[46] upon which it is crucially dependent for electoral mobilization.[47] It is unlikely to be amenable to the kinds

---

[46]   See Andersen and Damle, *The Brotherhood in Saffron*; Christophe Jaffrelot, *The Hindu Nationalist Movement in India*, New Delhi: Viking Penguin, 1996; Hansen, *The Saffron Wave;* Thomas Blom Hansen and Christophe Jaffrelot, *The BJP and the Compulsions of Politics in India*, New Delhi: Oxford University Press, 2001; Partha S. Ghosh, *The BJP and the Evolution of Hindu Nationalism: From Periphery to Centre*, New Delhi: Manohar, 2000.

[47]   This is clear from the literature on the BJP and RSS and was clear to me in an election survey in the 1999 elections that there is no BJP

of internal democracy discussed in this chapter. Due to its ideology, it cannot be expected to be accommodative of Muslim and Christian minorities beyond purely token and tactical gestures. However, it has tried to accommodate the OBCs and Dalits, as well as persons from regions like the south and east which, are not its traditional sphere of influence, through a process of 'social engineering' and stage-managed intraparty democracy, which has been electorally fairly successful.

Our principal conclusion is that, since the late 1960s, the umbrella Congress party has both failed to retain its traditional voter vase and failed to accommodate newly mobilized regional and caste groups, and this is crucially related to the erosion of the mechanisms of intraparty democracy. The lack of intraparty democracy has led to splits in the party, and likewise, splitting of other parties and the emergence of new parties based explicitly on region, language, and caste, state-wise, to give expression to the aspirations for empowerment of state-specific ethnic groups. However, splits are also due to clashes, factional, personality, or interest groups, in addition to the lack of accommodation of social diversity. Conversely, lack of internal democracy alone need not lead to splits. The most tightly organized but top–down parties of the ideological extremes have also been the least split-prone—the BJP, Shiv Sena, and the Left parties.

Thus, the pattern of accommodation of diversity has shifted from the classic umbrella party mechanism—Kothari's party of consensus[48]—to a politics of presence in which parties are based on specific ethnic groups. In other words, there is a shift to the representation of diversity by a host of parties rather than the negotiated accommodation of diversity within a few major parties. Electoral and governing coalitions of such parties are now the much less stable and more confrontational mechanism for the accommodation of diversity. This is in sharp contrast to the American pattern of two internally democratic and decentralized catch-all parties.

---

cadre distinct from the RSS cadre; the BJP is totally dependent on the RSS and its affiliates, not only for election campaigning but also for inter-election political work. The relative autonomy of the parliamentary party leadership is only relative and is under continuous pressure.

[48]   See Kothari, *Politics in India*.

We also conclude that the most important feature of internal democracy in the American parties—American-style primaries —are not feasible in the Indian parties because they presuppose state regulation of party processes; registration of voters with a declaration of party identification, a declaration most Indian voters will not be ready to make; a fairly stable two-party system, unlike the current flux in the Indian party system since 1989; and fairly high and stable party identification. None of these obtain in the Indian situation and are likely to in the foreseeable future, quite apart from the fact that primaries may lead to the further disintegration of already highly unstable and split-prone parties.

Even European-style primaries, managed by party managers under party rules, as was supposed to have existed, in theory, in the Congress party before the suspension of internal elections since 1972, are open to a great deal of abuse. In fact, the system began to break down in the 1960s precisely over the bogus membership issue, party membership being something that can be manipulated in what is still a largely rural and poor country.

However, even a return to such a system of internal democracy in what is a less poor, less illiterate, more politically aware electorate than in the 1960s, one in which it is easier to maintain verifiable membership records, given current information technology, and one in which elections to the third tier of local government give the public experience that can translate into party elections, can go a long way in democratizing parties. At the very least, it can help federalize, if not democratize from bottom–up, the structure of political parties. That is, decentralizing power within the leadership of parties so that power is not excessively concentrated at the national leadership level. This would be a very important first step. Some such institutionalization of internal democracy and accountability within political parties would also be necessary if any sort of state funding of elections is to be instituted. The latter is a step that can potentially push internal democracy much further.[49]

In the present situation of a near-total lack of democracy within parties, a return to internal party elections, by party rules, and under party management, where the selectorate are 'active members' by some organizational criteria, beginning from the

---

[49] E. Sridharan, 'Toward State Funding of Elections in India . . .'.

district and state levels, would be a very important first step. This would also provide incentives to newly mobilized social groups and would-be party formateurs to work within the rules of existing parties to try to capture a greater share of power in such parties, whether in terms of party offices or election nominations or influence in the shaping of party policy on issues of concern to them. Democratizing of parties could help to shift the process of accommodation of social diversity away from the formation of new parties, which try to win as many seats as possible and then bargain for power in (inevitably fractious) electoral and government coalitions, to one in which emergent groups try to work within, and are accommodated within, existing parties. This would also bolster the governance capacities of the party/ies in government and that of the state by making parties more inclusive.

NOTES AND REFERENCE

I would like to acknowledge the financial support of the Ford Foundation for this study and the project it is a part of. I would like to thank Pradeep Chhibber, Larry Diamond, Samuel Eldersveld, Scott Mainwaring, Jack Nagel, Marc Plattner, Austin Ranney, Ashutosh Varshney, and Ray Wolfinger who made time for me during a visit to the United States on this project for a month in October–November 2000, and particularly Douglas Verney who gave me detailed comments on a first draft. Neera Chandhoke, Peter de Souza, Nathan Glazer, Arend Lijphart, Juan Linz, Alfred Stepan, and Zoya Hasan gave me useful feedback and suggestions for follow-up after the mid-term and final workshops of the project. K.P. Vijayalakshmi suggested and gave me useful readings. I alone am responsible for the views expressed here.

7

Federalism, Multi-National Societies, and Negotiating a Democratic 'State Nation'
A Theoretical Framework, the Indian Model and a Tamil Case Study*

Alfred Stepan

INTRODUCTION

For many of its citizens, India is a 'nation state', for others, a 'state nation'. However, India also has some dimensions of a 'multinational society'. What do I mean, and not mean, by this later assertion?

All independent states have a degree of diversity, but for comparative purposes we can say that, at any given time, states may be divided analytically into three different categories:

1. States that have strong cultural diversity, some of which is territorially based and politically articulated by significant groups that in the name of nationalism and self-determination, advance claims of independence.
2. States that are quite culturally diverse, but whose diversity is nowhere organized by territorially-based politically significant groups, mobilizing nationalist claims for independence.
3. States that may appear to be relatively culturally homogeneous.

*   Support for Alfred Stepan's work on comparative federalism was provided by the Ford Foundation.

In this chapter I will call countries, part of whose territory falls into the first category, 'robustly politically multi-national'. Canada (owing to Quebec), Spain (especially owing to the Basque Country and Catalonia), and Belgium (owing to Flanders), are 'robustly politically multi-national'.[1] Switzerland and the US are both sociologically diverse and multicultural. However, since neither country has significant territorially based groups mobilizing claims for independence, both countries clearly fall into the second and not the first category. Countries such as Japan, Portugal, and the Scandinavian countries fall into the third category.

India, owing to the Kashmir Valley alone, merits classification under the first category as a polity with some 'robustly politically multi-national' dimensions.[2] Furthermore, at various times Nagaland and Mizoram in the Northeast, the Khalistan movement

---

[1]   The United Kingdom (UK) has the Scottish Nationalist Party which advocates independence for Scotland and is a politically significant force in Scotland. This alone makes the UK 'politically robustly multi-national'. With the exception of the UK, all longstanding democracies that are in this category are federal, and indeed *de facto* asymmetrically federal. The UK raises classification problems because it has no written constitution but combines both unitary features, and with the devolved Scottish and Welsh Assemblies, some *de facto* asymmetrical features. Unlike Canada, Belgium, or India there are no major territorially concentrated areas in the UK where a minority language is the majority language.

[2]   If we divide Jammu and Kashmir into its three zones (Kashmir, Ladakh, and Jammu) the Kashmir zone meets our definition of being 'politically robustly multi-national'. In a recent public opinion poll with 1,116 respondents in Kashmir (in a sample that tried to be close to a representative one) it is clear that the Kashmir Valley has a territorially concentrated linguistic–cultural majority of Muslims who speak Kashmiri; of the sample in the Valley, 91.9 per cent answered in Kashmiri, and 98.9 per cent self-identified as Muslim (only 1 per cent answered in Hindi, and only 4 per cent said they were Hindus). Most importantly, a significant armed group has devoted much of their political energies to achieving greater autonomy or even independence. In the survey only 8.2 per cent of those polled in the Kashmir Valley wanted to join Pakistan, but only 1.4 per cent agreed with the statement that 'Kashmir should remain with India as it is'. See *Jammu and Kashmir; Assembly Election 2002: Findings of a Post-Poll Survey* by Lokniti, Delhi, February 2003.

in the Punjab, and the Dravidian movement in the south have also given a multi-national dimension to Indian politics.[3] In addition, Indians have had to nurture, defend, and try to deepen democracy in a sociological and political context where this multi-national dimension interacts with more linguistic, religious, and socio-economic diversity than that found in any other longstanding democracy in the world.[4]

There is a long tradition in democratic social analysis that considers the term 'multi-national democracy' to be virtually an

[3]   On Kashmir see Sumatra Bose, *The Challenge in Kashmir*, London: Sage Publication, 1997; for independence movements and secessionist wars in the Northeast, see Sanjoy Hazarika, *Strangers of the Mist: Tales of War and Peace from India's Northeast*, London: Penguin Books, 1994, and Ved Marwah, *Uncivil Wars: Pathology of Terrorism in India*, New Delhi: Harper Collins, 1995. For a review of the literature on the Khalistan movement in the Punjab, see Surinder S. Jodhka, 'Looking Back at the Khalistan Movement: Some Recent Researches on its Rise and Decline', *Economic and Political Weekly*, 21–7 April 2001. For one of the most cited books about Tamil secession as a potential problem, see Eugene F. Irschick, *Politics and Social Conflict in South India: The Non-Brahmin Movement and Tamil Separatism, 1916–1929*, Berkeley and Los Angeles: University of California Press, 1969. For two important reviews of the literature of the Dravidian movements, see M.S.S. Pandian, 'Beyond Colonial Crumbs: Cambridge School, Identity Politics and Dravidian Movement(s)', *Economic and Political Weekly*, 18–25 February 1995, pp. 385–91, and N. Ram, 'Dravidian Movement in its Pre-Independence Phases', *Economic and Political Weekly*, February 1979, pp. 377–97.

[4]   For example, at Independence the Constitution-makers had to make decisions about what to do about the fact that at least ten different languages, almost all with mutually unintelligible scripts, were each spoken by at least thirteen million people (and at least twenty more languages had somewhere from thirteen to one million speakers). Also, at Independence, the dominant religion in India was Hinduism, but India, after Indonesia, and Pakistan had the third largest Muslim population in the world (currently close to 130 million); and therefore Nehru and the Constituent Assembly invented an 'equal distance, equal respect' new model of secularism to deal with Muslims, Sikhs, and Christians, all of whom now constitute a majority in at least one of India's states. All of these types of diversity, including degrees of caste stratification, and absolute poverty, can compound, or cross-cut, the possibility of mobilizing potential multi-national cleavages in India.

oxymoron.[5] This chapter contests this tradition, and will be primarily devoted to the theoretical and empirical inquiry into what helps increase, or decrease, the chances of democracy and social peace in polities with some multi-national dimension to their political life. A closely related goal of the chapter is to argue that Indian politics, properly understood, can teach social scientists, and indeed anyone interested in how democracy is crafted in countries with many languages, religions, cultures, and even 'nations' within their borders, an immense amount—both theoretically and politically.

I will attempt to carry out these tasks via the method of analysing how a potential problem of multi-nationalism, with possible secessionist potential in south India, the Dravidian movement, especially in what is now the state of Tamil Nadu, became a non-problem.

As with any potential problem that becomes a non-problem, there is always a possible question about how severe the original problem actually was, and throwing doubt on its severity may lead to a failure to examine *choices* that might have actually facilitated the management of the potential problem. It is true that the desire for secession never became a majority sentiment in south India, even at the height of the Dravidian movement from the 1920s to the 1940s, or even during the 1965 anti-Hindi language riots. It is also true that long after some Dravidian parties had abandoned their demands, or even possibly their desire for independence, they continued to deploy the language of separatism for purposes of voter mobilization inside electoral politics.[6]

But I note that even one of the leaders of the interpretive movement that stresses the instrumental uses of separatist rhetoric in the 1950s and 1960s, Narendra Subramanian, acknowledges that the Dravidian movement had separatist dimensions. For example, he states that 'the Dravidian movement in Tamil Nadu

---

[5] See Stepan's 'Modern Multinational Democracies: Transcending a Gellnerian Oxymoron,' in his *Arguing Comparative Politics*, Oxford and New York: Oxford University Press, 2001, pp. 181–99.

[6] All of these positions are articulated by Narendra Subramanian in his careful and well documented book, *Ethnicity and Populist Mobilization: Political Parties, Citizens and Democracy in South India*, Oxford: Oxford University Press, 1999, see for example pp. 15, 125, 131, and 313.

began during the 1910s by raising militant demands for secession and virulently opposed the upper Brahmin caste.'[7] Elsewhere he writes that 'Tamil Nadu was the first Indian state in which secessionist/autonomous impulses developed.'[8] The two great leaders of the Dravidian movement until the 1960s were Ramaswami Naicker (normally simply called Periar) and C.N. Annadurai.[9] Concerning Periar, Subramanian asserts: 'Periar called for the creation of a separate country in which the Dravidian-as-Sudra would enjoy primacy.'[10] On the Independence Day of India, Periar urged the burning of the Indian flag and non-recognition of the new Indian Constitution. Of C.N. Annadurai, who broke with Periar in 1947 to form a political party, Subramanian comments that this leader, who also shared Periar's discourse of Brahmins as alien and harmful north Indians 'argued that the Dravidians were oppressed by the Brahmin, the Bania (a north Indian merchant caste), and the British, and that the departure of one of the oppressors could only be an occasion to rejoice. He wished to continue the struggle for secession, to free Tamil Nadu of the other two oppressors.'[11]

If one accepts the accuracy of these assessments, the question that we must ask is: why did these articulations of separatist desires so dissipate by the early 1970s that the potential problem had become a 'non-problem'. We particularly need to examine how politically strategic decisions and choices can aggravate, or ameliorate, potential multi-national tensions. For example, in the *de facto* multi-national society of Sri Lanka, Sinhalese politicians eliminated English as a 'link language' for government posts, downgraded the language of the largest minority, the Tamils, insisted on maintaining a unitary state, and elevated Buddhism to the dominant and privileged religion of Sri Lanka. Most top Sinhalese policy-makers and most leading analysts that I have interviewed in Sri Lanka are now convinced that these choices contributed to turning the non-issue of Tamil separatism

[7]   Ibid., p. 7.

[8]   Ibid., p. 131.

[9]   Note: Periar is also often spelled Peryiar. Both are correct.

[10]   Ibid., p. 105.

[11]   Ibid., p. 122.

in the 1940s into one of the world's most intractable and bloody conflicts.[12]

In the period leading up to Independence, south India witnessed much more discussion of separatism than did what was then Ceylon (now Sri Lanka). However, as we shall see, on virtually all the strategic decisions facing multi-national India—the rejection of a unitary state, the acceptance of multiple but complementary political identities, the upgrading of regional languages, and the maintenance of a English as a link language, the maintenance of polity-wide careers, the constitutional espousal of 'equal distance and respect' for all religions, and the creation of mutually beneficial alliances between polity-wide and regional parties—India, unlike Sri Lanka, negotiated choices and alliances, especially in south India, that, I argue, increased the incentives for, and chances of, peaceful democracy in this potentially conflictual setting.[13]

Since I believe that relatively successful federal democratic experiences, in multi-national polities, have been under-analysed, I propose to explore the south Indian case. But first let me explore how and why multi-national democracies are poorly theorized, and attempt to construct a new conceptual framework for what works, and what does not work, when we consider the successful construction of democratic federations in polities with 'politically robust multi-national dimensions'.

[12]   For an excellent article on how bad political choices in Sri Lanka turned a near non-issue into a crisis, and how better political choices in Malaysia helped moderate multi-national tensions, see Donald I. Horowitz, 'Incentives and Behaviour in the Ethnic Politics of Sri Lanka and Malaysia', *Third World Quarterly*, October 1989, pp. 18–35.

[13]   However, as Dipankar Gupta tellingly documents and analyses, a series of bad political choices and actions by the government of Indira Gandhi helped turn the near non-issue of Sikh separatism in the Punjab into a bloody crisis that weakened for a while once-strong Sikh multiple and complementary identities and eroded the quality of democracy not only in the Punjab but in India. See his 'The Communalising of Punjab, 1980–1985', *Economic and Political Weekly*, 13 July 1985, pp. 1185–90. Kashmir, as a part of India, probably would have always been somewhat difficult, but even Nehru made some decisions that aggravated the situation by violating the agreed-upon constitutional formula.

CONSTRUCTING A USEABLE GRAMMAR FOR ANALYSING DEMOCRATIC FEDERATIONS IN MULTI-NATIONAL SOCIETIES

The Oxford Dictionary defines grammar as 'rules of a language's inflection or other means of showing relation between words.' Unfortunately, we do not yet have a conceptual and political grammar that captures the relationships that are most, and those that are least, useful in crafting supportive relations between the 'multi-national', 'democratic', and 'federal' fields of political force. There are eight phrases and/or concepts that must be culturally unpacked and then put together into coherent relationships to each other, before we can construct a theoretical language about federations in multi-national societies. They are:

1. Individual *and* Collective Rights.
2. 'Nations' that are culturally unassimilable *but* politically integratable.
3. Multiple *and* complementary identities.
4. 'Cultural nationalism' *versus* 'territorial nationalism'.
5. 'Coming together' *versus* 'holding together' federations.
6. A 'demos-enabling' *to* 'demos-constraining' continuum.
7. 'Asymmetrical' *instead of* 'symmetrical' federalism.
8. 'Polity-wide' *and* 'centric-regional' parties and careers.

I initially constructed these conceptual 'pairings' for general theoretical purposes.[14] However, all eight pairings (and of course the distinction made in the Linz/Stepan/Yadav chapter in this volume between 'nation state' and 'state nation', and our insistence that there is no democracy unless there is a 'useable state') come into analytical and political play when we analyse the Indian model of federalism. They also come into play in our attempt to explain why the potential issue of Dravidian, and especially Tamil, separatism in the 1940s became a 'non-issue' by the early 1970s.

Individual and Collective Rights

A polity cannot be a democracy unless the individual rights of all its citizens are enshrined in the constitution and a polity-wide system of horizontal and vertical controls is credibly established

---

[14]   Parts of the discussion of the first three pairs are drawn from a longer analysis found in the previously cited, Stepan, 'Modern Multinational Democracies'.

to enforce these rights. Whatever the rights of the national sub-units, they cannot constitutionally or politically violate the rights of individual citizens. The enforcement of individual rights can be an obligation of both the centre and the sub-units, but the centre cannot completely delegate responsibility for the establishment and maintenance of democratic rights and continue to be a democracy.

The above point insisted upon, it is also possible that in a multi-national polity, some groups can only participate fully as individual citizens, if as a group they acquire the right to have some schooling, mass media, religious, or even legal structures that respond to the specifics of their culture. Some of these rights might be called 'group specific' collective rights.

An assumption of many thinkers in the liberal tradition is that all rights are *individual* and *universal*. This assumption should properly be seen as a normative preference. Advocates of such a liberal approach are prone to see any deviation from individualism and universalism with suspicion.[15] Thinkers associated with the liberal tradition of rights are particularly skeptical of group rights, and thus, at least implicitly, of many of the 'consociational practices' that I, with thinkers such as Arend Lijphart, believe could be used to craft democracy in a multi-national polity. As a student of the historical development of democracies, and as an empirical democratic theorist, let me make four observations about what I think could be, and at times actually have been, democratic 'group specific rights', to use Will Kymlicka's phrase.

First, individuals are indeed the primary bearers of rights and no group right should violate individual rights in a democratic polity. In a democratic multi-national federal state, this means that something like a Bill of Individual Rights should be a property of the federal centre and that any laws and social policies that violate this polity-wide bill of individual rights must fall outside the constitutionally guaranteed policy scope of sub-units.

Second, while individual rights are universal, it is simply bad history to argue that in actual democracies *all* rights have been universal. Frequently, the struggle to reconcile the imperatives of political integration *and* to recognize the legitimate imperatives

---

[15] For a discussion of the liberal tradition and its discomfort with 'group rights', see Will Kymlicka, *Multicultural Citizenship: A Liberal Theory of Minority Rights*, Oxford: Clarendon Press, 1995, especially chapter 4.

of cultural difference has meant according group-specific rights such as those given to the Maori in New Zealand, and to religious and linguistic cultural councils in Belgium.[16] The key point is that it is the obligation of the democratic state to ensure that no group-specific right violates any universal individual right. As long as this political condition obtains, there is no contradiction between individual rights and group-specific rights.

Third, while individuals are the bearers of rights, there may well be concrete moments in the crafting of a democracy where individuals cannot develop and exercise their full rights until they are active members of a group that struggles for some collective goods common to most members of the group and that are being denied to them.[17] If Catalans (who under Franco were not allowed to organize Catalan organizations or to have Catalan language radio and television programmes) had not been given some group-specific rights, it is not clear that they could have developed as individual democratic activists. It was partially the group rights won by Catalans that contributed to their power to argue, vote, and negotiate for a form of devolution and power-sharing in the newly constructed Spanish federation.[18]

Fourth, the types of group specific rights I have discussed in the three points above may not be consistent with some nineteenth-century tenets of Anglo-Saxon liberal democracy, or the classic nineteenth-century French idea of citizenship in a nation state, but they are consistent with a polity in which group rights do not violate individual rights, where effective democratic citizenship and loyalty is broadened, and where a democratic state nation

[16] See Kymlicka, op.cit.; Lijphart, *Democracies...* op.cit.; and Lijphart, 'The Puzzle of Indian Democracy...', op.cit.

[17] An elegant development of this argument is found in the work of the Oxford legal theorist, Joseph Raz, *The Morality of Freedom*, Oxford: Oxford University Press, 1986, especially chapters 8 and 10; and his *Ethics in the Public Domain: Essays in the Morality of Law and Politics*, Oxford: Clarendon Press, 1994, preface and chapters 1, 6, and 8.

[18] For extensive argumentation and documentation of this point see Juan J. Linz and Alfred Stepan, *Problems of Democratic Transition and Consolidation: Southern Europe, South America, and Post-Communist Europe*, Baltimore and London: The Johns Hopkins University Press, 1996, chapters 2, 6, and 20.

exists. They are in fact often one of the few ways to craft democracy in the difficult and populous world of multi-national polities.

'Nations' that are Culturally Unassimilable but Politically Integratable

The bad news is that 'nation-building' and 'democracy-building' are complementary logics in a mono-national federation but, at least in the short run, conflicting logics in a newly democratic federation in a multi-national society. In the normative and sociological context of the modern world, assimilation of two or more cultural nations into one nation state, in two generations, is extremely difficult. Policies that are imposed to attempt to produce such rapid cultural assimilation will almost certainly tend to generate counter-movements of conflict, disloyalty, and structurally induced exit movements that work against the consolidation, or persistence, of democracy.

The good news is that cultural assimilation is not necessary in order to consolidate democracy. What is necessary is sufficient agreement about the legitimacy of institutions by which the demos, and all its demoi, can produce a central government *and* regional governments, all of which are bounded by a credible set of broadly accepted constitutional provisions and mechanisms to ensure that both the central and regional governments act within the law. The Catalans in Spain did not want to be, and could not have been, culturally assimilated into post-Franco Spain. However, as a result of their co-participation in a complex series of debates and votes resulting in a devolution of power in a previously unitary state, a sufficiently high degree of political integration was attained for the multi-national society of Spain to become a federal, democratic state nation.

Multiple and Complementary Identities

A democratic federal system by most definitions must have credible guarantees that there are some policy areas that are constitutionally beyond the scope of the centre, and some that are constitutionally beyond the scope of the sub-units. For example, for Dahl, federalism is 'a system in which some matters are exclusively *within* the competence of certain local units—cantons, states, provinces—and are constitutionally *beyond* the scope of the authority of the national government; and where certain other matters are constitutionally outside the scope of the authority of the smaller units.'[19]

If we accept some version of the above definition of federalism, then one must also accept the political fact that citizens in a democratic federal system are simultaneously subject to two different governments, each of which is sovereign in some areas.[20] Any democratic federal system, but especially a federal system in a territorially based multi-national society, can therefore experience centrifugal and/or centripetal pressures leading to the breakdown of the system. Extreme centrifugal pressures could manifest themselves by violent efforts by culturally distinctive sub-units to secede. Extreme centripetal pressures could be manifested by the coercive abolition by the centre of the constitutionally guaranteed areas of authority of the sub-units.

Given the above potential pressures threatening to cause a breakdown of multi-national federations, the more citizens in the sub-units feel there are polity-wide incentives and resources that they value, and benefit from, such as security, polity-wide careers, and participation in a large common market—while at the same time, securely enjoying autonomy in areas such as language, education, and communications—the more likely dual loyalty to the centre and the sub-units is politically possible, and the less likely secessionist efforts can be presented as absolutely necessary for the dignity and development of the nation or sub-unit. If an incentive and identity situation similar to what we have just described prevails, violent secessionists may exist, but they will tend to be weakly supported. A functioning democratic federal system in a multi-national society therefore is strengthened to the extent that its citizens have, or develop, multiple and complementary identities.

---

[19] Robert A. Dahl, 'Federalism and Democratic Process', in *Democracy, Identity and Equality*, Oslo: Norwegian University Press, 1986, pp. 114–26. Citation from p. 114. Emphasis in the original.

[20] This minimalist statement of sovereignty is consistent with acknowledging that in modern federalism there is much overlapping in jurisdictions. Martin Grodzin's famous analysis that American federalism is not so much a 'layer cake' as a 'marbeled cake' can be accepted, without rejecting Dahl's definition.

'Cultural Nationalism' versus 'Territorial Nationalism'

Conceptually and empirically we can imagine cultural
nationalism within a multi-national polity being responded to in
such a way so as to contribute to political integration, or to
political separatism. The political integration (but not
assimilation) outcome could be one in which individual rights
are respected, but substantial powers, especially in cultural areas
such as language, education, and communication, are devolved
to federal sub-units, with some protection for minorities or the
choices of individuals. If the most politically salient cultural
demands were met by this devolution, *and* many cultural
nationalists or their allies had political and non-political careers
and activities that were furthered by being active members of
the federation, polity-wide political integration and sub-national
cultural nationalism can be pursued simultaneously. In such a
context, territorial nationalists seeking independence would not
be widely supported, and should they use violence, they would
tend to be socially and legally marginalized by cultural
nationalists who are the democratic majority.

We can of course imagine the opposite dynamic starting from
identical cultural nationalist demands. If the cultural nationalist
demand, for example, is for the sub-unit to be administered in the
minority language and for some, mutually agreed 'link language'
to be used for communication with the centre (and indeed in
some cases for access to jobs in the centre) but the centre insists
that the multilingual polity functions as a monolingual federation,
territorial nationalists, who might have been in a small minority,
might begin to win many allies. Indeed, if the centre is perceived
as using illegitimate force against cultural nationalists, support
could grow quite rapidly for the use of violence by the once
small territorial nationalists.

'Coming Together' versus 'Holding Together' Federations

Much of the classic literature on federalism was influenced by
the model developed in Philadelphia in 1787. Indeed, for many
theorists not only did the US 'invent' federalism but it remains the
norm.[21] For such theorists, the essence of the US style of

---

[21]   See for example, William H. Riker, 'The Invention of Centralized
Federalism', in his *The Development of American Federalism*, Boston:

federalism is that the existing sovereign polities voluntarily enter into a federal bargain to pool their sovereignty in a federation. In this 'coming together' federation each of the existing sovereign units retain many of their self-governing rights. To enable those units to continue to play a major role in the governing of the new federation, the small states at Philadelphia refused to join the federation unless two other concessions to their continued sovereignty were made. The federation would have a bi-cameral legislature, one chamber based on the principle of population, the other chamber based on the principle of territory. In the territorial chamber, each of the existing sovereign states would receive, regardless of their great differences in population sizes, an equal number of votes. The second major concession made to the small states was that the upper chamber would have virtually the same competencies as the lower chamber.[22]

The most influential theorist of modern federalism in the English language, William H. Riker, argues that all federations in the world have made this US style, 'coming together' federal bargain. From a comparative perspective this is simply not so.[23] A major alternative is a 'holding together' federation. In 1975, when Franco died, Spain was a unitary state. But in the two years that followed his death it began increasingly clear to many leading political

---

Kluwer Academic Publishers, 1987, pp. 17–42; K.C. Wheare, *Federal Government*, Oxford: Oxford University Press, 1963, categorically asserts that 'The modern idea of what federal government is has been determined by the United States of America...', p. 1. Wheare not only measured all other federations against the US federation, but explicitly made the judgement that, 'the government of the United States is the most successful federal government in the world.' Ibid., p. 85.

[22] For an excellent discussion of how and why these compromises were made see Elaine K. Swift, *The Making of an American Senate: Reconstitutive Change in Congress, 1787–1841*, Ann Arbor: University of Michigan Press, 1996, pp. 1–94. Also see William H. Riker, *The Development of American Federalism*, pp. 17–42.

[23] See Alfred Stepan, 'Toward a New Comparative Politics of Federalism, Multi-Nationalism, and Democracy: Beyond Rikerian Federalism' in Alfred Stepan, *Arguing Comparative Politics*, Oxford and New York: Oxford University Press, 2001, pp. 315–61.

figures that if Spain were to 'hold together' peacefully, and to build a democracy, the centre had to agree to devolve power.[24] Belgium has historically been a unitary state, but in order to hold the Flemish and Walloon communities together, Belgium in 1993 adopted a federal Constitution.[25] Constitutions such as those of Spain and Belgium are examples of what are most usefully called, 'holding together' federalism.

It is possible that a 'holding together' federation could allow the demos to redraw the boundaries of the sub-units. The power of the demos at the centre to redraw the boundaries of the demoi of the sub-units is not something that an American style 'coming together', states-rights, type of constitution could easily tolerate.

The 'Demos-Enabling' to 'Demos-Constraining' Continuum

Regardless of whether a federation is close to the 'coming together' or 'holding together' pole it is necessarily somewhat demos-constraining in contrast to a democratic unitary system. This is so because, if we follow Dahl's definition, the policy agenda of the demos of the centre can not be completely *open* because some potential policy areas are constitutionally beyond its scope since they are the prerogative of the sub-units. However, democratic federations can, and do, vary greatly as to the degree to which the demos at the centre are constrained by the powers of the demoi in the sub-units. The US model, with its combination of *over-representation* of territory (a vote in Wyoming is worth around sixty-six votes in California for the election of an American federal

---

[24] For the new statutes in Spain, see Juan J. Linz, 'Spanish Democracy and the Estado de las Autonomías', in Robert A. Goldwin, Art Kaufman, and William A. Schambra, eds, *Forging Unity out of Diversity: The Approach of Eight Nations*, Washington DC: American Institute for Public Policy Research, 1989, pp. 260–326 and Robert Agronoff, 'Asymmetrical and Symmetrical Federalism in Spain: An Examination of Intergovernmental Policy', in Bertus de Villiers, ed., *Evaluating Federal Systems*, Pretoria: Juta, 1994, pp. 61–89.

[25] For Belgium's construction of a federal system with consociational characteristics, see Liesbeth Hooghe, 'Belgium: From Regionalism to Federalism', *Regional Politics and Policy*, 3 (Autumn 1993), pp. 44–69; Robert Senelle, 'The Reform of the Belgian State', in Joachim Jens Hesse and Vincent Wright, eds, *Federalizing Europe? The Costs, Benefits and Preconditions of Federal Political Systems*, Oxford: Oxford University Press, 1996, pp. 266–324.

Senator) and its *equality of legislative power* between the lower and upper houses, is at the high end of the demos-constraining end of the continuum. Other types of federalism, however, can be, and are, much less demos-constraining, in that the lower house is clearly the most powerful house in policy scope, and the upper house has some degree of PR. This does not mean that the demos at the centre might not agree to grant an impressive range of authority to the sub-units, especially in the areas of language, education, and communication. Indeed, the federation could be considered to be 'demos-enabling' if the majority at the centre is given significant powers to occasionally pass legislation it considers necessary to maintain the democratic integration of the federation.

A key question is whether federations in a mono-national society, or in a multinational society, can function equally well anywhere in the demos-constraining continuum. I think a strong *a priori* case can be made that a mono-national federation could function democratically more easily at the high end of the demos constraining continuum than can a federation in a multi-national society. I believe that a cluster of sub-units with a large population—say twenty times larger than the small sub-units—would not co-exist easily with a cluster of small units that had an equal vote with the larger sub-units on all policy issues. This would be especially so if the greatly under-represented states encompassed a religious or cultural majority in the federation.

I also think that a case could be made that a federation that is crafted as a multi-national 'holding together' federation, where fear of fragmentation is still a concern among political leaders at the centre, would be more likely to want to give 'demos-enabling' powers to the centre. These powers to the centre will allow the demos at the centre to structure devolution in such a way as not to threaten the capacity of the centre to pass binding legislation in the lower house by normal majorities, instead of by the norm of super majorities. A federation at the low end of the demos-constraining continuum would also prevent small blocking minorities in the upper chamber from impeding ordinary legislation, especially legislation that did not intrinsically relate to cultural issues of the sub-units.[26]

---

[26] For example, Austria only has one institutional veto player, and Germany, Spain, and Belgium have two. The US has four, and so the US is more 'majority' or 'demos-constraining'. See Alfred Stepan,

'Asymmetrical' instead of 'Symmetrical' Federalism

Many thinkers assume that the US style 'coming together' and 'symmetrical' federalism is both the quantitative and normative standard. It is neither. Since the French Revolution created the modern idea of a nation state, not a single nation state has yet freely yielded its sovereignty to join a 'coming together' symmetrical democratic federation. But four polities with a strong multi-national component—India, Canada, Belgium, and Spain— have created federations, all of which are 'asymmetrical'.

If the independent states of Europe, many of which are nation states, ever come together to make the EU, *rather than their own states*, the central locus of democratic power, such a democratic federation would almost certainly be 'asymmetrical. It would be constructed as 'asymmetrical' both to ensure some special prerogatives to the larger states without which it is doubtful they all would join and thus accept a much greater loss of autonomy than they have to date. Such an EU would also be 'asymmetrical' so as to constitutionally spell out, and embed, some of the culturally specific rights and prerogatives of members.

'Polity-Wide' and 'Centric-Regional' Parties (and Careers)

'Polity-wide' parties are parties with a strong organizational, electoral, and emotional presence in all, or virtually all, the member units of a federation. The presence or absence of 'polity-wide' parties (especially those that allow and indeed facilitate polity-wide careers, polity-wide loyalties, and free movement for all citizens) is correctly seen as a key variable in the literature on federalism, especially the literature on multi-national polities. In multi-national polities the presence of such strong polity-wide parties is correctly considered a politically integrating force and their relative absence a source of potential disintegration.

In contrast, 'regional parties' are parties that receive almost all their votes in one unit, or geographic space, in the federation. Such parties are normally seen as a threat to integration, particularly

---

'Electorally Generated Veto Players in Unitary and Federal Systems', in Edward Gibson, ed., *Federalism and Democracy in Latin America*, Baltimore: Johns Hopkins University Press, 2004, pp. 323–62.

if they receive a substantial amount of the total votes and seats in the federation and act as exclusionary institutions. I do not dissent from this general judgement. If no polity-wide party has a majority, 'regional parties' with no loyalty to the centre may be able to extract, as the price for their support, some disintegrating prerogatives or policies from the government. At times this has happened in Spain with some Catalan or Basque parties.

However, the vocabulary and theories of modern federalism would also benefit by an awareness of what I would term 'centric-regional' parties. By this I mean a party that does indeed get all of its seats to the federal legislature from one federal unit. If the political system is parliamentary, and no party has a majority, such a party might be able to enter into a valuable alliance with a polity-wide party. In return for the centric-regional party constituting part of its majority, the polity-wide party can make the centric-regional party a part of the governing coalition at the centre and gets votes, and policy fidelity, in return.

The polity-wide party could also act as a junior partner to the 'centric-regional' party in provincial or state elections. The alliance with a polity-wide party could thus directly generate votes, seats, and numerous federal-level jobs for the 'centric-regional' party. In such a situation, both from the viewpoint of politics and rational choice, it would seem that the alliance could create disincentives for the once regional party to support system disintegrative politics. For example, if the centric regional party became secessionist, or even semi-loyal towards the federal state, it would immediately risk becoming 'uncoalitionable' with its valuable polity-wide ally.

In a parliamentary federal system, there is also the possibility that a large number of once-regional parties could themselves constitute the central government and in the process become integrating 'centric-regional' parties.

A POTENTIAL ISSUE OF SEPARATISM BECOMING A NON-ISSUE: SOUTH INDIA

By Benedict Anderson's standards there would appear to have been more than enough raw material for territorial nationalists to imagine (and attain) separate independent nation(s) in south

India.[27] Useable cleavages abounded. In the last decades of the British Raj more than 90 per cent of the population in south India spoke languages in the Dravidian family, all of which had their own scripts and were unintelligible to the major language of the north, Hindi.[28]

Another useable cleavage grew out of religious-cultural differences. In the south the Brahmins were seen as northern in origin. Nationalists in the south, particularly near the important city of Madras, argued that traditional Dravidian culture had been more socially egalitarian than the version of Hinduism imported, and imposed upon Dravidians, by northern Brahmins. The potential of caste as a polarizing force was enhanced by the fact that under British rule, Brahmins were accorded a new higher social status that in effect lowered the social status of some previously quite socio-economically, and even religiously important, south Indian caste groups.[29] For some analysts, the two intermediate Hindu castes, Kshatriya and Vaishya, were virtually not present in south India and south Indians belonged, therefore, to either the lowest category of caste Hindu—the Shudras—or were untouchables, or even 'unseeable', outcasts and this increased the social and political distance of southern, from northern Indians.[30]

Modernity, á la Gellner, sharpened the south Indian sense of exclusion, and contributed to growing anti-Brahmin nationalist movements. The emerging Dravidian nationalist movements in the early decades of the twentieth century gained adherents as they documented and dramatized job-related statistics aiming to prove that non-Brahmins were second-class citizens in south

[27]   Benedict Anderson, *Imagined Communities: Reflections on the Origin and Spread of Nationalism*, London: Verso, 1983.

[28]   Jyotirindra Das Gupta, *Language Conflict and National Development: Group Politics and National Language Policy in India*, Berkeley and London: University of California Press, 1970, pp. 46–7.

[29]   See Nicholas B. Dirks, *Castes of Mind: Colonialism and the Making of Modern India*, Princeton: Princeton University Press, 2001, especially chapters 1 and 12.

[30]   For this argument see Marguerite Ross Barnett, *The Politics of Cultural Nationalism in South India*, Princeton: Princeton University Press, 1976, pp. 46–7.

India. For example, the famous 'Non-Brahmin Manifesto of 1916' argued that though Brahmins constituted less than 3 per cent of the population in the major administrative sub-unit of south India (the Presidency of Madras), all but one of the sixteen top civil service positions allocated to Indians in the Madras Presidency were held by Brahmins, all four of the Hindu judges to the Madras Supreme Court were Brahmins, and the major gatekeeper of modern careers, the University of Madras, was effectively controlled by them too.[31]

Would-be territorial nationalists had other valuable material. They could point to the fact that they were economically more developed than the Hindi belt of north India, which they saw as politically dominant; that south India was geographically contained, in that three of its four borders were oceans; and that they were populous enough to make a number of south Indian independent nations. At Independence this geographic, demographic, and imagined space contained 88 million speakers of Dravidian languages, the four largest of which in 1951 were Telugu (33 million), Tamil (27 million), Kannada (14 million), and Malayalam (13 million). The cultural capital of the Tamils was the city of Madras in the Madras presidency but the Dravidian movement also contained important advocates from the other three major Dravidian languages, many of whom also lived in the Madras presidency.[32]

A leading scholar of India, Lloyd I. Rudolph, who did extensive research in south India in the 1950s, graphically captures how the different components of territorial nationalism seemed to be compounding at the time of Independence:

With the coming of Independence, anti-Brahmanism was increasingly accompanied by an anti-North, Dravidian nationalist outlook.

---

[31] The manifesto is reproduced in its entirety in the previously cited Irschick, *Politics and Social Conflict in South India: The Non-Brahmin Movement and Tamil Separatism, 1916–1929*, pp. 358–67. From 1901 to 1911 Brahmins received 71 per cent of the degrees awarded by Madras University and controlled the key power centre in the university, the Senate, Barnett, *The Politics of Cultural Nationalism in South India*, p. 20.

[32] For the list of the major languages of India as of 1951 see Gupta, *Language Conflict and National Development*, pp. 46–7.

Opposition to Hindi as the national language, the destruction of the caste system, and threats of secession from the Indian Union became major political themes.[33]

THE CONSTITUTIONAL FORMULA: THE 'HOLDING-TOGETHER' AND 'DEMOS-ENABLING' DIMENSIONS

Why then, did the potential issues of 'territorial nationalism' and secession become non-issues? To explore these questions we have to turn to the incentive systems that were developed as part of Indian federalism. To analyse this process we will have to employ virtually all the grammar that we developed in the beginning of this chapter.

In terms of the analytic categories we have developed, India approaches the ideal type of a 'holding-together' and a 'demos-enabling' federation that creatively and consciously differs from the 'coming together' and 'bargaining' modalities associated with the formation of federalism in the US. In his address to the Constituent Assembly, the Chairman of the Drafting Committee, B.R. Ambedkar, assumed that India was already a diverse polity with substantial unity, but that to maintain this unity, under democratic conditions, a federation would be useful. Ambedkar told the members of the Assembly that: '... the use of the word Union is deliberate... The Drafting Committee wanted to make it clear that though India was to be a federation, *the Federation was not the result of an agreement by the States to join in a Federation.*[34]

Mohit Bhattacharya, in a careful review of the mindset of the founding fathers, argues that the central motivation of the Constitution drafters was to hold the centre together.

What ultimately emerged was a 'devolutionary federation' as a fundamentally unitary state devolved powers on the units through a long process of evolution... [Once] the problem of integration of the Princely States had disappeared after partition, ... [T] he bargaining

---

[33]   Lloyd I. Rudolph, 'Urban Life and Populist Radicalism: Dravidian Politics in Madras', *The Journal of Asian Studies*, vol. XX, no. 3, May 1961, pp. 286–7.

[34]   Ambedkar's speech is found in its entirety in India, *Constituent Assembly Debates*, New Delhi, 1951, vol. II, pp. 31–44. Emphasis added.

situation disappeared... The architects of the Constitution were sensitive pragmatists. Their attention was focused on ... the central authority that would hold the nation together.'[35]

Let me again quote from Ambedkar to illustrate how this was to be achieved in the federation.

The... Constitution has sought to forge means and methods whereby India will have Federation and at the same time will have uniformity in all basic matters which are essential to maintain the unity of the country. The means adopted by the Constitution are three: (1) A single judiciary, (2) Uniformity in fundamental laws, civil and criminal, and (3) A common All-India Civil Service to man important posts.[36]

In relation to the demos-constraining versus demos-enabling continuum, India chose one of the most demos-enabling formulas found in any democratic federation, whether in a mono-national or a multi-national society. The US formula, which did grow out of a 'coming together' bargaining process, gave each state equal representation in the upper house, and gave the upper house somewhat greater legal competencies than the lower house. India's 'holding-together' federation was fundamentally different in both respects. The lower chamber, which was based on the principle of population, had the exclusive right to form the government and was vastly more important in legislative competence than the upper chamber, which represented the states. Also there was a significant degree of PR in the upper chamber. The demos at the centre, aided by the choice of a Westminster-type of fused executive-legislative parliamentary model, was thus nowhere near as constrained in independent India as was the demos at the centre in the divided government, Presidential model, chosen in the US.

A major controversy in the Constituent Assembly was over the languages that would be used in the federation. Precisely because the members of the Constituent Assembly knew that the

[35]   Mohit Bhattacharya, 'The Mind of the Founding Fathers', in Nirmal Mukarji and Balveer Arora, eds, *Federalism in India: Origins and Development*, New Delhi: Vikas, 1992, pp. 87–104, quotes from pp. 101–2.

[36]   Ambedkar, previously cited address to the Constituent Assembly.

most controversial issue surrounding Indian unity in the future would be language policy, and because there was a desire on the part of many delegates to eventually reorganize the states along more linguistic lines, the language of the Constitution was extremely demos-enabling.[37] Future parliaments were given the right to completely redraw state boundaries. Article 3 of the Constitution is categorical. With a simple majority 'Parliament may by law a) form a state by separation of territory from any state or by uniting two or more states...; c) diminish the area of any state... e) alter the name of any state.' In a 'coming together' federation such as the US the sovereign states would obviously have been able to bargain successfully for a much more demos-constraining constitution to protect states' rights.[38]

The fact that the demos, as represented in the Constituent Assembly, gave the parliament the right to work with the numerous linguistic demoi of India to reformulate the states turned out to play a very important role in allowing the demos of India, and the demoi of India, to 'hold together' in a multi-national democratic federal system. I will not retell that story because it has been well analysed by other writers.[39] The key point I want to stress here is that in 1955, the parliament authorized a States Reorganization Commission. As a result of that commission

[37] An important precedent was Gandhi's reorganization in 1920 of the Indian National Congress into 20 PCCs *based on language*. British India was still organized along quite different administrative lines.

[38] See Alfred Stepan, 'Federalism and Democracy: Beyond the US Model', *Journal of Democracy* 10, Fall 1999, pp. 19–34. Indeed, it was precisely this feature of the Indian Constitution that led the then leading theorist of federalism in the world, K.C. Wheare of Oxford, to argue that 'What makes one doubt that the Constitution of India is strictly and fully federal, however, are the powers of intervention in the affairs of the state given by the Constitution to the central government and parliament. To begin with, the parliament of India may form new states; it may increase or diminish the area of any state and it may alter the boundaries or name of any state.' See his *Federal Government*, 1963, p. 27.

[39] See especially Jyotirindra Das Gupta, *Language Conflict and National Development*, p. 33 and Paul Brass, *Language, Religion, and Politics in North India*, Cambridge: Cambridge University Press, 1974.

eventually most of the units of the Indian federation were geographically and sociologically reconfigured to achieve a greater congruence between languages and state governments and each state was allowed to carry out its state administration in the dominant language of the state. This major constitutional change meant that a significant degree of politically-legitimated linguistic and cultural nationalism had been achieved *inside* India's federal polity.

Let us now attempt to analyse how the demos-enabling constitutional and linguistic formula was utilized in the attempt to hold together the Hindi-speaking north with the speakers of Dravidian family languages in the south. Here we have to turn to the complex question of a polity-wide party, and its relationship to cultural nationalist parties, and the possibility of multiple and complementary identities.

THE IMPORTANCE OF A 'POLITY-WIDE' PARTY WITH MULTIPLE AND COMPLEMENTARY IDENTITIES

In the immediate pre-and post-Independence era, what was the relationship between culturally nationalist 'regional parties' or movements, and a 'polity-wide' party? In 1944, an offshoot of previous Dravidian movements, The Self-Respect Movement and the Justice Party, was renamed the Dravida Kazhagam (DK). According to Irschick, the DK had 'as its primary aim the realisation of a separate non-Brahmin or Dravidian country.'[40] It was led by the charismatic, autocratic, nationalist leader, Periar, who a leading specialist called 'one of the most dynamic and colourful political leaders South India has ever produced.' Periar 'boycotted independence day celebrations, refused to honour the national flag, just as he later refused to recognise the Indian Constitution.'[41]

For our analytical purposes, it is important to note that this regional nationalist movement had to compete with the polity-wide party, the Indian National Congress. Under the leadership of Jawaharlal Nehru, and the great mobilizer Mahatma Gandhi,

[40]   Irschick, *Politics and Social Conflict in South India*, p. 347.

[41]   See Robert L. Hardgrave Jr., 'Religion, Politics and the DMK', in Donald Eugene Smith, ed., *South Asian Politics and Religion*, Princeton: Princeton University Press, 1966, quotations from p. 216 and p. 223.

the Congress party had an All-Indian institutional presence since its formation in 1885. This polity-wide party had acquired great legitimacy and experience owing to its leadership role in the Indian independence movement. However, the Congress party originally made the mistake of recruiting most of its leaders in the Madras presidency from the small and culturally alien Brahmin community.[42] Nonetheless, the regional nationalist movement, the DK, led by Periar, never became a party. In 1949, the DK lost some important followers when an equally charismatic, but more democratic, leader, C.N. Annadurai, left the DK to form a political party called the DMK. The DMK was not yet able to compete successfully with the Congress party in the founding polity-wide elections. In the first post-Independence elections in 1952, the Congress party won twelve of the fourteen parliamentary seats from the state of Madras, but only a plurality, 152 of the 375 seats, to the Madras state assembly. The DMK, even though a culturally nationalist party with territorial nationalist goals, supported a United Democratic Front coalition of parties, some of which, the communists and the Socialists, were polity-wide parties.

The original leader of the Congress-led government in Madras after the first post-Independence elections of 1952 had been a Brahmin, C. Rajagopalachari, who was perceived to be insensitive to lower caste and Tamil cultural aspirations. But in the new, very competitive electoral context, Kamaraj Nadar, a lower caste, Tamil-speaking, professional Congress party organizer became a crucial leader linking Tamils and the Congress party. Kamaraj did not have the benefit of much formal education, and did not speak Hindi or English, but he combined strong All Indian nationalist *and* Tamil nationalist roots. Kamaraj, who had spent more than 3,000 days in jail for his pro-Independent activities, emerged as the kingmaker in the Madras Congress party. By 1954, he had become the chief minister of Madras. Significantly there was not one Brahmin in his first cabinet.[43]

---

[42]   Indeed the previously cited 'Non-Brahmin Manifesto' explicitly laments that fourteen of the fifteen members of the Madras Congress Party Committee were Brahmins; see Irschick, *Politics and Social Conflict in South India*, p. 361.

[43]   See Duncan B. Forrester, 'Kamaraj: A Study in Percolation of Style', *Modern Asian Studies*, vol. 4 (1), 1970, p. 54.

Jawaharlal Nehru employed a leadership style that, both as prime minister of the government and as president of the Congress party, relied heavily on the consensual support of regional leaders. Nehru and Kamaraj related to each other in ways that made centre-periphery relations cordial. As a major party regional boss, Kamaraj had political resources at the centre and indeed, he became one of the five members of the group called the 'syndicate' that co-ruled the Congress party with Nehru. Moreover, after the death of Nehru, Kamaraj became the president of the Congress party. Kamaraj was effective as a leader of a polity-wide party partly because his autonomy as a Tamil political and cultural leader was respected by Nehru. Nehru, by ideological preference, would have preferred a strong Indian central government which generated an increasingly homogeneous nation state culture, but politically, he knew he had to depend upon a core of Congress party members who represented, and led, India's major regions with their diverse languages and cultures. In essence Nehru followed a 'strong centre, strong sub-unit' policy.

In this type of federal politics, Kamaraj was a regional leader in Tamil-speaking India who commanded enough strength and respect in the centre for him for to be allowed to deliver upon many 'cultural nationalist' demands. As a regional boss of a large state, Kamaraj could also deliver valuable votes and support to the polity-wide party. Lloyd Rudolph summarizes Kamaraj's contribution to the strength, inside the state of Madras, of the polity-wide Congress party: 'Between 1952 and 1957 Congress increased its share of the popular vote from 35.5 per cent to 45.3 per cent largely by identifying itself more closely with the [Tamil] populist appeal... The growth in Congress strength can be attributed largely to the leadership qualities of Mr. Kamaraj.'[44]

In the discussion of the new 'grammar' of federalism I argued that it is necessary to analyse some important democratic

---

[44]   Lloyd I. Rudolph, 'Urban Life and Populist Radicalism: Dravidian Politics in Madras', *The Journal of Asian Studies*, vol. XX (3), May 1961, p. 294. On the 'cultural nationalist' and 'polity-wide party' appeals of Kamaraj, also see Robert L. Hardgrave Jr., 'Religion, Politics and the DMK', in Donald Eugene Smith, ed., *South Asian Politics and Religion*, Princeton: Princeton University Press, 1966, pp. 226–7.

federations, such as Spain, Belgium, Canada, and India, in their multi-national context. Thus I stressed the importance of 'multiple and complementary identities.' I think this concept is valid, and indeed necessary, but perhaps it does not quite capture the dual, but nonetheless occasionally competing, identities many nationalists feel. Most Tamil-speakers were very interested in Tamil cultural nationalist goals and from the 1930s on many were members of parties or movements that periodically articulated separatist aspirations. However, many Tamils were *also* interested in the struggle for Indian Independence. Since the most effective mass-based, pro-Independent organization was the polity-wide Congress party, notwithstanding the fact that many Tamils were cultural nationalists, precisely because they also identified with the Congress party, many of these Tamils were not necessarily territorial nationalists.[45] As the chief minister of Madras, Kamaraj (and the Congress party) received some cultural nationalist credit for the creation of special quotas for lower caste Tamils and for their support for the Tamil language. A leader like Kamaraj reduced the potential tension between the polity-wide and the cultural nationalist goals. But, without a polity-wide party, he could not have played such a role.

The fact that the three other major Dravidian-speaking areas of India had, by the late 1950s, also been given a state in which the language of the government was their own, ended any possibility of a successful movement for a single, independent, Dravidian-speaking country. This was so because, by the late 1950s, linguistic cultural nationalist claims for the then 37 million Telugu speakers were organized and articulated by the state of Andhra Pradesh, by the Madras state (which changed its name to Tamil Nadu in 1968) for the 30 million speakers of Tamil, by

[45] In electoral terms, in the 1920s, the Congress party, with its pan-Indian ideology, and the Dravidian cultural nationalist Justice party, would seemed to have been in a zero sum relationship. However, the existential reality of people who simultaneously wanted to affirm support for cultural nationalism *and* pan-Indianism is beautifully shown by a quote from Subramanian: 'Congress was so popular that by 1927 the Justice Party was forced for reasons of survival to allow its members to have parallel membership in Congress.' See his *Ethnicity and Populist Mobilization*, p. 125.

Karnataka, for the 17 million Kannada speakers, and by the state of Kerala, for the 17 million Malayalam speakers.[46]

But, if the 1955 States Reorganization Commission Report effectively ended all chance of a united, separatist, Dravidian movement based in a single country, there were still some advocates of a territorially independent country of Tamil Nadu. Why then did the Tamil 'cultural nationalists' defeat the Tamil 'territorial nationalists'?

FROM TERRITORIAL NATIONALISM AND SEPARATISM TO CULTURAL NATIONALISM AND POLITICAL INTEGRATION

The constitutional decision to make India a federation made it possible for political activists like Kamaraj to be a cultural nationalist leader at the state level and an All-India leader at the centre. Furthermore, the decisions to craft a 'demos-enabling' and 'asymmetrical' federation allowed the parliament at the centre to go forward with the fundamental redrawing of the political boundaries of the federation to reflect the cultural nationalists' demands concerning language rights. And, of course, the political activity and organization of the Congress party since 1885 allowed a polity-wide party to compete effectively in the elections against cultural nationalists, even in the newly-created linguistic states.

The creation of a Tamil-speaking state in a context where cultural nationalism was very strong gave the chance to the two Tamil nationalist political organizations, the DMK and the DK, to win control of the state by waging cultural nationalist campaigns. The DMK participated in the election for state and federal legislatures in 1957, but owing to the popularity of Congress and Kamaraj, it did not do very well. The DK, as a non-party, did not compete in the election but continued with its formal demand for a sovereign and independent country. In 1959, the DMK, with a campaign focused adroitly on local government, finally won political control of Madras, the largest city, and capital of the state of Madras.[47]

---

[46] The number of speakers of these languages is from the Census of India, 1961, reproduced in Das Gupta, *Language Conflict and National Development*, p. 46.

[47] Barnett, *The Politics of Cultural Nationalism in South India*, p. 105.

After 1959 the nationalist DMK increasingly began to believe it could win control of the state assembly and the state government and some of its leaders and followers even harboured ambitions for greater political autonomy. However, DMK parlamentarians in Delhi sent back warnings that separatist parties might be made illegal, and that territorial nationalist demands in the state of Madras were unfeasible and dangerous. Not wanting to jeopardize their chance to win control of the state of Madras, the top DMK leaders in 1960, in a closed private meeting, made a decision to implicitly, but not explicitly, to drop their territorial nationalist aspirations.[48] They made this explicit after China attacked India in October 1962. The DMK rallied to India's defence as Indian nationalists and patriots, and also as prudent party leaders not wanting to run afoul of the newly-passed sixteenth amendment, Article 19, which authorized sanctions for challenges to the 'integrity of India'.

In 1967, the DMK defeated the Congress party, and won control of the state.[49] From 1967 on the DMK never gave up its cultural nationalism, but it did become increasingly integrated into the politics and norms of the Indian federation.

THE STRUGGLE TO MAINTAIN MULTIPLE AND COMPLEMENTARY IDENTITIES: THE ROLE OF CAREER OPPORTUNITIES

One of the elements that can help sustain a politics of multiple and complementary identities in a polity with some multi-national dimensions are material interests, especially polity-wide career opportunities. In 1965 and 1970 in Tamil-speaking India, there were two protest movements. Both in essence were struggles to maintain India-wide career opportunities. In one case there was

[48]   Ibid., pp. 102–15.

[49]   For the growing integration of Tamil politics into Indian federal politics, see the dissertation by a leading specialist on Indian federalism, Balveer Arora, *Specificite Ethnique, Conscience Regionale et Developpment National: Langues et Federalism en Inde*, (Thèse pour le Doctorat de Recherches, Fondation Nationale des Sciences Politiques, Paris, 1972), esp. pp. 193–406. Also see Subramanian, *Ethnicity and Populist Mobilization*, pp. 160–72.

a struggle against language policies that were threatening to be imposed by the centre, while in the other case, the struggle was against excessive cultural nationalist policies of the regional government. In both cases, some of the same activists participated.

What was at stake in the first protest movement was that 26 January 1965 was the fifteenth anniversary of the Constitution of India. The 1950 Constitution stipulated that 'it was the duty of the Union to promote the spread of the Hindi language, to develop it so that it may serve as a medium of expression for all elements of the composite culture of India.'[50] Moreover, English was accepted as a 'link language' of the federation for fifteen years, a period that lapsed in 1965. There were widespread demands in the northern Hindi heartland to make Hindi the official language of the Union. In the south, particularly among Tamil elites, there were intense fears that English would become marginalized and that Hindi would become the only acceptable language for entrance examinations to the coveted and powerful Indian Administrative Service (IAS), and for exclusive use in India's courts. A long-time observer of south-Indian politics, who was based in Madras in 1965, nicely captured middle-class fears about career prospects in this period.

Students, lawyers, and businessmen, indeed the Madras middle class generally, see their interests as tied to the continuance of English as the medium for the Union Public Service Commission's competitive examinations. Northerners and Southerners start from the same point in English; the introduction of Hindi would impose a serious hardship on those for whom it is not their mother tongue.[51]

Faced with the threat of losing these career opportunities, students, supported by lawyers and many other groups, waged—for much

50   Constitution of India, Article 351.
51   Duncan B. Forrester, 'The Madras Anti-Hindi Agitation, 1965: Political Protest and its Effect on Language Policy in India', *Pacific Affairs*, Spring-Summer 1966, pp. 19–36, quote from p. 23. Forrester, on the same page, gives a telling detail. From 1948–62, Madras state won 23.3 per cent of all places allocated in the IAS, more than any other state in the Union. If English had been eliminated as a link language for federal examinations this figure would have been radically reduced, as it was for Tamils in Sri Lanka when English was marginalized.

of January and February 1965—the biggest protests in Madras since the anti-British 'Quit India' protests of the 1940s. These protests rapidly became riots and government police and army troops opened fire in twenty-one towns in the state, arrested over 10,000 people, and probably killed over 100 people.[52] The two Tamil-speaking ministers of the central government (for Agriculture and Petroleum) submitted their resignations.

To stop this growing crisis of multi-national India, on 11 February 1965, prime minister Lal Bahadur Shastri announced a crucial decision on an India-wide broadcast:

For an indefinite period...I would have English an associate language...because I do not wish the people of the non-Hindi areas to feel that certain doors of advancement are closed to them... I would have [English] as an alternative language as long as people require it, and the decision [to maintain or revoke English as a link language] I would leave not to the Hindi-knowing people, but to the non-Hindi knowing people.[53]

More than forty years later Shastri's decision remains the *de facto* policy of the federal government. Both the protests, and the centre's reaction, contributed to the maintenance of polity-wide careers that help under-gird multiple and complementary identities in Tamil Nadu.

What if Hindi had been imposed as the only official language of the Indian federation in 1965? I asked C. Subramanian, one of the Tamil-speaking Union Ministers, who had submitted his resignation, this question. Subramanian responded that the President of India virtually refused to accept his resignation from

[52]   For much of these two months the leading newspaper in Madras, *Hindu* carried two or three articles a day on these increasingly bloody and dramatic events such as the self-immolation of a headmaster and others in defence of the Tamil language and also in defence of the use of English, not only Hindi, for careers in the federal government.

[53]   Cited in Barnett, *Politics of Cultural Nationalism in South India*, p. 134. For the 1965 protests see pp. 131–5 in Barnett, Richard L. Hardgrave, Jr., 'The Riots in Tamilnad: Problems and Prospects of India's Language Crisis', *Asia Survey*, vol. 5, August 1965, pp. 399–407 and the previously cited article by Forrester.

prime minister Shastri and asked Shastri, 'Do you want to lose Tamil Nadu from India? If not, kindly take back your recommendation.'[54] Subramanian went on to speculate that if Hindi had been imposed, and English eliminated as a link language, the protest movements would have been more virulent, and the once moribund secessionist movement would have suddenly become greatly reinvigorated and possibly have won.[55] It is impossible to say if Subramanian's speculations would have been borne out. However the DMK, which as we have seen had become 'cultural nationalist'— instead of 'territorial nationalist'—might have come under increasing pressure to reintroduce a territorial nationalist discourse so as not to lose control over Tamil-nationalism. Significantly, Barnett says that during the anti-Hindi mobilizations, the DMK, for the first time in many years, lost control over the leadership of the most important Tamil and Dravidian protest movements and could not keep them within constitutional limits.[56] At the very least it would appear that the combination of Hindi imposition, and the removal of English as a link language for civil service examinations, would have been a disincentive, as in Sri Lanka, to the polity-wide careers, and multiple and complementary identities, that are so useful in maintaining peaceful and democratic federalism in multi-national settings.

In 1967, the DMK political party won the provincial elections, and became the first cultural nationalist party to assume control of an Indian state. The question of career opportunities once again assumed great importance, but in this case students put pressure on the DMK chief minister, C.N. Annadurai, not to close off their career paths in the Indian polity and market. Here the desire of a political party's followers to maintain their access to polity-wide careers throughout the federation helped transform a potential exclusionary nationalist 'regional party' into 'centric-regional' party that allowed dual identities.

Barnett's book, *The Politics of Cultural Nationalism in South India*, shows how political struggle can be waged in the name of keeping open the possibility of multiple and complementary identities.

[54] Interview with C. Subramanian, Chennai (Madras), 1 April 1998.

[55] Ibid.

[56] Barnett, *Politics of Cultural Nationalism in South India*, pp. 132–5.

Barnett argues that Annadurai's problems resulted from his proposed policy of progressively making Tamil the dominant, possibly the exclusive, medium of instruction in government colleges. 'However, many students protested, demanding a free choice of medium of instruction. This caused colleges to close in late 1970 and early 1971. Many students were interested in high quality English medium instruction, believing it would improve their employment opportunities. They did not see this as a Tamil nationalist issue, and resented the DMK's efforts to define it as such.'[57]

With elections on the horizon, and fearing damaging demonstrations, the Tamil Nadu chief minister hastily set up a panel to respond to students' demands. A month and a half before the elections, the chief minister defused the potential crisis by accepting the panel's recommendation that 'the opportunity to choose the medium of instruction should be available to students.'[58]

'CENTRIC-REGIONAL' AND 'POLITY-WIDE' PARTIES: AN ANALYSIS OF COALITIONAL INCENTIVES

Prime minister Jawaharlal Nehru died in 1964 and closely fought elections became increasingly important after 1967. Indeed, in 1967, the Congress party lost power in what is now Tamil Nadu, and has never again formed the government by itself in that state. However, in the vast majority of states, India's combination of numerous political parties, and a FPTP, single-member-constituency, electoral system means that, since 1967, a single party running alone often loses to a candidate supported by a multiparty alliance, and a single party by itself normally does not get a majority in the provincial legislature which would allow it to form a single-party government.

As long as the above conditions exist in a parliamentary context, and as long as state and federal elections are held, and

---

[57] Barnett, *Politics of Cultural Nationalism in South India*, p. 291. For the tone of this conflict, which was shorter and less intense than that of 1965, but nonetheless important for policy outcomes, see two page 1 articles in *Hindu*, 1 January 1971.

[58] Ibid., p. 291.

offices and appointments flow from electoral results, there will be *strong incentives to form multiparty electoral coalitions.*[59]

Surprisingly, this proposition holds even for coalitions that combine polity-wide parties and parties that would seem to be potentially separatist regional parties. But, and this is the crucial point, the mutual electoral benefit of coalitions can only be obtained if both the potentially separatist regional parties and the polity-wide parties adjust their behaviour (and votes) to make the alliance possible.

The incentive system of this type of electoral bargaining is the following. A polity-wide party would be severely constrained against entering into an electoral alliance with a territorial nationalist party, which articulates, or is widely believed to harbour, secessionist ambitions, because it would be attacked throughout the rest of India by polity-wide parties for contributing to the 'disintegration' of India. For its part, a regional-cultural nationalist party would be severely constrained against entering into an alliance with any polity-wide party that voted in the federal legislature for the imposition of assimilationist policies, because it would fear losing votes to other cultural, or even territorial, nationalist parties.

Tamil Nadu in 1971 illustrates the complex electoral and policy trade-offs that can make an apparently cultural nationalist 'regional' party, in effect, 'centric-regional', and a 'polity-wide' party, in effect, supportive of regional cultural nationalism. Let me explore this complicated, but absolutely crucial, aspect of Indian federalism.

By the late 1960s, the Congress party had split into a Congress (R) faction, led by Indira Gandhi, and a Congress (O) faction. The Tamil cultural nationalist parties had also divided into the

[59]   See the article on political parties by E. Sridharan 'The Fragmentation of the Indian Party System, 1952–1999: Seven Competing Explanations', in Zoya Hasan, ed., *Parties and Politics in India*, Oxford and Delhi: Oxford University Press, 2002. Also see Balveer Arora, 'Negotiating Differences: Federal Coalitions and National Cohesion', in Francine R. Frankel, Zoya Hasan, Rajeev Bhargava, and Balveer Arora, eds, *Transforming India: Social and Political Dynamics of Democracy*, Oxford and Delhi: Oxford University Press, 2000, pp. 176–206.

DMK and another group that later became the ADMK in 1972 (and later the AIADMK). Congress (R) was primarily interested in how it did in the federal Lok Sabha elections, and the DMK was primarily interested in how it did in the Tamil Nadu state assembly elections. Both the Congress (R) and the DMK felt they would be greatly helped in forming a strong government in their respective spheres of greatest interest if they could work out an electoral alliance. In the end Congress (R) agreed in 1971 not to compete against DMK in state assembly races but to form a DMK-led coalition. Even though the DMK-Congress (R) coalition only won 53 per cent of the votes, they won an overwhelming 78 per cent of the seats to the state assembly. The alliance thus meant that the DMK won strong control over the political arena—the provincial legislative assembly—most vital to *its* goals.

In return, the DMK agreed to help the Congress (R) by not running against them (and urging their followers to support them) in selected federal seat constituencies where Congress (R) could, with DMK support, win more federal seats, and also by supporting Congress with DMK votes in the Lok Sabha. Due to this agreement of non-competition and mutual support, the Congress (R)-DMK alliance won a total of thirty-five out of thirty-nine Lok Sabha seats, the DMK won twenty-five seats, and Congress (R) won the ten constituencies where the DMK agreed not to run a candidate. Furthermore, in the federal lower chamber, the DMK lent its twenty-five votes to Congress (R) on all key issues such as bank nationalization and budgets as long as it did not hurt its power base back home in Tamil Nadu. Thus, this alliance meant that the Congress (R) was significantly strengthened in *its* most important arena—the lower house of the federal centre, the Lok Sabha.[60]

Barnett succinctly captures the reinforcing incentives by which the leading cultural nationalist party in Tamil Nadu—indeed then in all of India—became what I would call a 'centric-regional' party deeply integrated into the federal political system.

[60]   The 1971 election was not an exception but a precedent. Since 1977 the DMK has had to compete with a spin-off party, the AIADMK. In a large majority of these elections since 1977, one or both of these once Dravidian parties have been in alliances with non-Dravidian, polity-wide parties.

Although the DMK alliance with Indira Gandhi's Congress (R) seems paradoxical, given previous DMK separatist tendencies, it is in fact consistent with DMK priorities and cultural nationalist orientation. In analysing DMK political activities and policies on the national level, it is essential to remember that the primary party priority was consolidation of their state-level base.

After the November 1969 Congress party split, a unique opportunity was created for the DMK to enhance its national image, improve relations with the centre, and most importantly, consolidate its state support base by linking itself to the left-leaning economic and social policies of Indira Gandhi.[61]

Since 1971 the DMK has been solidly 'centric-regional'. Given the coalitional incentive system I have just described, even the DMK's major cultural nationalist competitor, the AIADMK, routinely enters alliances with polity-wide parties, so it too, is subject to the same 'centric-regional' incentive system.

TAMIL NADU: 1968–2005: CULTURAL ASSIMILATION, NO, POLITICAL AND CAREER INTEGRATION, YES

By 1968, Tamil-speaking India controlled a major political entity of India named after the Tamils (Tamil Nadu) and administered that state in Tamil. There has never been any cultural nationalist assimilation into Hindi-speaking India in Ernest Gellner's, or John Stuart Mills', terms. As we have seen there is a strong intellectual and political body of opinion that is worried that such 'cultural conquests' will go down the slippery slope towards 'territorial nationalism', and eventual violent demands for separatism and independence.

In the Tamil Nadu case however, we have seen that many cultural nationalists, such as students and lawyers, who sparked off the 1965 anti-Hindi movement also had material interests in maintaining access to All India-wide political, administrative, and legal careers.[62] Tamil businessmen also had interests in continued access to the Indian common market. However, if their

---

[61] Barnett, *The Politics of Cultural Nationalism*, ibid., pp. 292–3.

[62] Thus, Narendra Subramanian, writing about Tamil Nadu, correctly asserts that 'the material interests of many core DMK supporters were not directly linked to secessionism'. See his *Ethnicity and Populist Mobilization*, p. 313.

cultural nationalist demands regarding a separate political state with its own language had been thwarted, if English had been eliminated as a link language for the Indian federation, and Hindi imposed as the sole official language of the federation as a whole, cultural nationalism might easily have begun to merge into territorial nationalism, as it did in Sri Lanka. Even as late as 1965, if the centre had insisted on Hindi-only cultural assimilation, no provincial government would have supported it, because in the words of the Madras-based observer, Forrester, 'No Madras government could in present circumstances make the study of Hindi in schools compulsory and survive.'[63] But, once the centre renounced the goal of Hindi dominance in the federation, once English was *de facto* accepted as a permanent link language, and once the Tamil language was made secure as the language of regional power, virtually no key Tamil leaders ever again spent major resources on the goal of achieving independence and a separate independent country. In fact, in terms of the definitions advanced earlier, Tamil India remained deeply multicultural, but was no longer 'politically robustly multinational.'

Barnett administered a poll in Tamil Nadu to DMK and Congress party activists in 1968. Of the 459 local DMK party leaders who were asked the question: 'What do you consider the most important problem in your district?', only 2 per cent mentioned issues of language as the first problem, and none mentioned independence. Of the thirty-eight members of the DMK general council who were asked about their reasons for being active in the DMK movement, none mentioned Tamil Nadu separatism as the first reason, but 7.8 per cent did mention Tamil language and culture, and 10.5 per cent mentioned the two-language policy.[64]

In this context, worries about cultural nationalism, or threats to integration, were not salient even for the 120 state-level Congress party leaders interviewed in Tamil Nadu. Indeed, in 1968 only 2.5 per cent listed as their first worry 'threats to national integration'.[65] The responses to these questions, by both DMK and Congress party activists, are further support for my overall

[63] Forrester, 'The Madras Anti-Hindi Agitation, 1965', p. 34.

[64] Barnett, *The Politics of Cultural Nationalism in South India*, pp. 203–5.

[65] Ibid.

argument that a potential issue of separatism in Tamil Nadu, had by the early 1970s, become a non-issue in India's 'state nation'.[66]

In 2004–5, this was more so than ever. The DMK was a classic 'centric-regional' party. The DMK and two Dravidian allies— helped by their alliance with Congress—not only controlled the Tamil Nadu Assembly but, in terms of seats, they were the third largest party in the Congress-led ruling coalition at the centre. For this, they were rewarded with the federal cabinet portfolio of the Ministry of Finance, and five of the other twenty-seven cabinet posts.

Public opinion in Tamil Nadu, far from sliding down any slippery slope to separatism, was *above* the Indian average on three of the key indicators that help a multi-national polity to be a well functioning democratic 'state nation': 'a great deal of trust in the central government' (54 per cent to 27 per cent), 'satisfaction with the way democracy works in India' (69 per cent to 56 per cent), and 'very proud of being Indian' (68 per cent to 63 per cent).[67]

[66] For a discussion of how the DMK abandoned 'secession, and exclusionary emphases on Tamil and non-Brahmin identities' from the 1970s to the present, see Narendra Subramanian, 'Beyond Ethnicity and Populism? Changes and Continuities in Tamil Nadu's Electoral Map', in Paul Wallace and Ramashray Roy, eds, *India's 1999 Elections and 20th Century Politics*, New Delhi and London: Sage Publications, 2003, pp. 50–93, quote from p. 57. Indeed, by 1989, a major Dravidian party, AIADMK, was led by a Brahman, J. Jayalalitha, who became chief minister. Furthermore, since the late 1990s, there have been tactical alliances between major Dravidian parties and the BJP. For a lamentation of these trends see V. Geetha and S.V. Rajadurai, 'Dravidian Politics: End of an Era', *Economic and Political Weekly*, 29 June 1991, pp. 1591–2.

[67] *State of Democracy in South Asia: Survey Component*, 2005, Lokniti, Coordinator Yogendra Yadav.

8

Decentralization
Explorations of Local Government in India and the United States

Peter Ronald deSouza*

In recent years, decentralization has grown, quietly and steadily, as an instrument of governance across the world, providing innovative solutions to the bottlenecks that national and state governments face in their attempts to meet the rising expectations and impatience of their citizens. While globalization has weakened the capacities of national governments to meet citizen needs, and to satisfy the plurality of demands being made on the state, decentralization has emerged as a possible response to these pressures from below since it promises to bring citizens and communities more actively into the governance process. The global landscape of decentralization is beginning to be dotted

* I wish to thank K. Shankar Bajpai, E. Sridharan, Alfred Stepan, Neera Chandhoke, Nathan Glazer, Arend Lijphart, Moolchand Sharma, Juan J. Linz, Niraja Gopal Jayal, and Kuldeep Mathur, for giving me the benefit of their comments several times during the making of this paper. The perspective on local government in India and the US that I have presented here has benefited immensely from their interrogations. I also wish to place on record my gratitude to Alan Altshuler, Director, Alfred Taubman Centre, Kennedy School of Government, Harvard University for inviting me to be a visiting scholar at the Centre during this study. Although I have gained from the conversations I have had with several scholars, I alone, however, am responsible for the arguments in this chapter.

with bold and imaginative experiments in designing local government institutions, in planning local delivery of services in a merciless and competitive market for public goods, in initiating local civic actions to energize communities, in creating legal instruments that are seen as protection against possible abuses of political power,[1] and more recently in producing new perspectives on localism.

From the Porto Alegre experiment in people's budgeting in Brazil,[2] to the People's Campaign for Decentralized Planning in Kerala,[3] to the Enterprise Zones, Tax Increment Finance Districts, and Business Improvement Districts (BIDs) in the US,[4] to the recognition of multiple levels of citizenship in Austria,[5] to the growing importance of sub-national governments in post-apartheid South Africa,[6] the institutions and processes that comprise the decentralization initiative worldwide are producing a portfolio of new experiments in governance that have significant implications for the discourse on decentralization. It has begun to engage with a variety of new intellectual streams ranging from the post-modern debate on the decentred city,[7] to rational choice

[1] For example, California's proposition 13 which gave the impetus for instruments such as the popular referendum.

[2] 'Participation, Activism, and Politics: The Porto Alegre Experiment and Deliberative Democratic Theory', in Archong Fung *et al.*, *Deepening Democracy: Institutional Innovations in Empowered Participatory Governance*, The Utopias Project, vol. VI, London: Verso Press, 2001.

[3] Thomas Issac and Richard Falk, *Local Democracy and Development: People's Campaign For Decentralized Planning in Kerala*, New Delhi: Leftword, 2000.

[4] Richard Briffault, 'The Rise of Sub-local Structures in Urban Governance', 82, *Minnesota Law Review* 504, December 1997.

[5] Rainer Baubock, 'Reinventing Urban Citizenship', IWE, Working Paper Series, no. 18, June 2001.

[6] Steven Friedman and Caroline Kihoto, 'Decentralization, Civil Society and Democratic Governance.' South Africa background paper, (Johannesburg). Centre For Policy Studies.

[7] Gerald Frug, 'Decentering Decentralization,'60, *University of Chicago Law Review*, Spring 1993.

debates on the calculus exhibited by the citizen as consumer,[8] to the civic republicanism debates on empowered communities,[9] to feminist debates on a situated and contextualized subjectivity,[10] to new public management debates on reforming state bureaucracies, and of building partnerships of local government with the private sector.[11] Decentralization has, in recent years, moved out of the shadows and into the contested terrain of social theory.

This extensive global literature that is growing on decentralization can be seen to participate in at least five major discourses. The first discourse is on democracy where issues of citizen participation, representation of excluded groups, federalism as a structure of power, civic republicanism, and plurality of interests, etc., are considered. The second discourse is about development and the concomitant failure of existing state initiatives to meet the basic needs of its citizens. Here policy issues such as those relating to programmes of poverty alleviation, bottom-up planning, effective targeting of beneficiaries, asset creation for the poor, stakeholder commitment, etc., are of concern. The third discourse is on justice and equity where the nature of the societal structures that distribute resources between state and locality, and also within localities, is at issue. This third discourse on justice and equity also engages with issues of segregation and discrimination between groups, of gender justice, and of equity between localities. The fourth discourse is on new public management where market-friendly strategies are examined for the delivery of public services. Here the concern is with reinventing the state, downsizing its

---

[8]   Pranab Bardhan and Dilip Mookerjee, 'Capture and Governance at Local and National Levels', *AEA Papers and Proceedings*, May 2000, pp. 135–9.

[9]   Joshua Cohen and Joel Rogers, 'Secondary Associations and Democratic Governance', in *Associations and Democracy*, Erik Olin Wright, ed., The Real Utopias Project, vol. I, London: Verso Press, 1995.

[10] Seyla Benhabib, *Situating the Self: Gender, Community and Post-Modernism in Contemporary Ethics*, New York: Routledge, 1992.

[11] Alan Altshuler and Robert D. Behn, eds, *Innovation in American Government: Challenges, Opportunities and Dilemmas*, Washington: Brookings, 1997.

bureaucracies, privatizing its activities, and generally reducing its functions to a minimal regulatory role. The fifth discourse in which the new thinking on decentralization participates is of legal theory where constituting the subject of law, the local government unit, in terms of boundaries, jurisdictions, power and authority, rights, etc., is of concern. The decentralization debate has hence become very exciting since it now has to make sense of a multiplicity of experiments taking place all over the world.

Two of the most interesting are the decentralization experiences of India and the US.

This study will attempt a comparison of these two experiences. While they are connected in and through theory, the two have dissimilar histories. Further, because they are located in different societies that bring a diverse bundle of resources—cultural, social, economic, technological, management, political—to bear on them, the decentralization experiment resonates differently in each of them. The drivers of decentralization too are dissimilar and therefore the dynamics they produce are also dissimilar. Yet they have many concerns that are common. In this study I shall attempt to reflect on what is common and what is different. The chapter has three parts. Part I will attempt a conceptual clarification of the terms 'decentralized administration' and 'decentralized democracy'. It will also explore some of the normative issues that underlie these discussions. Part II will, in summary form, present the main features of the Indian and American terrain of decentralization. And Part III will draw, with broad brush strokes, some comparisons between the two experiences of decentralization.

I

The idea of decentralization has undergone a subtle but significant shift in the intellectual landscape of the last four decades. In an earlier period, what I like to call the neo-classical period of democratic debate, the language of decentralized democracy was a language of critique. It represented a political challenge to liberal democracy as representative democracy. It suggested a holistic alternative based upon the idea of redesigning the institutions of democracy so that there was more (tending to maximum) not less participation of ordinary citizens.[12] This alternative was the radical model of democracy.[13] Today, in contrast, discussions on decentralized democracy present decentralization as an extension of, not as an alternative to, representative democracy.[14] Whereas earlier the ethical principles of a decentralized democracy could not be accommodated by, and within, liberal democracy, because the latter was seen as based on domination[15] and manipulation,[16] today its ethical principles are regarded not as antagonistic but as complementary to liberal democracy.[17] It was this holistic way of looking at the world that was the basis of Gandhi's alternative vision of the 'oceanic circle', and of Fromm's dream of re-establishing 'the Town meeting'.[18] They, and others who argued in similar vein, saw

[12] See the works of Fromm, Marcuse, Schumacher, Gandhi.

[13] D. Held. *Models of Democracy*, Cambridge: Polity Press, 1987; C.Pateman, *Participation and Democratic Theory*, Cambridge: Cambridge University Press, 1970; C.B. Macpherson, *The Life and Times of Liberal Democracy*, Oxford: Oxford University Press,1977.

[14] Richard.C. Crook and James Manor, *Democracy and Decentralization in South Asia and West Africa*, Cambridge: Cambridge University Press, 1988; Abdul Aziz and David D. Arnold, eds, *Decentralized Governance in Asian Countries*, Sage, New Delhi, 1996.

[15] H. Marcuse: *One Dimensional Man*, London: Routledge and Kegan Paul, 1964. This was the view of the early Frankfurt School.

[16] 'Party rivalries ... give birth to demagoguery, depress political ethics, put a premium on unscrupulousness and aptitude for manipulation and intrigue. Parties create dissensions where unity is called for, exaggerate differences where they should be minimized. Parties often put party interests over the national interests. Because centralization of power prevents the citizen from participating in government, the parties, that is to say, small caucuses of politicians rule in the name of the people and create the illusion of democracy and self-government.' J.P.Narayan, 'A Plea for the Reconstruction of the Indian Polity', in Bimal Prasad, ed., *A Revolutionary Quest: Selected Writings of Jayaprakash Narayan*, New Delhi: Oxford University Press, 1959, p. 226.

[17] Peter R. deSouza, *Leadership, Participation and Democratic Theory*, unpublished D. Phil dissertation, University of Sussex, December 1986.

[18] 'Unless planning from the top is blended with active participation from below, unless the stream of social life continuously flows

decentralized democracy as a privileging of the local over the distant, of bringing people back into the affairs of the state, of removing the impediments to the emergence of the good society. Weber's realism on the impracticability of direct democracy had no place in this critique.[19]

Today, however, the discussion on decentralized democracy has shifted from seeking a holistic alternative to liberal democracy to merely searching for a segmental solution to some of the problems of politics and public administration that emerge within it. The focus here is on filling in the unoccupied democratic spaces of liberal democracy, on designing initiatives and searching for innovations that improve the quality of governance within it. This shift which has occurred is quite fundamental in that the broad normative vantage point from which the framework of democratic politics was constructed, of the 'good society', has given way to a narrower vantage point, of 'good governance'. This latter position is concerned with the functioning of government with respect to aspects such as accountability, autonomy, responsiveness, delivery efficiencies, transparency, accessibility, simplicity, etc. The justification for the practices of politics now comes from the goals of 'good governance' and not from those of the 'good society'. Gandhi's 'village swaraj' and Fromm's 'sane society' are not

---

from below upwards, a planned economy will lead to renewed manipulation of the people.' E.Fromm, *The Fear of Freedom*, London: Routledge and Kegan Paul, 1955, p. 237. This he believed was not an insoluble difficulty, and could be overcome by organizing 'the whole population into small groups of say five hundred people, according to local residence, or place of work, and as far as possible these groups should have a certain diversification in their social composition.' E.Fromm, *The Sane Society*, New York: Fawcett Premier, 1955. p. 297.

[19]   The necessary conditions for direct democracy for Weber are '(1) it must be local or otherwise limited in the number of members; (2) the social positions of the members must not greatly differ from each other; (3) the administrative functions must be relatively simple and stable; and (4) however, there must be a certain minimum of development of training in objectively determining ways and means.' Max Weber, *Economy and Society*, 2 vols, Guenther Roth and Claus Wittich, eds, Berkeley: University Of California Press, 1978, p. 949.

reference points any more. I have referred to this shift here merely to fix the contemporary debate on decentralization within the 'good governance' camp. For the purposes of this chapter I will, therefore, accept this narrower normative grounding.

Let me now attempt a second clarification. The contemporary debate on decentralization needs to distinguish between decentralized administration and decentralized democracy. Making this distinction is necessary because the two are often conflated in the literature and because what makes them different is the conception of politics contained within them. Decentralized administration is primarily a 'managerial idea', which holds that one can increase the efficiency of service delivery by adopting a strategy of administrative decentralization. The preoccupation here is with looking at managerial strategies, with designing an administrative structure where some degree of decision-making is shifted from the higher levels, the apex of the pyramid, to the lower levels, the base.[20] This shift is accompanied by a commensurate change in the mechanisms of managerial control. The concern in decentralized administration is with management solutions for improving service delivery.[21] In this model the decision-makers are the administrative personnel. All that has happened is that those at the lower levels have now greater powers and wider jurisdictions within which to function. There are now more issues on which they can make authoritative decisions. Within the idea of administrative decentralization the citizens exist only as beneficiaries of an administrative structure that is 'arguably' more efficient and effective than one that is more centralized. Citizens here are primarily consumers of services responding to decisions with their cheque books and their feet. Not with their arguments and voices.

[20] The term 'deconcentration' is sometimes used to refer to this exercise of dispersal. The point to be noted with respect to deconcentration, however, is that the lower level offices, that now have wider jurisdiction and powers, continue to be accountable to the central authority.

[21] The details of the various management options are elaborately laid out in a study of the America experiment in local government by Richard Briffault in 'Our Localism: The Structure of Local Government Law', 90, *Columbia Law Review*, 1 January 1990.

Decentralized democracy,[22] in contrast, is a political idea that seeks to promote two distinct and independent objectives of equal value: (1) citizen participation in decision-making, where such participation involves deliberation and the consideration of reasons,[23] and (2) effective service delivery. While the thinking on decentralized democracy is concerned with an instrumental calculus that is, it concedes the importance of redesigning the structure of administration to provide efficient and effective service, this calculus can sometimes be trumped by the other equally important value of citizen participation. In other words, one may be willing to settle for a lower level of administrative efficiency if one can, through this compromise, achieve a higher level of citizen participation in decision-making. Within this idea of decentralized democracy citizen participation is both an intrinsic goal, that is, participation is valuable because it is integral to the quality of citizenship, and an instrumental goal, that is, participation is valuable because it produces good outcomes. The innovation in the thinking here is to see citizen participation as promoting effective service delivery. Here itself, citizen participation is part of the instrumental calculus. While the discussions on decentralization in India and the US engage with both decentralized administration and decentralized democracy, it is necessary to make this analytic distinction to recognize the different roles present in the two ideas of the citizen 'as consumer' and 'as participant' in politics.

II

In India the concern with empowering local government institutions is over a century old. The debate went through four major phases.

[22] Here too a conceptual distinction must be made between 'decentralized democracy' and 'democratic decentralization'. The former is concerned with democratic practices that exist at the base whereas the latter is concerned with democratic practices that promote the base. The first concerns the *location* and the second the *direction* of democratic activity. See Peter, R. deSouza 'Democratic Decentralization of Power in India,' in D.D. Khanna and G.W. Kueck, eds, *Principles, Power and Politics*, New Delhi: Macmillan, 1999.

[23] Seyla Benhabib, ed., *Democracy and Difference: Contesting the Borders of the Political*, Princeton, New Jersey: Princeton University Press, 1996.

The first phase goes back to the colonial period beginning with Lord Ripon's Resolution of 18 May 1882, which advocated decentralization to promote the goals of 'administrative efficiency', 'political education', and 'human development'. Paragraphs 5 and 6 of the Resolution, in fact, state these goals quite ambiguously: 'It is not primarily with a view to improvement in administration that this measure is put forward and supported. It is chiefly designed as an instrument of political and popular education' ... And '... as education advances there is rapidly growing up all over the country an intelligent class of public spirited men who it is not only bad policy but sheer waste of power to fail to utilize.'[24] The second phase is the debates in the Constitutent Assembly where a Constitution, based on the Gandhian vision of village *swaraj*, was proposed. This was vehemently opposed by Ambedkar the chairman of the drafting committee who wanted a more conventional Constitution.[25] What was at stake were two visions of an independent India, one centred on the village as the basic unit of politics (the Gandhian vision) and the other based on the individual as a rights bearer (the Nehru-Ambedkar vision), and two readings on the scope of the locality with Gandhi seeing it in romantic terms as an idyllic village community in contrast to Ambedkar who saw it as a site of oppression and discrimination. The compromise that was finally reached placed the article on panchayats in the chapter on Directive Principles in the Constitution.[26] The third phase was the post-

---

[24] H. Tinker, *The Foundations of Local Self-Government in India, Pakistan and Burma*, Bombay: Lalvani Publishing House, 1967, p. 44–5.

[25] 'It is said that the new Constitution should have been drafted on the ancient Hindu model of a state and that instead of incorporating Western theories the new Constitution should have been built upon village panchayats and District panchayats. ... They just want India to contain so many village governments. The love of the intellectual Indian for the village community is of course infinite if not pathetic... I hold that the village republic have been the ruination of India. I am therefore surprised that those who condemn provincialism and Communalism should come forward as champions of the village.' *Constituent Assembly Debates*, 4 November 1948, p. 38–9.

[26] Amendment 31-A, which became Article 40 of the Constitution, directs: 'That the state shall take steps to organize village panchayats

Independence period where several committees, such as the Balwantrai Mehta Committee (1957), K. Santhanam Committee (1963), Asoka Mehta Committee (1978), M.L. Dantwala Group of the Planning Commission (1978), G.V.K. Rao Committee (1985), and the L.M. Singhvi Committee (1986), sought to identify policy instruments and administrative structures that would make decentralization more effective.

The fourth and final phase is the period around the passing of the constitutional 73 and 74 Amendments[27] and the decade after. The 73rd Amendment concerns local government institutions in rural India whereas the 74th Amendment concerns local government in urban India. These two amendments seek to create a third tier of local government in both rural and urban India.[28] A district planning committee is envisaged that will integrate the development plans of the rural and urban tiers into an integrated plan for the district. The enactment of these two amendments and the political dynamics that they have set into motion constitutes what I call the 'second wind' of Indian democracy since it seeks to address, initially through a constitutional amendment, five major problems that were faced by earlier attempts at establishing institutions of local self-government. (I shall focus in this chapter on local government in rural India.) These are: (1) irregular elections and supercession of panchayats, (2) insufficient devolution of powers to them, (3) resistance of the bureaucracy to report, and be accountable, to the elected politicians of these panchayati raj institutions (PRIs), (4) domination by rural elites, who have always been able to corner most of the

---

and endow them with such powers and authority as may be necessary to enable them to function as units of self-government.'

27 I will present the features only of the 73rd Amendment since that is the one on which I am currently most familiar.

28 In both the rural and urban domains the third tier is in turn split up into three tiers. Rural local government—PRIs—have the gram panchayat (village council) at the lowest tier, the panchayat samiti, as the intermediate tier, and Zilla Parishad (district council) at the highest tier. Urban local government has nagar panchayats at the lowest tier, muncipal councils at the intermediate level, and city corporations at the highest level.

benefits of the developmental state[29], and (5) the unsatisfactory working of the village assembly, the gram sabha.[30]

The 73rd Amendment, that finally came into force on 24 April 1993, tries to address some of the problems encountered by PRIs in previous years. This it does by (1) granting PRIs constitutional status, (2) empowering socially and economically disadvantaged groups, for example, Dalits, Adivasis, and women, (3) ensuring free, fair, and regular elections, (4) keeping terms fixed, (5) identifying a list of items which would come under the jurisdiction of PRIs,[31] and (6) addressing the issue of PRI finance.[32] These last two items are the most contested. A review of the extent of decentralization across India has shown that while there may be political decentralization, this is not accompanied by commensurate administrative and fiscal decentralization. The fact that there are parallel government bodies to these local government institutions in rural India, such as rural development agencies (RDAs) and MP local area development schemes (MPLADSs) and also that line departments of the state governments continue to exercise jurisdiction, shows that there is still resistance to administrative decentralization. There is even less decentralization on the fiscal front with little untied funds being available from state resources.

There are many interesting aspects[33] to the 73rd amendment but here I shall discuss only three which, I believe, have the

[29] The first *India: Rural Development Report: Regional Disparities in Development and Poverty, 1999*, when reflecting on the overall failure of rural development, since there are still 200 million rural people in poverty in the 1990s, observes that an 'elaborate system of patronage, thriving on the disempowerment of the poor and hapless, distributes largesse to a chosen few at the cost of multitudes and characterizes rural India.' Hyderabad: NIRD, 1999.

[30] S.P. Jain 'The Gram Sabha: Gateway to Grassroots Democracy', *Journal of Rural Development*, vol. 16 (4), pp. 557–73.

[31] In this list, 29 items have been specified the eleventh schedule (article 243G). These range from agriculture to health and sanitation to maintenance of community assets.

[32] Shika Jha, 'Strengthening local government: Rural fiscal decentralization in India', *Economic and Political Weekly*, 29 June 2002, pp. 2611–23.

[33] The main features are as follows: (1) The centrality of the gram sabha, as a deliberative and deciding body, to decentralized governance;

potential to deepen and strengthen democracy in India. The first
is the reservation route to representation that has been adopted
to give vulnerable groups in the village, that is, Dalits, Adivasis,
and women, a voice. Here seats are reserved for these groups in
the gram panchayat (the panchayat executive) and among the

---

(2) A uniform 32-tier PRI structure across the country, with the village,
block, and district as the appropriate levels. States with populations
of less than 20 lakhs have an option not to introduce the intermediate
level; (3) Direct election to all seats for all members at all levels. In
addition, the chairpersons of the village panchayats may be made
members of the panchayats at the intermediate level and
chairpersons of panchayats at the intermediate level may be
members at the district level. MPs, MLAs, and MLCs may also be
members of panchayats at the intermediate and the district levels,
(4) In all the panchayats seats are to be reserved for SCs (henceforth
Dalits) and STs (henceforth Adivasis) in proportion to their
population and one-third of the total seats to be reserved for women.
One third of the seats reserved for SCs and STs will also be reserved
for women; (5) Offices of the chairpersons of the panchayats at all
levels will be reserved in favour of SCs and STs in proportion to their
population in the state. One-third office of chairpersons of panchayats
at all levels will also be reserved for women; (6) The legislature of
the state is at liberty to provide reservation of seats and offices of
chairpersons in panchayats in favour of backward class of citizens;
(7) An average panchayat will have a uniform five-year term and
elections to constitute new bodies will be completed before the
expiry of the term. In the event of dissolution, elections will be
compulsorily held within six months. The reconstituted panchayat
will serve for the remaining period of the five-year term, (8) It will
not be possible to dissolve the existing panchayats by amendment
of any act before the expiry of its duration; (9) A person who is
disqualified under any law for elections to the legislature of the
state or under any law of the state will not be entitled to become a
member of a panchayat; (10) An independent State Election
Commission (SEC) to be established for superintendence, direction,
and control of the electoral process and preparation of electoral
rolls; (11) Devolution of powers and responsibilities by the state in
the preparation and implementation and development plans; (12)
Setting up of a state finance commission once in five-years to revise
the financial position of these PRIs and to make suitable
recommendations to the state on the distribution of funds among
panchayats.

total number of sarpanchas (chief executive of the gram panchayat) in the state. This strategy is intended to empower these groups that have hitherto lived at the margins of the village. Reservation of places in the institutions of power seeks to give them a presence in the political sphere and to make them significant stakeholders in the development of the village.

This reservation route to representation, creates an 'opportunity space' for groups, that have hitherto always been marginalized, to contest the rules of their exclusion from both the symbolic and the material world. This is an uneven contest since the odds are stacked heavily against them. India still remains a very casteist and patriarchal society; asymmetries of power and resources are persistent and cumulative.[34] The hope that these can be undone by the creation of an 'institutional opportunity space' is a little innocent. The biggest challenge that this new institutional opportunity space faces is of it being occupied by 'proxies' of village elites, either proxy women or proxy Dalits. Dominant elites, loathe to concede power to groups that have hitherto had no place in the firmament of power, respond to these attempts to

---

[34]   Al Stepan invited me to mention that India is the only major democracy where elementary education is not compulsory. As a consequence of this in 1995, 35 million children did not go to primary school and of those who went 38 per cent dropped out before grade 5. This has resulted in only 52 per cent of the adult population being literate (male 66 per cent , female 33 per cent). Table 8, 'Education Profile', *Human Development in South Asia: The Crises of Governance*, Oxford: The Mahbub Ul Haq Human Development Centre, 1999, p. 198. This condition stems from a lack of political will as has been argued by A.Vaidyanathan and P.R. Gopinathan Nair, eds, *Elementary Education in Rural India: A Grassroots View*, New Delhi, Sage, 2001. 'Achieving universal primary education within ten years was included as one of the Directive principles of State Policy in the Constitution of the Indian Republic. The rhetoric continues but the goal remains elusive even after fifty years of planning. Governments both at the centre and in the states, irrespective of their ideology, have not pursued this objective seriously and with vigour. Resources allocated to education have been woefully inadequate and, with higher education absorbing a rising proportion of allocations, elementary education has remained on a semi-starvation diet; Introduction', ch. 1, p. 23.

weaken them and give disadvantaged groups a voice by choosing women and Dalits who they can control and who, by being proxies for the rural elites, sustain the rural power structure. In spite of this, the small window that has opened up has become a space for resistance to the old patterns of domination. There are several instances across the country of resistance and defiance as there are also as many instances of violence and retaliation.[35] The struggle to transform the terms of social discourse has begun.[36]

The second innovative feature is the granting of constitutional status to the SEC which is charged with the conduct of panchayat elections. This should considerably reduce the widespread election malpractices that have characterized elections to panchayats in an earlier period.[37] Hence the benefits of accountability and genuine representation which were not

---

[35] The best known case is the Melavalavu case where both resistance and challenge are evident, on the one hand, as is violence and retaliation, on the other. '...what happened at Melavalavu village on 30 June 1997 was the epitome of intolerance by high caste people. On that day just because the Dalits stood for elections to the village panchayat (Melavalavu being a reserved constituency), the high caste people of the village brutally murdered six persons, including the president and vice-president of the panchayat, in broad daylight. They severed the head of the panchayat president and threw it inside a well ... The post of panchayat president in this village was reserved for the Dalits during the recent panchayat elections. The high caste people, unable to face this encroachment on what they traditionally considered their domain, protested against it and threatened the Dalits with reprisal if they contested for the post. They burnt even their houses.' The murders were a result of the Dalits contesting the elections. Mohan Larbeer, 'Atrocities in Melavalavu Panchayat', *Panchayati Raj Update*, July 1997, no. 43, p. 6.

[36] See *Panchayati Raj Update*.

[37] Because of the fearless and firm manner in which the central election commission has been operating, the prestige of the election commission, as an institution, has been growing in recent years and some of this prestige may rub off on the SECs.

available to local government now becomes available.[38] The establishment of an SEC to oversee the election process, when seen together with the reservation of seats will, I expect, produce a representative outcome that should promote the interests of the weaker groups in rural India. Regular elections have radical potentialities, particularly because of power asymmetries in rural India since they could (1) produce challenges to the existing power structure, or (2) expand the composition of the rural elite since new challenges could result in a strategy of cooption of the new challengers into the power structure (a la Pareto), or (3) create as a result, internal contradictions among the power elite between the old and new groups. The presence of the SEC set into motion a new dynamic that needs to be mapped particularly with respect to its impact on the rural power structure. Reports in 2002 from most states on the conduct of elections to local government bodies show a marked improvement over earlier periods. The second round of panchayat elections, after the 73rd amendment, had taken place in that year.

The third innovative feature is the empowering of the gram sabha, the village assembly. As a deliberative space the gram sabha is intended to introduce the idea of self-government to local government. It seeks to create a system of cohabitation between representative and direct democracy.[39] By seeing it as one of the main instruments for promoting rural development, the 73rd amendment recognizes the importance of participatory decision-making at the level of local government. The gram sabha hence becomes an important site for building consensus and the gram panchayat and gram sabha, together, combine the principles of representative and direct democracy. This poses a challenge to theorists of decentralization who have to understand the

---

[38]   In the state of Tamil Nadu before the amendment, elections had not been held for nearly twenty years. The reasons for postponement ranged from drought, floods, cyclones, school examinations, etc. This was not a unique case of infrequent elections to PRIs in the pre-amendment period since PRIs had become patronage bodies for state-level leaders who kept their henchmen in these bodies so that their bidding in the locality could be carried out.

[39]   R.C. Choudhury and S.P. Jain, eds, *Strengthening Village Democracy*, Hyderabad: NIRD, 1999.

dynamics of the encounter between an enabling institution, the gram sabha premised on deliberation, inclusion, and community, and a traditional social structure based on the contrary principles of a segmented society where the absence of dialogue between segments prevails and where these segments, essentially caste and class, are located along a hierarchy of power which determines the rules of social intercourse. In this encounter, the empowering potential of the gram sabha is in contest with the resistance of rural elites who use every strategy available to them to retain their hold on power. Evidence from the states shows that the gram sabha has served to both empower disadvantaged groups—as reported by the Mazdoor Kisan Shakti Sangathan (MKSS), the NGO that is spearheading the freedom of information movement in Rajasthan—and to further the domination of rural elites[40] who are more adept at manipulating the procedures to be followed for the gram sabha as laid out in the conformity acts.[41]

[40]   G.K. Lieten and Ravi Srivastava, *Unequal Partners: Power Relations, Devolution and Development in Uttar Pradesh*, IDPAD 23, New Delhi: Sage, 1999.

[41]   The record of the gram sabha meetings, from various studies so far, has not been very encouraging. In a study of 195 gram sabha meetings in six states of Gujarat, Haryana, Himachal Pradesh, Kerala, Madhya Pradesh, and Uttar Pradesh, PRIA and its Network of Collaborating Regional Support Organizations (NCRSO) (organizations that have been studying PRIs) have found that 'in the vast majority of these Gram Sabha meetings, the *minimum required quorum as prescribed by each state was rarely fulfilled*. However, in nearly one-third of the cases under study, *records of the Gram Sabha meetings were completed even when the meetings were either not held or quorum were not completed*. (Emphasis mine.) This experience is endorsed by other observers. Some of the experiences can be listed.

- Sarpanchas convened these meetings under pressure from higher levels of administration, such as the panchayat samiti or zilla parishad.
- Meetings mostly called without prior or adequate notice.
- Very few panchayats convened the minimum prescribed number of meetings.
- Thin attendance.

The above is merely an outline of the uniform all-India structure of local self-government that has emerged from the 73rd Amendment. On this structure is superimposed the variations that each state has introduced through its conformity legislation and government orders (that is, delegated legislation). It is at these second and third levels of law that the subversion of the decentralization intended by the 73rd Amendment takes place. It is here where rules are introduced—the 'should' and 'may' clauses, that have the effect of retaining power in the hands of the higher tiers of government.[42] The innovation that the 73rd Amendment has brought about is to introduce a new dialectical relationship between institution and process in the exercise of building democracy in India. As mentioned earlier, various interesting experiments are underway in the different states of the union depending on their own locus of power. While West

---

- The participation of women was nominal and conspicuously absent in places where purdah is observed. Hence, gram sabha meetings were not representative of all sections of rural society.
- Appropriate rules for conduct of meetings not framed.
- No agenda was generally prepared in advance.
- Gram sabha never consulted in planning for the villages of the panchayat area.
- Since most people unaware of their role they attended the meetings as silent listeners.
- Proceedings mostly not recorded properly and never reported to the panchayat or panchayat samiti.
- Violence.
- PRIA and NCRSO 1997, 'Local Self-Governance: Myth or Reality of Gram Panchayat and Gram Sabha', paper prepared for the seminar *Strengthening Panchayati Raj Institutions in India*, IIC, 30 August 1997.

[42] Peter R. deSouza 'Decentralization and local government: The "second wind" of democracy in India', in Z. Hasan *et al India's Living Constitution: Ideas, Practices, Controversiess*, New Delhi: Permanent Black, 2002; 'Decentralization and Panchayati Raj in India: Pursuing the Holy Grail of Devolution', in Paul Flather, ed., *Recasting Indian Politics: Essays on a Working Democracy*, forthcoming.

Bengal has adopted the route of land reform in tandem with political reform, and Kerala has experimented with decentralized planning, Madhya Pradesh has opted for a significant devolution of powers to the local level including the wards, and Andhra Pradesh has initiated a parallel structure of decentralized administration, the *Janmbhoomi* programme, what is common to all state experiments on decentralization is the desire to redress the development deficit that plagues independent India, where the extent of rural poverty remains a source of shame and where the demands for the 'goods of development' are growing more strident.

In the last decade there has been a growth of the number of bodies that have sought to address the concerns of rural society. The nature of the relationship between some of them, such as community-based organizations (CBOs), NGOs, self-help groups (SHGs), and PRIs varies from being competitive with each other to cooperating with each other. In addition to these civil society-based initiatives that impact PRI performance, there are also parallel structures of power that distribute resources to rural groups. The most subversive of these, from the viewpoint of PRIs, is the MPLADS where MPs get Rs 2 crore for development schemes in their constituency. The district collector is the authority who processes applications received by the MP in a chain of decision that excludes the PRI network, which remains starved of funds. This MPLADS has recently been seen to function as a source of patronage and corruption.[43]

The decentralization experiment in India can, therefore, be seen to be primarily within the discourse on development with the other discourses of democracy—equity, rights, new public management, etc.,—merely as supportive discourses.[44] This reflects the fact

---

[43]   In Uttar Pradesh, in early 2003, the Mayawati government was charged with asking its MLAs/MPs to siphon off money from these schemes for the party.

[44]   Niraja Gopal Jayal, who was the discussant for this paper when it was presented in a workshop in January 2003, has rightly pointed out that the issue of primary discourse and secondary discourse depends on from whose viewpoint one is making the observation. For example, from the viewpoint of the state, decentralization is primarily a development discourse but from the viewpoint of the Dalit Sarpanch the democracy, equity, and rights discourses may be no less important.

that state thinking and policy-making is driven by development concerns. The decentralization experience in the US, in contrast, spans almost equally all the five discourses of democracy referred to earlier—citizen participation, development, equity and justice, new public management, and law. This is a measure of the self-confidence of the state and civil society in the US with respect to their capacity to deliver public goods.

In the US, discussions on decentralization refer to both the state and the local level of government. As an idea, decentralization belongs to the intellectual and political tradition in the US which is suspicious of power and the possible tyranny contained within it. Its genealogy can be traced to the Declaration of Independence, drafted by Thomas Jefferson, which embodies the belief that a people have a right to revolt when a government is denying them their legitimate rights. The declaration states 'that to secure these rights, Governments are instituted among Men, deriving their just powers from the consent of the governed. That whenever any Form of Government becomes destructive of these ends, it is the Right of the People to alter or to abolish it, and to institute new Government, laying its foundation on such Principles and organizing its Powers on such form, as to them shall seem most likely to effect their Safety and Happiness'.[45] To institutionalize this suspicion the founding persons of the American system devised a structure of government which, as Madison stated in *The Federalist Papers*, is protected against the 'usurpation of power', by a 'division of government into distinct and separate departments'. The federal system was designed to make 'ambition ...counteract ambition'. It is this suspicion of government that has produced the range of experiments that currently mark the landscape of decentralization in the US.

In this chapter I shall limit the discussion on decentralization only to the issues of local government. It is important to note at the outset that the American state does not precede local government but succeeded it.[46]

---

[45]   Kenneth Janda *et al.*, *The Challenge of Democracy: Government in America*, 3rd edn, Boston: Houghton Miffin Company, 1992, p. 71.

[46]   I am grateful to Nathan Glazer for reminding me to mention this historical point at the outset of my discussion on local government in the US.

Local governments in the United States should hence be seen as having evolved over several centuries as a response to local contingencies and developments. They have no common structure since a number of legal routes have served their evolution.

Local government units, unlike state and federal governments, are not products of constitutional design, but of historical developments, originating in English Law. The number and types of local government units continued to grow through successive stages of urbanization to perform ever increasing services and regulation. The modern patchwork of boroughs, towns, cities, counties, and special districts must be understood in the light of their particular uses in each of the states... Though similarly named, the legal incidents and powers of particular classes of local government vary, depending on their enabling charter laws, whether or not they are 'incorporated', and rights gained by custom or prescription.[47]

Local governments are not 'true sovereign governments, but political creatures and subdivisions of sovereign state governments. As such they possess no independent sovereign powers or authority, save those delegated to them by state constitutions and laws'.[48] They can be classified according to structure, that is, municipalities (which would include cities, boroughs, villages, and towns), counties, townships, and special districts, or they can be classified according to functions, that is, in terms of whether they are general function units such as municipalities or special function units such as special districts. The powers they have concern the following: (1) the authority to tax property, which has become one of the main drivers of local government development, (2) to spend on local resources, and (3) to regulate land use through zoning. A significant right they have is to protect local autonomy from absorption into another locality and, finally, the right to come into governmental existence.[49] Many aspects of local

[47]   William D. Valente, *Local Government Law: Cases and Materials*, third edn, American Casebook Series, St Paul, Minn: West Publishing Co., 1987. p. 2.

[48]   Ibid., p. 2.

[49]   Richard Briffault, 'Our Localism: Part 1—The Structure of Local Government Law', 90 *Columbia Law Review*, January 1990, and 'Our Localism: Part II—Localism and Legal Theory', 90 *Columbia Law Review*, March 1990.

government law have developed over this long and diverse history of the evolution of local government. Aspects such as the relationship between cities, and state and local government; relationship among neighbouring cities; relationship between cities and citizens; judicial and legislative control of local government; local police powers; financing of local government; staffing; etc., have emerged as significant issues of local government. In the following pages I shall, however, discuss only four sets of issues which I think define the terrain of local government in the US.

The first set of issues is in the domain of law. Three aspects here are particularly noteworthy. The first two, which are more narrowly legal—the sources of local government authority and the dual legal nature of the city—require an elaboration based on existing case law, whereas the third—a post-modern perspective on the city—is an invitation to reconstitute local government law so that its assumptions are more in keeping with the times, with the social geography of contemporary America where populations are mobile, and citizens have multiple obligations based on their place of residence, work, shopping, transit, and leisure.

With respect to the first aspect, the sources of local government authority, two possible sources are identified—that which comes from the state government, referred to as 'Dillon's Rule', and that which comes from the citizen's themselves, referred to as 'Home Rule'. Dillon's Rule states that:

It is a general and undisputed proposition of law that a municipal corporation possesses and can exercise the following powers, and no others. First, those granted in express words, second those necessarily or fairly implied in or incident to the powers expressly granted, third those essential to the accomplishment of the declared objects and purposes of the corporation... Neither the corporation nor its officers can do any act, or make any contract, or incur any liability, not authorized thereby, or by some legislative act applicable thereto. All acts beyond the scope of the powers granted are void.[50]

This restriction of local government power by Dillon's Rule is sought to be countered by the 'Home Rule Initiative' which seeks to give cities a general grant of authority from the state instead

---

[50]   John Dillon 'Municipal Corporation', in Gerald Frug, *Local Government Law*, pp. 53–4.

of 'requiring them to rely on individualized delegation for particular purposes'. The further aim was to give cities an 'area of autonomy immune from state control'.[51] The legal topography of local government has evolved through an unending negotiation between these two rules. An extensive review of the local government case law has shown that although local governments are creatures, delegates, or agents of the state, and thereby have limited legal independence since they can be overruled and even dissolved by the state, in practice, local governments wield significant power particularly in the fields of zoning, school education, property taxes, and delivery of public services.[52] The analysis of cases at both the state level and the federal level shows that both the political elites and the courts have demonstrated a commitment to allowing local governments to exercise powers fairly autonomously even though theoretically they do not draw these powers from either state or the federal constitutions. The independent exercise of power, in the above mentioned areas, allowed to local governments, stems from both a pragmatic recognition that local governments are more efficient at delivering these goods and also a normative commitment that citizens as communities have a right to govern themselves. How far local communities actually embody the qualities of 'community' from which they draw their legitimacy, particularly in the face of the high mobility of American families, is a moot point, but the romanticism of 'community', nonetheless, provides the normative grounding for political and legal decision-making in the US.[53]

Related to this is the second aspect of law identified earlier which concerns the dual legal nature of the city. When they exercise power, cities do so as public or as private entities, that is, as governments or as corporations. In the former case, they exercise the coercive power of government whereas in the latter case they can be seen as 'collective entities organized to pursue not the interests of the state but the interests of the people who live within them. Although cities are created by state law, they are partly created by city residents seeking to exercise their own

---

[51]   Ibid., p. 70.

[52]   Richard Briffault, 'Our Localism...' see fn 39.

[53]   Richard Briffault, 'Our Localism...' ibid.

power independent of national or state control'.[54] In cases of conflict of authority, on whether a particular municipal activity is 'propriety' or 'governmental', on whether corporate or constitutional law is involved, discretionary law-making by the courts has played a part in providing an answer.

The third aspect of law that I hope to discuss is more radical in its implications than the previous two. It is based on a post-modern construction of the city as an 'ageographical city', the equivalent of the 0-800 telephone number, a number without a place. The modern city in the US, as seen in post modern terms, challenges the basic assumption of local government law, which is that citizens reside and work and shop and draw resources all from one locality. This emphasis on 'residency' in local government law is the basis of the discourse on rights and obligations. However, it neglects the reality of modern America, a reality made possible by new technologies of communication, travel, work, and entertainment. A person may live in one locality, work at another, shop at a third, transit daily through a fourth, and pursue hobbies in a fifth. This multi-locational existence is compounded by a high mobility where, it is argued, an average American relocates residence several times (five) during his/her lifetime.[55] In such a scenario what is the picture of community on which local government law can draw its legitimacy. It is convincingly argued that the citizen thereby has obligations to multiple jurisdictions since she enjoys the services provided by these multiple localities.[56] It is hence necessary to reformulate local government law as the old assumption of 'residency' is no longer valid and since the social

[54] Gerald Frug, 'The City as a Legal Concept', in *Local Government Law*.

[55] I am grateful to Philip Oldenburg for pointing out to me the contrasting mobility of the Indian citizen, who may appear rooted, but if one looks at the population movement in the small towns and urban centres that are growing in India one sees a different kind of mobility. Because these towns are the main sources for employment in areas where there is considerable underemployment, one sees, every morning, hordes of people on cycles commuting to the towns for work and returning to the villages in the evening. This too has implications for the residency assumption of local government democracy.

[56] Gerald Frug, 'Decentering Decentralization'.

topography of everyday life can no longer be defined in terms of boundaries, inclusion and exclusion, and unitary selves.

This attempt to match citizen rights with local government duties gets further muddied when one factors in the growing suburbanization of the US and its implications for both the traditional city and for the assumption of residency. The areas where this suburbanization has had the strongest impact are those of zoning and school management, the second set of issues concerning local government which I hope to discuss here. While zoning is a common practice in all local authorities, in the US it has come to be seen as a discriminatory practice to create exclusive neighbourhoods. Exclusionary zoning has grown as a land-use regulatory tool with the growth of suburban localities in the US. The justification for such zoning policies was that they would protect the exclusive interests of local residents. Concerns such as the defence of private property values, the control of public service costs and the local tax rate, the preservation of the beauty and calm of the locality, the maintenance of the bonds of community, the desire to have neighbours like oneself, etc., are some of the arguments advanced in justification of exclusionary zoning. Its increasing use by a growing suburban movement in the US is producing, together with the dynamics that develops in the 'race to the bottom', a patchwork segregationist society where there is great inter-local inequality, and where there are legal and fiscal gates to the choice of place of work and residence. Exclusionary zoning creates the conflict that is endemic to the US, between the drive for autonomy of local government on the one hand, and the over-riding of this autonomy by the courts, to safeguard citizen rights, on the other. As a result the 'courts in several states have rejected the view that the validity of local zoning is to be assessed solely in terms of its effects on the 'welfare of the particular community' and have required municipalities to take the regional implications of their actions into account'.[57] The issue of exclusionary zoning has generated an interesting discussion on inter-local equity, on how to balance the interests of contiguous localities, so that the costs of the policies of one are not borne by the other, and also over how to balance the interests of residents against the interests of non-

[57] Richard Briffault, ' Our Localism:...', pp. 41–2.

residents who want to share in the benefits that life in the suburbs has to offer. It has also generated a debate on the resultant discrimination that emerges from this suburbanization because when social faces are put on localities one finds that the poor and blacks are largely resident in run-down localities such as inner city centres.[58] A parallel discussion has taken place on schools since the funding of schools comes largely from local government budgets and hence local governments that have a capacity to raise resources through property taxes, are able to devote more resources for school education. The right to education is thus unequally enjoyed by citizens in the US.

This discussion of the implications of the suburbanization of the US leads to the third set of issues, the budgetary pressures on local governments. One response to confronting increasing costs is to reform local government structures. There are three groups of reforms suggested: (1) civil service reforms which seek to reduce bureaucratic rigidities, (2) employee empowerment which seeks to emphasize greater employee initiative and active participation in decision-making and operations, and (3) private sector reforms which seek competition in service delivery arrangements.[59] Another response to these budgetary pressures centres around the policies of taxation followed by various local governments. Since the major share of local government revenue comes from these taxes, especially property tax, maintaining a wide tax base, in the face of a mobile population of citizens and corporates, is a tricky exercise. These taxes are necessary to provide services such as education, police, fire services, waste disposal, welfare, etc. The need to retain their taxpayers causes local governments to lower taxes thereby reducing their capacity to cross-subsidize and provide services to poor localities where minorities are generally resident, especially in the cities. The run-down inner cities are the inegalitarian consequences of this lowering of taxes. If local governments raise taxes, to execute their progressive policies, there is a flight of both capital and

---

[58]   Guy Stuart, 'Segregation in the Boston Metropolitan Area at the end of the 20th Century', February 2000, The Civil Rights Project at Harvard University.

[59]   Anirudh Ruhil et al., 'Institutions and Reform: Re-Inventing Local Government', Urban Affairs Review, January 1999, vol. 34 (3), p. 43.

affluent citizens thereby reducing their tax base and triggering what has become in political jargon a 'race to the bottom'. Local governments find themselves thus having to balance the 'electoral threat' against the 'exit threat'. This situation gets accentuated by the competition, between states, for investment. Such competition is increasingly becoming the norm. Under this approach of 'market preserving federalism' 'if any state were to impose rent-seeking regulations, capital owners and workers alike would move to different jurisdictions offering more investment-friendly environments and, only those economic restrictions that citizens are willing to pay for will survive'.[60]

Caught in this 'damned-if-you-do-damned-if-you-don't' paradox local governments find themselves increasingly having to rely on federal grants or the capital markets for funds. Over time the net result of this taxation policy is a demographic shift of populations with affluent mobile whites being resident in the suburbs whereas the aged, low-income, non-white populations having to live in inner cities. So while the whole of the US may be the melting pot of races and communities, the reality of the localities—where most people live—is of a more segregationist society. This is a disturbing trend for democracy and equal citizenship since such enclaves are impediments to building the wider, more just, political community.

The fourth set of issues that merit attention is the 'strategic partnerships' to improve local governance, between local government and local businesses on the one hand and local government and civic associations on the other. Relying on the opportunities and instruments of the market an increased contracting out of public services, sale of public assets, permission given to private contractors to bid against local agencies, etc., has been relied upon by local governments to improve their goods and services. One innovative new instrument that has found favour with local governments is the BID. This is a territorially defined district within a city, which is created by the city to finance and improve services within a district. BIDs perform a range of activities from sanitation, street maintenance, public security to sponsoring festivals and other special events. The main purpose of a BID is to attract and retain businesses within the district,

[60]   J. Rodden and Susan Rose-Ackerman, op.cit. p. 1531.

which they sometimes do by creating distinct marketable images of the district.[61]

The other strategic partnership, between local government and civic associations, has also a unique place in American democracy. From the time of Tocqueville's America till date, the thick network of civic associations has produced a certain social capital that has been useful for local government in the US. This has inspired several innovations such as community policing, parent involvement in school services, voluntary care for the elderly, and soon, Although some have argued that there is a decline of social capital in the US,[62] others have contended that 'the tale is not only of decline; unprecedented group innovation and proliferation have happened too' since 'contemporary Americans ... may be organizing more than ever before but they have fashioned a very new civic universe'.[63] Several new arrangements are emerging from these new paths of public governance that are being attempted such as

community policing: a strategy for enhancing public security that features a return of police officers to particular beats, regular discussions between them and organized bodies in the communities they are policing, and regular coordination between those bodies and agencies providing other services that bear on controlling crime. Or consider forms of school decentralization that—while shrinking school size and permitting parents to choose schools—also replace close controls by central bureaucracies with governance mechanisms in which teachers and parents play a central role.[64]

---

[61] Richard Briffault, 'The Rise of Sublocal Structures in Urban Governance', *82 Minn L Rev*, 503, pp. 517–21.

[62] Robert Putnam, 'Bowling Alone'.

[63] Theda Skocpol, 'Advocates without Members: The Recent Transformation of American Civic Life,' in Theda Skocpol and Morris P. Fiorina, eds, *Civic Engagement in American Democracy*, Russell Sage Foundation Washington/New York: Brookings, 1999, p. 463.

[64] Joshua Cohen and Charles Sabel, 'Directly Deliberative Polyarchy'.

III

The foregoing sketch provides us with a backdrop for a comparison between the two decentralization initiatives of India and the US. I suppose one should begin this comparison with the recognition that in both democracies the decentralized political space is an important space for citizen voice and participation. While in India the expansion of this space was a product, at each stage, of policy decisions taken at the top, not as a result of demands coming from below. In fact, the centralized instrument of a constitutional amendment was enacted forty-three years after the adoption of the Constitution to give decentralization a basis in primary law. In the US the space has evolved organically, from the time of the founding of the Republic, through a continuous negotiation between the value of autonomy and that of citizen rights. In India, decentralization in the first four decades belonged basically to the realm of administration with it developing a participative democratic character only after the 73rd and 74th constitutional amendments of 1993. In the US, decentralization has always had a strong democratic identity being premised on the Madisonian ambition 'to break and control the violence of faction' as outlined in *The Federalist*. While there are considerable variations in the working of local government in India, depending on which political party controls the state, these decentralized units, have a set of uniform features at their core.[65] Such uniformity is absent among local governments in the US since not only do they trace their genealogies to different starting points, but also because they are 'creatures', 'delegates', or 'agents' of the states and hence take on a form that the individual state decides. An all-American pattern is, therefore non-existent. In both democracies the number of local governments is very large, with there being about 234,078 panchayats in India[66] and approximately 82,290 local government structures in the US.[67] The number of local governments is growing as America becomes a more suburbanized socio-geographical landscape and also since

[65]   See no. 10, fn 31.
[66]   *Panchayati Raj Update*, July 1998, 55, p. 6.
[67]   William D. Valente, *Local Government Law*...p. 2.

suburbs have the power to break away from cities within a metropolitan area and form their own local government units.[68]

A survey of the functioning and initiative of local government in the US would show a tremendous propensity to innovate, not just in the creation of forms of administration, or in the acceptance of different strategies to deliver services (which is where the heat is) but also in the adoption of structures of local government authority that are able to combine the regulatory functions of the state, with the efficiencies of the market, together with the resources of trust of civil society. Examples of such innovative forms are the enterprise zones, tax increment finance districts, business improvement districts, community policing initiatives, etc. The capacity for innovation in India, in contrast, is hampered by the culture of the 'mai-baap' state which has become pervasive in the last fifty years or more. Citizens have thereby developed a dependency on this developmental state. This is manifested in a high level of inertia and a hesitancy to innovate. In the US innovation, both as a strategy of survival and as a way of maximizing profit is a constitutive part of the public culture. This comprises the cultural capital that is available to the various initiatives that make up the set of local government initiatives. It is the source of many of the innovations in government that one can find in the US.[69]

The survey also points to the centrality of the domain of law in the evolution and functioning of local government in the US. The observation that I am making here is more than the trite one that the US is a rule-governed society, or that it is a litigious society, but that many of the conflicts over resources or jurisdictions or consequences, or profiles, or practices of local government are played out in the law courts. The impressive body of case law discussed by Gerald Frug and William D. Valente

[68] Ajit Mozoomdar has made the valuable observation that perhaps the resistance of the bureaucracy in India to decentralized democracy, as compared to the US, is because in India the administrative structure has a single line whereas in the USA it is a broken line which means ambitions are correspondingly vertically rather than horizontally directed.

[69] Alan Altshuler and Robert Behn, *Innovation in American Government: Challenges, Opportunities, and Dilemmas*, Washington Brookings, 1997.

in their respective case law books, and by Richard Briffault and others in the series of articles in law journals, corroborates this point.[70] In India there is no such body of litigation.[71] The Conformity Acts that each state has passed have not yet become major sites of legal disputation. This is a reflection either of the fact that interests in India have not yet seen the field of law as a site of articulation, or that the conflict of interests is settled in the realm of politics rather than that of law, or that the state, at the levels of the first and the second tier, is so powerful vis-à-vis the third tier that the latter does not see the law as being either a protective or an enabling instrument. Further, perhaps another reason for why law has not become a major site for disputation in India is because 'law and order' is not and will not be devolved as is the case in the US. Hence, in India decentralization will be limited to service delivery and nothing else.

Another interesting aspect on which a comparison should be made is with respect to the contrasting forces of decentralization in India and the US. In India the momentum for decentralization developed from the recognition that the state had failed to

---

[70]   Besides the two case law books on *Local Government Law*, one by Gerald. E. Frug and the other by William. D. Valente, both of which have very interesting case material, some of the most fascinating discussions on local government are found in law journals. Some examples are: Gerald E. Frug, 'Decentering Decentralization.' 60 *University of Chicago Law Review*, Spring 1993; Richard Briffault, 'Our Localism: The Structure of Local Government Law', Part 1 and January 1990 and 'Our Localism: Localism and Legal Theory', 90 *Columbia Law Review*, March 1990; Robert P. Inman and Daniel L. Rubinfeld, 'Making Sense of the anti-Trust State Action Doctrine: Resolving the Tension between Political Participation and Economic Efficiency', 75 *Texas Law Review*, 1997; George A. Bergmann, 'Taking Subsidiarity Seriously: Federalism in the European Community and the US', 94 *Columbia Law Review*, 1994; Lino A. Graglia, 'Revitalizing Democracy,' 24 *Harvard Journal of Law and Public Policy*, Fall 2000; J.Rodden and Susan Rose-Ackerman, 'Does Federalism Preserve Markets?' 83 *Virginia Law Review*, 1997.

[71]   I am grateful to Ajit Mozoomdar for drawing my attention to the fact that not only is there little case law with respect to local government in India but there is also little case law with respect to federal issues of centre–state relations in India.

significantly tackle the problem of rural poverty. It was held that the 'slow rate of benefits flowing from the infrastructure already built up, as indicated by the slow growth of productivity, and, (the) ... insufficient percolation of benefits to the poor and the socially disadvantaged sections, despite the proliferation of several poverty alleviation programmes',[72] meant that a new strategy was required. Decentralization was seen as this new strategy since it gave rural society a 'voice' vis-à-vis urban society, and since it gave the poor, within rural society, a 'voice' vis-à-vis the rich. This empowerment of rural society it is hoped would produce a range of benefits that would help in the alleviation of poverty.[73] In the US, in contrast, the motivation of decentralization is a combination of factors, all of which reflect the societal dynamics of a rich society. Some of these are the increasing

[72]   C.H. Hanumantha Rao, 'Decentralized Planning: An overview of Experience and Prospects', *Economic and Political Weekly*, 25 February 1989, p. 411.

[73]   Some of these are: (1) breaking the hold of rural elites over resource use and distribution in rural areas, (2) providing a greater say of the hitherto marginalized in the distribution of state welfare schemes, (3) creating a deeper involvement in the planning, implementation, and monitoring of those developmental processes that have an impact on rural areas, (4) ensuring a more balanced and sustainable use of local resources, (5) providing a better maintenance of local assets created through participatory processes, (6) locally and regionally innovating diverse solutions, (7) increasing the accountability of local officials, (8) increasing the pressure on government to concentrate on the priority concerns of local groups and finally, (9) reducing the costs of delivery and a rise in efficiency of government, (10) ensuring greater representation of various political, religious, ethnic, and tribal groups in development decision-making that could lead to greater equity in the allocation of government resources and investments, (11) increasing the efficiency of senior bureaucracy by relieving them of routine tasks that can be more effectively performed by lower officials, (12) allowing better political and administrative penetration of central and state policies into areas remote from these levels, (13) leading to development of greater administrative capability among local government, and (14) leading to an improvement in the self-esteem of exploited and suppressed groups through the activity of participation Peter R. deSouza in *Multi-State Study...*, report to the World Bank.

suburbanization of the US, the rise of a middle class that is upwardly mobile and that has adopted a consumerist culture, the desire of this class to live in little enclaves along with people similar to itself, the play of market forces, the political culture of individual choice, the resistance to the tyranny of centralized power, etc. While the intended outcome of the Indian project is the ending of the obnoxious segregation that has been the defining feature of a caste society, through reservation of places in local government for Dalits and Advasis, the unintended outcome of the US project will be the strengthening of segregation.[74] 'Typically the more affluent mobile whites move to the surburbs while the aged, low income and non-white groups move to and remain in the city'.[75] While in both places the citizen is primarily a consumer of local government services, the citizen in the US does so from a position of strength whereas the citizen in India does so from a position of weakness. In the former case, the citizen can go elsewhere if the services are poor; the goal of local government is therefore to ensure that the consumer of their services remains within the locality.[76] In the latter case the citizen is too poor to be so mobile and therefore she has to just suffer the poor quality of services. Service providers are far less accountable— they only have to face political protest and not a loss of tax revenue. So while it is poverty alleviation which is the driver of decentralization in India, it is the growing affluence of the middle class which is the driver behind decentralization in the US.

Another aspect, linked to the above, is the contrasting roles of the state and the market in both countries. In India the state is the predominant instrument of decentralization since it provides not just the personnel, and the schemes, but also the resources required by local government through the provision of grants. The tax base of local government in rural India is very poor and resources therefore must come through grants. In the US the

---

[74] Perhaps segregation is intended by individuals but it is certainly not the intended policy of the state. In fact this is an area of considerable dispute between the federal and state and local governments.

[75] William D.Valente, *Local Government Law...*, p. 11.

[76] Charles Tiebout, 'A Pure Theory of Local Expenditures', *Journal of Political Economy*, 1956.

market plays an important role in partnering the state.[77] Since a considerable amount of local government revenue comes from taxes, the need to reduce government expenditure, and thereby taxes, is strongly felt. This is done by contracting out many of the services of local government to private service providers.

As mentioned in brief earlier the partnership between local government and civic associations is another point of comparison worthy of investigation. While there is a consensus of the significance of civic associations for the democratic project in the US, there is less agreement on whether this social capital remains as robust as it was in an earlier period.[78] Robert Putnam's observation that during the last few decades 'the United States has undergone a less sanguine transformation: its citizens have become remarkably less civic, less politically engaged, less socially connected, less trusting, and less committed to the common good'[79] has provoked a debate on the status of civic associations.[80]

In India this debate on democracy and social capital is growing, through a series of case studies, some of which connect up with the activity of local government.[81] An argument similar to that made in the US, of a vibrant civil society being good for PRI Governance, is gaining adherents.[82] The question, however, remains of how the civil society resources can be deployed in the new opportunity space opened up by the panchayati raj

---

[77] J. Rodden and Susan Rose-Ackerman, 'Does Federalism Preserve Markets?' *Virginia Law Review*, vol. 83, 1997, pp. 1521–72.

[78] Theda Skocpol and Morris, P, Fiorina, *Civic Engagement and American Democracy*, New York: Brookings/Russell Foundation, 1999; Robert Putnam, 'Civic Engagement in America', *Government and Opposition*, vol. 36 (2), Spring 2001; Erik Olin Wright, ed., *Associations and Democracy: The Real Utopias Project*, vol. 1, London: Verso Press, 1995.

[79] Robert. D. Putnam, ibid., p. 135. On this proposition there is an intense debate as is evident from the collection of articles in the Skocpol/Fiorina book listed above.

[80] See fn. 60.

[81] 'Democracy and Social Capital', a special section with seven articles in the *Economic and Political Weekly*, vol. xxxvi, no. 8, 24 February, 2 March 2001.

[82] George Matthew, 'Decentralized Institutions: Government and Voluntary Sector', *Economic and Political Weekly*, 27 February 1999, p. 533.

structure. This is a question that haunts the debate, especially in the context of Ambedkar's view still remaining relevant, of the village as a 'sink of localism, a den of ignorance, narrow-mindedness and communalism'. There are disturbing news reports of traditional caste and patriarchial authority being used, through panchayats, to discipline social behaviour. A recent case of an unwed mother in Uttar Pradesh, who had just given birth to her child, being beaten to death because she was unwed, by the panchayat members, who first asked her father to do the job and then did so only when he refused, is just one example among the myriad cases of oppression that also characterize the stock of social capital in India.[83] The American discussion on social capital does not resonate very well in India where the values of feudalism, caste[84], and patriarchy[85] run deeply through the life-world of society in India, especially that of rural India.

To undermine this social structure of exclusion and exploitation, the new decentralization initiative has reserved seats for disadvantaged groups. Three groups in particular—women, Dalits, and Adivasis—are eligible for these seats in recognition of their social and economic condition, which results in them being denied a 'voice' in the public sphere. It is further recognized that these disadvantages are built into the system and hence cannot be overcome through the normal structures of opportunity that are available. Reservations of places in the gram panchayat, and for the post of the sarpanch, are therefore called for in the absence of which these groups would be permanently handicapped. This reservation route to equal citizenship has no equivalent within the structures of local government in the US, which perhaps uses other instruments, seeking a diversity and a discrimination profile, to arrive at the same goal.

The final comparison that I would like to make concerns the consequences, for the dynamics of local government, of the different systems of democratic governance adopted by the US

---

[83] Manabi Mazumdar, 'The Unlawful Culture', The *Hindu*, 29 August 2001.

[84] Ghanshyam Shah, ed., *Dalit Identity and Politics*, New Delhi: Sage, 2001.

[85] Nivedita Menon, ed., *Gender and Politics in India*, New Delhi: Oxford University Press, 1999.

and India. The last decade of politics in India has, paradoxically, increased the importance of local government. This is not because of any great change of heart among the political class, an altruistic turn, but because of the hard-nosed realism that India has entered a phase of politics where only coalitions can come to power at the Union level in Delhi, in contrast to the states which are increasingly moving towards an alternating two-party system. To win the government of the Union, therefore, political parties have to secure the states. To secure the states parties in power must deliver. The delivery route of the last fifty years or more has proved to be marginally effective, if not ineffective, and therefore new routes are being sought that will give an increasingly restless and cynical electorate a sense of good governance. The decentralization route is the one being embraced by all political parties in India today. It is the optimum delivery path available: delivering services to the citizen in one direction and delivering control of government to the political party in the other. The dynamics of local government has therefore become a key element in the calculus of parties.

There is a second calculus within which local government has a prominent place. Since today all state governments in India are in a perilous financial position they have, increasingly, come to rely on aid and grants from international donor agencies. For these agencies 'decentralization' has become, what 'civil society' is for the academy, the 'promise' word in which lies the solution to many of the problems of contemporary India. State governments are trying therefore to showcase their decentralization efforts to procure soft loans from agencies such as the World Bank.

There is also a third calculus within which decentralization finds favour. This is the aspiration of the new political leadership that has emerged as a result of the 73rd and 74rd constitutional amendments. It is estimated that in both rural and urban local government institutions, three million new representatives have found a place. The representative density has thereby increased considerably in India. These lower level representatives, who are really the workers of the higher level representation create a web of interlinked representatives that need the institutions of local government to provide patronage to their supporters. This is a powerful force and has introduced a new dynamics into the processes of political mobilization and transformation. Hence, the evolution of the parliamentary system in India is in the direction of local government. In the US, because the federal government is somewhat free from the politics of coalition-making, the politics of local government does not affect it very much and the link between securing states and forming the government at the federal level would need to be established in terms of the logic of electoral politics in the US. In the context of this electoral calculus, the interesting question is to see how far the dynamics of local government travel. In the Indian case it travels very far.

Contributors

Alfred Stepan, Wallace Sayre Professor of Political Science, Columbia University.

Arend Lijphart, Research Professor Emeritus of Political Science, University of California, San Diego.

E. Sridharan, Academic Director, University of Pennsylvania Institute for the Advanced Study of India.

Juan J. Linz, Professor Emeritus of Political Science, Yale University.

K. Shankar Bajpai, Chairman, Delhi Policy Group, New Delhi.

Nathan Glazer, Professor Emeritus of Sociology, Harvard University.

Neera Chandhoke, Professor of Political Science, University of Delhi.

Peter Ronald deSouza, Senior Fellow and Co-Director, *Lokniti* Programme of Comparative Democracy, Centre for the Study of Developing Societies, Delhi.

Yogendra Yadav, Senior Fellow and Co-Director, *Lokniti* Programme of Comparative Democracy, Centre for the Study of Developing Societies, Delhi.

Index